THE LEADERSHIP TRILOGY

UPGRADE YOUR MINDSET

UPSKILL YOUR LEADERSHIP

UPLIFT YOUR TEAMS

LEADERSHIP LESSONS FROM LEADERSHIP SPECIALIST

ANTON GUINEA

First published by The Rural Publishing Company.

eBook: 978-0-6458801-9-9
Print: 978-0-6459180-1-4

The Rural Publishing Company
Email: hello@theruralpublishingcompany.com.au
Website: https://theruralpublishingcompany.com.au

THIS IS THE MOST IMPORTANT BOOK DEDICATION YOU WILL READ.

This book is dedicated to all of those leaders out there who have never received leadership coaching. Who've never been supported to upgrade themselves. Who've never understood just how important it is to learn, grow, lead, in that order. This is the group of leaders who I wrote this book for. Don't worry, we've got you covered, if you're willing to come on a little journey with me to upgrade your mindset.

This book is also dedicated to old-school leaders. Leaders who didn't have to think about political correctness, who didn't have to think about offending people, and who didn't have to worry about raising their voices in meetings. Because you could do that in the 1900s. This is the other group of leaders who I wrote this book for. Never fear, we've got you covered, too, if you're willing to buy into the challenges of leading with heart and care factor, not just into taking an 'I'm not here to win friends' approach.

This book is dedicated to the teams that were impacted by the leaders mentioned above.

> **I was one of those workers, in one of those teams. I suffered through poor leadership, and I'm committed to helping the old-school leaders who are willing to learn how to think differently about leadership and about humans.**

Upgrading your mindset is thinking differently. It's about reacting differently. And, it's about responding differently. At its simplest, upgrading your mindset is about becoming reflective, so that you can answer the big questions about why you're a leader. At its more complex, upgrading your mindset is about knowing that every human is unique, every human is different, and every human has a very specific set of personal and professional needs.

If you read the paragraphs above, and you're a little freaked out, don't be. You have two options: you can put this book down and never look at it again, or you can work through it, and see what happens to your mindset, and to your approach to leadership. And see what happens to your team, and your team members, after you apply what you've learnt.

This book is also dedicated to all of the amazing mentors, coaches and trainers, who I've learnt so much from over the years. I've invested hundreds of thousands of dollars into my professional education, not only to be the leader that my team and business needs, but so I can share what I've learnt with you—the leader who's ready to upgrade their mindset!

Finally, this book is also dedicated to my amazing family, Mrs G (the amazing teacher), Toby (Son 1—engineer), and Zac (Son 2—future pilot) who've been on this crazy journey with me since 2004. They are my tribe, my number 1 team, and they are my motivation to be the best human and leader that I can be.

HOW TO USE THIS BOOK

This book is a playbook, not a story book.

It comprises a series of standalone ideas, elements, and tips and tricks to help you. It comes with actions to take to become a better thinker, a better leader, and a better advocate for your team's professional development. You'll also find a series of prompts and questions to encourage you to reflect honestly on your leadership skills and practices, and to think of ways to upgrade, upskill, and uplift yourself and your team.

Happy reading! You're on the way to being the best leader that YOU can be.

CONTENTS

CONTENTS

CONTENTS

THE LEADERSHIP TRILOGY

BOOK 1

UPGRADE

YOUR MINDSET

LEADERSHIP LESSONS FROM LEADERSHIP SPECIALIST

ANTON GUINEA

UPGRADE
YOUR MINDSET

WITH THE UPGRADE MODEL

This model was developed as a strategic tool for putting theory into practice to upgrade your mindset.

The model draws on various psychological theories relating to attitude, perception, and emotional experience in the workplace, and structures this information into a practical framework to guide leaders through the process of upgrading their mindsets to become better leaders.

It was developed over nearly 20 years of theoretical analysis combined with real-world experience, and it underpins the Guinea Group's winning formula for creating effective leaders, high-performing teams, and workplaces that are both physically and psychologically safe for workers.

Refer back to this model while reading this book. It'll help you form a concrete framework in your mind that will, over time, become a natural reference point as you grow and develop in your attitudes and behaviours, and move you closer to being the leader you want to be.

To make the most of this resource, contact us via our website at antonguinea.com.au for a self-diagnostic tool and action plan to review and improve your skills against the model.

01 START WITH A **FUTURE FOCUS**

Skillset: As a leader, decide who you're becoming

02 DEVELOP A **POSITIVE PERSPECTIVE**

Skillset: Practice the art of putting things into perspective

03 THINK ABOUT **YOUR THOUGHTS**

Skillset: Develop and practice the skill of introspection

04 LEAD **UNDER PRESSURE**

Skillset: Manage the pressure; don't let it manage you

05 KNOW YOUR **LEADERSHIP STYLE**

Skillset: Find your leadership style, and lean into it

INTRODUCTION:
UPGRADE YOUR MINDSET

Upgrading your mindset is one of the most important steps to take in life. It can help you reach your goals, make better decisions, and become a better version of yourself. It can help you to become a better leader—as good a leader as those who've inspired you, or the leader you wished you had.

Changing your mindset isn't easy. It's a difficult job, and it requires dedication and hard work. It requires introspection.

But it it's worth it. Investing in it can help you become more resilient, confident, and happy—and a better leader for all the people who are looking to you for guidance and support so they can be their best, too.

This book was written for all of those leaders ready to upgrade their mindsets and move into the future as a better leader. It was written because so many leaders out there haven't received leadership coaching, and because so many don't even know that it's a thing. It was written because so many leaders don't understand that to be a better leader, they need to learn, grow, and then lead—in that order.

This book was also written because old-school leadership still exists. Even in this day and age, there are leaders who don't understand political correctness, and whose ideology and behaviour align with the problematic ways of leading we've been trying to let go of in the last decades. It was written because it's time for leaders to think differently about people and about leadership, and to lead with heart and care factor—because their teams need it to perform at their best.

Upgrading your mindset is how leaders can begin thinking differently. It's about reacting differently, and about responding differently. Throughout this book, I'll walk you through a process of instrospection, encouraging you to become more reflective so you can get to the core of the big questions about why you're a leader, and why you lead like you do. I'll encourage you to think about your leadership style, and how you can upgrade it to a style that allows you to be more resilient, better able to lead under pressure, and better relate to your teams—who need your leadership to perform at their best for you and your organisation.

Upgrading your mindset can be a complex process. But it's worth it—for you as a leader, and for the unique humans who make up the diverse teams you're leading.

Throughout this book you'll find activities, real-life anecdotes, and evidence-based leadership tips to help you upgrade your mindset. I encourage you to spend real time reflecting on what you're learning as you work through the book on your way to becoming a better leader—one with strength as well as care factor.

In the meantime, here's how you'll upgrade your mindset.

ONE IDENTIFY YOUR LIMITING BELIEFS.

The first step to upgrading your mindset is to identify your limiting beliefs. These are the beliefs that hold you back from achieving your goals and reaching your potential. Take the time to think about what these beliefs are, and how they're impacting on your life. Once you've identified them, you can start to challenge them, and begin to change them.

TWO SET GOALS.

One of the best ways to upgrade your mindset is to set goals. Having goals will help you focus your efforts and give you something to strive for. Make sure that your goals are realistic and achievable, and that they align with your values and beliefs.

THREE DEVELOP SELF-AWARENESS.

Self-awareness is key to upgrading your mindset. Take the time to understand yourself better, including your strengths and weaknesses, your values and beliefs, and your goals and motivations. This will help you become aware of how your thoughts and beliefs are impacting on your life, and help you begin to see how you can make positive changes.

FOUR PRACTICE POSITIVE THINKING.

Once you've identified your limiting beliefs and developed your self-awareness, it's time to practice positive thinking. Positive thinking helps to replace negative thoughts with more positive ones, which can help to upgrade your mindset by reframing the way you approach challenges.

FIVE TAKE ACTION.

It's important to take action to upgrade your mindset. If you find yourself stuck in a rut, or if you want to reach a goal, taking action is the only way to make progress. Make sure to set specific goals, and to put all of your effort into reaching them.

SIX SEEK HELP.

If you find yourself struggling to upgrade your mindset, it's important to seek help. This could be from a coach, a mentor, a therapist, or anyone else you trust. Talking to someone can help you identify any patterns or roadblocks that might be standing between you and your goals.

SEVEN DEVELOP SELF-DISCIPLINE.

Self-discipline is a key factor in upgrading your mindset. It's important to be able to stay focused and motivated, and to be able to push yourself to reach your goals. Developing self-discipline will help you stay on track, and to do what you need to do to get where you want to be.

By following these steps, you can upgrade your mindset and become the best version of yourself. It requires dedication and hard work, but the rewards are worth it. Upgrade your mindset today and take control of your life, and your leadership.

SKILL 1
START WITH A
FUTURE FOCUS

I WAS NOT A NICE HUMAN WHEN I WAS YOUNGER.

I was angry, I had a log (not a chip) on both shoulders, and I was very quick to escalate a conversation. From controlled to crazy out-of-control. Highly emotional. I had zero emotional control, and I didn't care.

When I reflect on being a younger man, and the less nice human that I was, I couldn't have told you what my mission was. After a lot of personal and professional development work, I'm now very clear on my purpose, and that is simply to leave people better than I found them. Simple, but a great driver of behaviour.

Back then, I was a tradie, so it didn't seem like a big deal. Everyone was like that. Or were they? There weren't too many on my crew that had the lack of emotional control that I did. But I made it OK. Until one day it just lost it. I had a massive stand-up blue in the workshop, with the boilermaker on our shift. It was so uncool! Let's just say that the language we used towards each other was colourful.

My lovely wife remembers the conversation that evening, and it was about me baring my soul and being brutally honest about my lack of people skills. I don't remember the exact words I used, but Mrs G remembers me saying that I was sick of not being able to get on with people, and that I was totally committed to changing my approach. And to learning new communication skills. But where do you start in this elusive quest for better connection with others?

With a future focus.

Mine started at Monash University, studying Engineering. Then I did a HR degree, and a postgraduate diploma at CQU. That'll fix it, I thought. The study was useful, and so was the work that I was doing on trying to understand humans. Understanding others was about watching and listening. Looking and learning. What made people tick? And what made them crack?

The journey has never stopped, and I recently completed a psychology degree. In saying that, the best thing I ever studied was NLP (Neuro-Linguistic Programming)—love it or loathe it, that program was an eye opener into the human species, and how we all connect.

Having studied people for nearly thirty years (I'm now doing a PhD in behavioural science), I share with leaders some of the simple techniques that they can use to improve their leadership and their connection. Especially when they're under pressure, which is the hardest time to connect.

Here are the three biggest lessons I've learnt about becoming the best human I can be (and failing plenty of times along the way).

ONE BE CLEAR ON WHO YOU WANT TO BE OR BECOME.

If you're happy where you are, stay there. But if you'd like to change something about how you behave, or who you are, decide what that new version of you looks like. Here's the challenge you'll face: if I asked you what your life's purpose is, you may or may not know that. 90% of the leaders that I ask this question to freak out and can't answer it. Which is cool. But if you can answer it, you'll be better placed to lean into behaviours that help you live your purpose.

If you don't know what your purpose is, the next best step is to understand how you'd like to be remembered. That's generally an easier thing to get your head around. Do you want to be remembered for the person that lifted others, or saw potential in others, or someone who was the toe-cutter or the Chief Twit? (Elon sacking thousands, as a case in point.)

When it comes to being remembered, I think back to all of the stories people have shared with me about their poor leaders. Some of those people share stories from decades ago, and how they still remember how bad those leaders made them feel. Yes, people remember conversations that hurt them, for thirty years and more. That's a long time...

LEADER ACTION

When you know what your purpose is (preferred) or at least how you want to be remembered, you can become the person and the leader who achieves that purpose.

TWO YOU REALLY DO NEED TO MAKE IT A PRIORITY.

Here's my next question for you: are you interested in or committed to becoming the leader that you want to be?

I see two types of leaders come through my programs. Type one went to university after leaving school. They move through their career, learning leadership on the job, spending three to five years at each level of the business, on their way to GM or CEO, and over time they become good leaders. Or not. Depending on the leaders that they're exposed to or the organisations that they join.

Type two leaders that I come across are those that do what it takes to become who they want to be. They get educated. They study humans. They stay in their leadership role for as long as it takes to master it. They know that it might take more than five years, or less, to develop the skills they need to progress their career. Some don't want to progress their career, they're happy at the level they're at, and they look for horizontal challenges and not vertical ascendance.

The thing that I know about leaders who become who they want to be is that they're clear on their direction. They do what it takes to get there. They sacrifice, they commit, and they dedicate themselves to the mission.

LEADER ACTION

Don't just be interested in becoming the leader you want to. Make it a priority and commit to it. Do something today to move you forward.

THREE BE COMFORTABLE WITH DISCOMFORT.

The challenge you'll face as you go after what you want to achieve as a leader is that you'll face trials and find yourself in uncomfortable situations. This is part and parcel of the growth and the development process.

This point reminds me of the great Australian world champion triathlete, @Chris McCormack.[37] When Macca turned up to race at the Ironman World Championships in Kona for the very first time, he was asked by the media if he was ready for the race. He scoffed, and said, 'Ready?...I'm here to win.' Which most people thought was a bit cocky at the time.

Macca couldn't even finish that race.

But he knew what he wanted to achieve, and over the next ten years, he turned himself into a three-time Ironman World Champion, and one of Australia's greatest ever triathletes. After all of that, Macca looked back over his career and wrote the book I'm Here to Win[37] to honour where he'd come from in the very first race.

In that book, Macca wrote a lot about being able to 'embrace the suck'. In other words, being uncomfortable with discomfort. His theory is 'the person that can hurt the most during the race will win.' Just like leaders who develop themselves, getting out of your comfort zone and challenging yourself is part of the process of becoming an effective leader.

On the other side of discomfort comes growth. The more comfortable you can be with being challenged, the more you'll develop your leadership skills. And the better you'll learn to lead under pressure.

LEADER ACTION

Actively seek out opportunities to stretch yourself. Put yourself into positions or roles that challenge you and stretch your current skill set.

Having a future focus means deciding early in the journey who you want to become as a leader, and committing to making the changes that will be required for you to get there. It's also about finding opportunities to get out of your comfort zone on the way to becoming that leader and that human— and there will be plenty. Here's some of mine.

WHAT I LEARNT FROM DOING 700 LEADERSHIP COACHING SESSIONS

In January 2020, just before the pandemic whipped up its frenzy, Facebook started sending me ads for a thing called Remarkable. The metaverse must have been listening to my conversations (or maybe just my phone), and must have known that I write a lot, and that I've got piles of old books full of notes from meetings and coaching sessions.

The Remarkable looked cool, so I purchased one, and on January 24, 2020, I started documenting my coaching sessions in it, instead of in workbooks. Recently, I clocked over 700 coaching sessions, all documented in the Remarkable. Remarkable!

700 one-on-one coaching sessions, sitting with leaders at all levels of organisations, talking through their challenges or their wins. I've coached global managers and CEOs, and I've worked with team leaders. Both face-to-face and online. Either fortnightly or monthly, or weekly, even daily sometimes. Our coaching programs offer 24/7 support, which some leaders need at times. Some sessions take as little as fifteen minutes, but I've also spent full days with some leaders.

It's been a journey for me, and for the leaders I coach. The learnings on both sides have been amazing, and the conversations are documented, and sent out as part of the close out for every session.

In relation to my reflections, and the common themes that have come

through during those 700 sessions, here's three that stand out.

ONE LEADERSHIP CAN BE LONELY.

In our coaching sessions, I've seen (and experienced) every emotion, and then some. And what I've learnt about leaders is that things can change in a heartbeat. Life can be humming, and suddenly it gets uncomfortable. And, at times, lonely.

Leadership is such a rewarding experience for most, but at the same time, it can present such a challenge. And regardless of how much or how little support the leader is getting from their leader, there are times when leadership can cause feelings of isolation and loneliness.

Big decisions need to be made. Hard conversations must be had. All while there are teams and team members involved in and impacted by those decisions. It's so easy for a leader to say the wrong word, or use the wrong tone, or the wrong body language, and the relationship with a team or team member is strained for the next period.

My reflection is that leaders need a coach, and someone in their corner, who's external to the organisation, who they can talk openly to about their challenges. And of course, their wins. Don't worry, we celebrate success as much as we talk through issues, but at the same time, there's a confidentiality with coaching that makes it a hugely supportive process— where leaders feel like they've got a friend, as well as a coach.

My coaching on this is: if you find leadership lonely, reach out to a coach or mentor (or your leader), and be willing to have real conversations about your leadership and your team. These conversations will help you feel like you're not in this on your own. You're loved, and we're here for you when you need to chat. Life (and leadership) is a team sport.

TWO LEADERSHIP IS VALUES-BASED.

The clearer that leaders are on their values, the better results they get. Period.

Value alignment is such a key part of leadership because it's the thing that leaders go to consciously when they need to make tough decisions. Yes, our beliefs and conditioning drive our behaviour, but these are more subconscious, and we don't think about these too much (although we should do that, too).

Our values are the behavioural drivers that we go to when we're under pressure. If your value is honesty, you'll be driven by telling the truth. If it's caring, you'll lean into compassion and empathetic leadership. And if it's integrity, you'll be the leader who makes a commitment and follows through (not the one who commits and forgets).

My reflection on this one is that a lot of leaders haven't done a values exercise, and they aren't sure on their values, which makes it difficult for them. In several ways. Firstly, a leader's values need to align with the values of the organisation. It's not uncommon for me to hear a leader leave an organisation because their values aren't aligned with their business. This shows up with they're asked to do something that 'doesn't feel right'. Yes, leaders need to support business decisions, but at the same time, they'll feel challenged if how they're expected to behave is out of alignment with their caring value or their integrity value, for example.

My next reflection on this one is that if you ask someone about their leader, they'll generally talk in values-based words. So, our values are what we're remembered for. That's because values drive behaviour, and our behaviour is always on show.

And in case you're wondering, what's the one big overarching value that should drive leader behaviour? It's integrity. We've surveyed teams and asked them what they respect (and expect) from their leaders, and it's integrity. Which means the two elements of integrity—firstly, doing what's right, and secondly, doing what you said you would do.

THREE LEADERSHIP IS ABOUT CONTROL.

It's about control—in a good way, not in the power-hungry way. It's about internal control. Or more specifically, conscious control.

We get some great outcomes for the leaders that come through our programs, and I think the biggest compliment I could get is when leaders share that they have learnt the skill of 'responding, not reacting'. In other words, they've learnt to channel their emotional state, and breathe through the pressure of the situation.

Leaders that can create conscious control are able to control their behavioural responses. Which helps them control situations. And to control high-pressure situations. Which is when it's most important to be responsive, not reactive.

Emotional states are contagious. Leaders that can stay calm can help their team members stay calm. Some leaders I've coached have a poker face and try hard not to show when they're struggling emotionally. They try to 'shield' their teams from any pressure they might be facing.

The best leaders realise that their teams, and team members, are a reflection of their leader. If the leader is reactive, the team members will become that way, too. If the leader is in control, ditto (in general terms).

And again, in case you're wondering, one of the character traits that people are looking for from their leaders is consistency. Consistency means that the leader's emotional state isn't all over the place. It's consistent. Teams don't like working with leaders who are volatile or erratic. It's just uncool.

The other thing that rates highly from a team member perspective is care factor. Consistency and care factor are the two things your team is looking for from you, in relation to behaviour at least.

Finally, the very first coaching session that I recorded on my Remarkable was David Mallia on January 24, 2020. The 500th coaching session that I recorded on my Remarkable was Jayden Baker, on 5 September, 2022. If you do the numbers and count the working days during that period (670), then divide that by 500, you will get about 75%. So on average, I do three coaching sessions every four working days. That's between three and four coaching sessions every week—week in and week out.

It's been a blast, and my thanks and gratitude goes out to all the leaders that have trusted me to be in their lives. Their advice has helped support my future focus, and sometimes, even changed it.

But there's isn't the only advice that's helped. I've also gotten great advice in places beyond the profession, that's been just as invaluable.

THE BEST ADVICE I EVER GOT

The best advice I ever got was life advice from my favourite schoolteacher of all time. She's currently a grade six teacher. And I was never in any of her classes. I married her instead. This section is a shout out to Mrs. Guinea (as her students—and now, I—call her!), or Mrs. G for short.

When I met Mrs. G, she wasn't a schoolteacher. She was working in admin for the Queensland Police Service. Like me, she wasn't overly 'committed' at school. She didn't trouble the scorers when it came to report card time, and she's fairly open about the fact that school was more of a social affair for her (like much of her life still is). I was an electrician, and Mrs. G was a clerk. How things have changed in the 30-something years since we first met and fell in love and built an amazing life together.

Amazing for me—remember that Mrs. G married an entrepreneur—always a roller coaster ride for a supportive spouse. We've supported each other's goals over time, but I am lucky to say that Mrs G has always been there,

through the good and bad times in business, for which I am forever grateful. I sometimes say that I'm not sure how I got her to hang around so long. I'm glad she has, because she's taught me some amazing life lessons, and here are the best three (and if you're a leader out there, feel free to grab these and run with them—I do)!

ONE BE KINDER THAN IS NECESSARY.

This is my favourite Mrs G line of all time. Being kinder than is necessary is a great motto for life. It's about knowing what you should do, and then going above and beyond, because you care enough to. It's about paying it forward, it's about going out of your way to help others when you don't really have to. Or when you're not expected to. It's about smiling when you feel like frowning, and encouraging when you struggle to get the words out. It's about knowing that you don't like everyone, but you're still kind, regardless of the human you're dealing with.

TWO THEY WON'T REMEMBER WHAT I TAUGHT THEM.

Possibly the best line I have heard during my time on planet Earth. If you're a leader, they won't remember what you showed them; they'll only remember how you made them feel.

Mrs G steps into this and makes the effort with all her students. She's amazing at creating smiles. I love that about her, and about this advice.

I've taken this advice one step further, and in our business, my mission is to 'leave people better than I found them'. Many people have heard me say that in programs or in coaching. And if you ever hear me saying it, you'll know that we've got Mrs G to thank for that piece of wisdom—and for me, showing up with that as a goal and a life purpose is my 'why'.

THREE THERE'S GOOD IN EVERYONE.

The beautiful thing about this is that Mrs G really believes it, and leans into it. Because our beliefs drive our behaviour. How we think and feel shows up in how we act. When this is a strong belief, strong actions follow. One of the things that Mrs G is somewhat known for is being good with 'bouncy boys'. Aka, those boys that other teachers may not like to have in their class, due to how rowdy or excitable they can be. I love Mrs G's response to the question about how hard it might be to teach some of those boys—'I raised bouncy boys; they just need someone to see the best in them, to see their potential, and treat them accordingly. And they will blossom'. Isn't that beautiful? Go Mrs G.

Leaders, I apply these lessons as much as I can, especially when I'm under pressure. I hope they can help you out.

And if you ever see Mrs G, reach out and say hi! Love ya Jules.

HOW I SURVIVED A LEADERSHIP ROLE I WASN'T READY FOR

Having a future focus is important. It helps to reveal the steps you need to take to get where you want to go. But sometimes, you think you're ready for the next step, when you're not.

I thought I was ready. Some others (very few) thought I was ready. That is, ready for a demanding leadership role. But I wasn't. Not even close. But I took the role anyway. And pretty much failed.

CAN LEADERSHIP BE LEARNT, OR IS IT INHERITED?

Both. Leadership is a skill set. It can certainly be learnt. And it's inherited too (for the few lucky ones—studies have isolated the rs4950 genotype, the gift that nature has given some born leaders). I didn't get that gene...I've had to learn the hard way.

This really is the nature or nurture debate, and it's about how much of each is required for leadership. My theory is that you could be born with zero innate leadership abilities, but you can learn them—if you're committed enough. My experience is that most people aren't committed enough to doing the level of work that it takes to become a strong leader. Leadership learning is an important process. And it's a process that I didn't go through prior to taking on a high-stress leadership role.

I was a tradesperson. I could lead other tradespeople, right? Can't be that hard. I had a degree in human resources—that should have been all I needed to know, right? I was committed, and willing to work really hard and even do the work myself if I had to. That would get me through any difficult situation...right?

It should have pretty much been a NO to the three questions above. But I thought I was ready, and I thought I was right. Tip to young and future leaders: stop. Slow down. You've got heaps of time to build your career. I know you want that job tomorrow, but you don't need that job tomorrow. It'll come in time, when you're really ready for it.

No one could have told me, but if I could have been wise enough at the ripe old age of 29, when I got my first real leadership role, I would have read more. Watched more. Questioned more. Written more. And basically, I would have made leadership a study (not a university study, but a real-life study—which is what I'm doing now). And I would have gotten myself ready for the demands and the pressure of leading other humans, at least from a theoretical perspective.

During one of our leadership programs in 2021, we had a leader in a session who had been a leader for thirty years, who said 'It's great to be here, but I didn't know leadership training was a thing.'

WHAT HAPPENS WHEN LEADERSHIP GOES WRONG?

Yes, if you're reading this, and you've been a leader for a while, you'll say that no reading or training will set you up for the experiences you need to have as a leader, to develop your resilience, or your skills at leading with control, care factor, and courage. And you're right. Ish...

Leadership training and coaching does work. Some of my coaching is with future leaders, not just current leaders. And here is my experience from seventeen years of leadership coaching: future leaders are so much better at reflection and review than current leaders. Very few leaders spend time sitting, reflecting, reassessing and reinvigorating. Leaders, strangely enough, think that the experience itself will do the job for them. Just turn up, learn on the job, and we're all good.

That's when leadership goes wrong. Because leaders haven't learnt from the last time the same thing happened. And they keep hurting humans. Uncool.

And they let themselves lose control. Your burning question, like ours, should be 'why is important that I stay calm and in control as a leader, and how can I do that?' Tip to young and future leaders: reflect, review and reassess. And journal. Write stuff down. Commit to learning as much as you can about leading humans, and why it's so important.

But why, when leadership is the most important role on planet Earth—after parenting—don't we spend more time working on it?

Because leaders are too busy. Fun fact—most of my coaching sessions start with questions like:

> **Anton:** G'day, how are you today?
>
> **Coachee:** Oh, I'm so busy (or a derivative like busy, too busy, crazy busy, flat out, under the pump...etc).
>
> **Anton:** How have you gone with your actions from the last session (which are usually about working on their leadership)?
>
> **Coachee:** Scroll back up, and see the answer to question 1.

For me, I really have sympathy and empathy for the people I led in those early days. My apologies to all of them, and big thanks for being patient. It went wrong, a lot.

HOW DO YOU SURVIVE A LEADERSHIP ROLE YOU'RE NOT READY FOR?

I have no real pearls of wisdom as an answer to this question. In short, I bluffed my way through it. Mind you, I didn't bluff many other people. Poor leadership is usually glaringly obvious. Which it would have been for me.

And isn't that sad to say. There were humans involved. And I was bluffing. I had zero idea how to engage people, or motive them, at that time. Tip to young and future leaders: if you're in a role that you know deep down you're not really prepared for, please reach out. I'm here to help. And it's really OK to ask for help!

WHICH LEADERSHIP STYLE IS BEST?

Your style is best. As long as you can put your hand on your heart and say that you're doing the work, you're learning, and you're leading—on purpose. And doing no harm along the way.

And when you can also say you're working with a clear future focus—and you're actually doing the work it takes to get there.

WHEN IS NOW THE RIGHT TIME TO STOP PROCRASTINATING?

I've written 10,000 words of my next book. And they are great—really. But every time I go to write the rest of it, the fridge needs cleaning. Or I suddenly feel the urge to go for a run. Or a swim. Or to do anything else except book writing. Wednesday, Thursday, Friday (aka: WTF) is going on...

I'm being akratic, is what's happening. In other words, procrastinating. When we're under pressure constantly, we opt for easy and quick wins, instead of the important work. Beating procrastination is about self-discipline, and being in conscious control.

Firstly, let's go back in time to, oh, about 2,600 years ago, and unpack the origins of the word akratic, and how it's developed into what we now know as procrastination.

The concept of akrasia dates back to the time of the great Greek philosopher, Plato. Plato was perplexed (in the 300s BCE that is): 'why, if one judges action A to be the best course of action, would one do anything other than A?' Apparently, we procrastinated, even back then.

Aristotle also weighed in on the debate. He weighed in on things back then (before social media), and determined that the opposite to being akratic would be enkratic. Which was defined as having 'power over oneself.'

To top off the 4th Century BCE debate on why we don't get into action, we must go back to Socrates. Socrates must have been an action taker, as he's credited with founding Western philosophy. Socrates couldn't buy into akrasia, because for him, akrasia didn't even exist. His take on it was that 'no one moves willingly towards the bad.'

I wonder what Socrates would think if he was alive today, and he picked up one of the many books in bookstores on procrastination and how to get into action. I love his take on it, though—procrastination is moving towards the bad. Just knowing that might be enough to get some people into action.

And is procrastination moving towards the bad? Absolutely. Just think for a moment about how crapola (technical term) it feels to put things off day after day. And then imagining the intense pleasure and satisfaction that you would have felt if you'd stepped into that robust conversation, that book writing, that other-language learning, or the myriad other things that you would love to achieve but are putting off for some reason. I'm busy too. I get that. But we're not talking about a time issue here.

If it's not a time issue, then what is it? Why do we procrastinate?

Fear, generally. The fear of not doing it right (for the perfectionists). The fear of the response (for the people pleasers). Or the fear of the experience itself—like boredom from a long-term project (for the instant pleasure seekers). Procrastination can generally be attributed to one of these three, and if you can unpack the reason for yourself, you can get yourself into action, by doing one of the following—and these are a summarised version of tips from the great business philosopher (aka, author of **Atomic Habits**) **@JamesClear**.[13]

ONE FIND A WAY TO REWARD YOURSELF SOONER.

The issue with procrastination, or what some people have termed the 'intention-action gap' (I prefer Akrasia, it just sounds cooler), is that there is a short-term reward. There's some instant gratification, that you use to make yourself feel better in the moment. But you sacrifice the feeling of satisfaction (which would be far greater) from doing the thing you're putting off. Find a way to reward yourself sooner for doing the hard things.

TWO HAVE SOME DISCIPLINE.

This is the conscious control piece. In the book **Extreme Ownership** by

@LeifBabin and @JockoWillink,[59] they talk about the word discipline. And what they mean is personal discipline. Personal commitment to a plan. Personal commitment to an action. Personal commitment to completion. In their world, discipline equals freedom. But discipline takes effort. It takes consistency, and it takes consideration of what your big goals (and small goals) are, and why they're important to you. Plan your days. Plan your weeks. Be disciplined with your time, and with your planning. Be on purpose. Ask yourself regularly, 'is this serving or sabotaging me?'

THREE LOOK ON THE BRIGHT SIDE OF LIFE.

This is the under-pressure piece. Pressure can push us towards negative thinking. We tend to (even in general terms) move by default to a negative. Or what might go wrong. 'What's the worst possible thing that could happen if I do this?' We blow up the negatives until they're huge—we think that 'I might not get it right', 'I could get ridiculed', or 'I have to do something that's rudimentary'. And those things might be true. What could also be true is the opposite of those, and the amazing positive outcomes and emotions that you'll feel, if you get it done. Focus on the positives and feel and see what could go right, not what could go wrong.

The great business philosopher (aka singer) @EricIdle nailed it when he shared with the planet the great advice to 'always look on the bright side of life'. Here are some of the lyrics from that song, which I think sum it up:

> I mean, what have you got to lose?
> You know, you come from nothing
> You're going back to nothing
> What have you lost? Nothing
> Always look on the right side of life
> Nothing will come from nothing, ya know what they say
> Cheer up ya old bugga c'mon give us a grin (Always look on the right side of life)
> There ya are, see
> It's the end of the film.

When you have the discipline and the attitude, the next part of future focus is putting it into practice—by dealing with other humans. For this part, you need more schooling, and it's learning emotional literacy.

LEARNING EMOTIONAL LITERACY

We're born. We go to school. We mature physically and sexually. We leave school. We go to work or university. And we think we've reached emotional maturation. Despite that we haven't learnt some of the fundamental skills of emotional control, and emotional channelling. And maybe never will.

In his book **The School of Life—An Emotional Education**, Alain De Botton[17] explains that:

> We aren't ever done with the odd business of becoming that most extraordinary and prized of things, an emotionally mature person—or, to put it a simpler way, an almost grown-up adult. In an ideal society, it would be not only children who were known to need an education. All adults would recognise that they inevitably required continuing education of an emotional kind and would remain active followers of a psychological curriculum.

Firstly, though—what is an emotional education, or emotional maturity? An emotional education is one where we can put a name to the emotion we're experiencing. And we're self-aware enough at the time to do that. An emotional education is about being able to read the emotional states of other humans, and know what impact you're having on them, and why. It's about understanding that our moods matter, and that we (leaders especially) impact the emotional state of their team, just by the way we show up.

The universe is a mirror, and it reflects back to us what we put out there into the world. If you find yourself surrounded by people that are not always in a great emotional state, be brave enough to ask yourself the question of what contribution you've made to that. An emotional maturity will give you the confidence to know that other people's emotional states are not your responsibility, in general terms. But it's the confidence to know that if you're leading them, it's in your best interests to help them feel happier, rather than sadder, when they're at work. And that might take effort. To understand others, and to understand yourself.

Emotional maturity is understanding what your triggers are, and why you can't keep your emotions in check at times. We all have emotional triggers, and the emotional part of our brain fires within a second when triggers show up. Be prepared for triggers, and you'll be able to use your smart brain to respond, rather than react. You'll start to create conscious control.

Here are three things you can start doing right now to begin learning at emotional maturity school.

ONE REFLECTION.

As opposed to rumination. Reflection is about unpacking what happened (generally in a pressure situation), and what you can learn from it. It's a positive process that helps you to reframe a situation, and know that when faced with it again, you'll act in a more emotionally mature way. When we lose our emotional control, we can spend days (yes, days) ruminating on what happened, and why. We spiral negatively out of control, and it can make the situation worse. Or make it appear worse than it was or is. Reflection is a short process, that helps your subconscious mind to be prepared to do better in the future.

TWO INTROSPECTION.

The beautiful skill of going beyond reflection. Instead of just trying to understand how to behave differently into the future, introspection is about understanding how and why you process information in the world in the way you do. What are your belief systems? What are your values? Why do you do what you do, and what are your habits or patterns? What do you believe is acceptable, and what isn't? And why? These are big questions that most people never really consider.

THREE EXTROSPECTION.

The equally beautiful skill of not only understanding yourself, but also understanding others. Why do people do what they do? What must they believe to behave in that way? This is next level, and it takes that amazing skill of being able to read others while engaging with them at a deeper level.

With some reflection, some introspection, and some extrospection on a regular basis, you're back in school—the school of emotional control and emotional channelling. I say channelling very specifically, as emotional maturity is not about emotional suppression; it's about emotional direction.

Regardless of your emotional state, the goal always is to 'leave people better than you found them' (my purpose on planet Earth). If you use your emotional state to help, not harm, and to heal, not hurt, you're on a winner.

But working towards the future you're focused on isn't just about what you do for other people. It's about what they do for you, which is just as important. You can't make it on your own—you need to be ready to lean into help, even before you need it.

GETTING HELP BEFORE YOU NEED IT

I visited sunny Perth recently to speak at the *AusIMM Minesafe International Conference* and share some leadership insights with the mining community.

But there was one insight I didn't share in my talks, that I think is one of the most important of all: as leaders, especially in mining, we have to reach out and get help before we need it.

Let's rewind a little.

My mining career started at the ripe young age of 21. I was a young tradie who had just been released from a burns unit after more than a month of healing from a BOOM incident. I remember being in hospital and making the decision that I wouldn't be working as an electrician for any longer than I absolutely had to. That meant I needed to find something else to do with my career, and fast!

Within a year of starting work in the little mining town called Pannawonica in 1994, I heard about this thing called mines rescue. I was in. Probably for the wrong reasons at first, as I thought it might be a new career. But then, the enormity of the work dawned on me. And, not long after completing what felt like a decade (about two months) of training, I ended up as the captain of the mines rescue team on C Shift.

I was confident, but careful. I was focused, and fearful. I was alert, but anxious. I was the first port of call (with my team) for any incident that occurred on that mine site. A big role, with heaps of responsibility. There are so many roles on mine sites that can take their toll on people, and this is one of them. I was lucky, though...

I can still remember the two 190-tonne haul trucks crashing into each other, causing serious injury. The grinder that carved a path through Dave Partington's thumb. The head injury in the workshop after a fainting episode due to a fear of blood. The vehicle roll-over, that left two people badly hurt. And strangely enough I can still remember the insect in Ken McQueen's ear one night shift that we couldn't get out (that was a funny one). There were many more.

And knowing about psychology now, I know that these images (aka, episodic memories) get lodged in your hippocampus, neocortex, and amygdala. They start in your occipital lobe, and then get stored for later recollection. That is, whether or not you want to recall them.

My time in mining taught me that the terrible things you see (and feel) in life don't go away. They stay with you. And since that time, I've really understood how PTSD occurs. I get it. Big time. There must be a point when there are too many images and memories in there. And it gets too much.

And that would be the same for leaders, not just mines rescue team leaders. Mining can be pressure packed. I'm lucky that I had people around me to help. The secret for me, was to reach out and to debrief quickly after the incidents. To be open and honest about what I felt, which despite my youth, I actually was able to unpack.

Until (and sorry, don't read on if you're squeamish) the day I was playing football with Mick Fursman, when his foot turned around and was left facing the wrong way. Horrible. In that moment (and sorry Mick) I said, 'sorry mate, you're on your own,' and I had to walk away. I resigned from mines rescue straight away, and never attended another incident. To this day, blood and gore I can handle, but body parts out of place...that's really not OK.

I wonder if I really did reach out enough prior to that incident, or if it was fate. Who knows. But as a leadership coach, my advice is to reach out for support before you need to, and don't let one incident stop you from reaching the future you're focused on.

LEAN INTO MEN'S HEALTH

Recently, I was lucky enough to share some of my insights into men's mental health at a men's circle event at Agnes Water. The issue of men's mental health is a major issue in Australia: a LOT of men die by suicide each year in this country. And we need to do something about it.

I shared my experience of having a serious workplace incident, and the impacts that experience had on my life. The good, the bad and the ugly. I shared what 100 days of anxiety looked like for me, and how hard that process was. From the seeing a doctor for a script, and not getting it filled, to talking myself through the process.

Recently, and maybe since I've turned 50, I've started to feel compelled to share more of my experiences and challenges, in the hope that others might just learn something from my story. Although, in general terms, I've been very blessed in my life, there have been one or two little hurdles along the way that have been very difficult to deal with. And without my supportive wife and kids, the stories might have been different.

With 44% of Australians being diagnosed with a mental health condition in their lifetime, it's important to lean into men's mental health and make it OK for men to open up to others—not just so you're equipped to keep on tracking toward your future, but for resilience throughout your whole life.

But I don't think men have trouble sharing their feelings. What I think the problem is, is that other men aren't good listeners, and they don't hold the space. They try to fix stuff up. That's not supportive.

Here are some things that I would share with men everywhere to help them reach out when they need to.

ONE BE VULNERABLE.

When I talk to groups about any topics, including mental health, I try to provide practical advice and tips that can be implemented straight away.

Topics like being vulnerable are very broad topics. And most people can describe what it means to share your inner struggles with another human—even if it means that they know deep personal stuff about you—but it's harder to actually practice it.

Vulnerability takes a whole lot of courage for men. This is about exposing your underbelly and giving people information about you that they could share or 'use against you' in the future. Which is what one man in the men's circle said was his biggest issue with sharing personal information.

LEADER ACTION

The action, or the process, of being vulnerable always starts with words like 'I am feeling', 'I feel like', 'I am experiencing', 'I am hurting', or...'I need someone to talk to.'

TWO BE EMPATHETIC.

Vulnerability is for the person speaking, whereas empathy is for the person listening. Listening with care factor.

Empathy is about stepping into the same emotional experience that the other person is having. Which is very achievable for any man, if they're willing to make the effort. There are times when empathy starts at sympathy, which is a natural response, and in those cases, it's easier to feel what someone else is feeling.

There are times though, when you need to come to empathy from apathy (low care factor) because their challenges don't seem big enough. That's where the real effort comes in. And that's OK.

LEADER ACTION

The action, or the process, of being vulnerable always starts with words like 'thanks for trusting me', 'thanks for sharing', 'congrats for being courageous', or 'I'm here for you.'

THREE BE PRESENT.

To me, this is the most important skill set, when it comes to supporting someone who's struggling. Being present means being in the conversation. It means holding the space (thanks, **Brene Brown**).[7] And it means keeping your mind focused on not only the words being said, but also the message behind them.

Being present is a little like leadership listening, when you're listening to understand, not to respond. And yes, if you think back to empathy, it's nearly impossible to be empathetic if you're not present.

Presence can mean not even talking at times. It can be just sitting with someone who's hurting. It can be about just being there. If the person has things to share, it's about lingering in the conversation. Not changing the topic, not deflecting. Being available.

LEADER ACTION

The action, or the process, of being present is simply about 'tell me more', 'talk me through it', 'what I'm hearing is...'

Every man has a story. And at some stage, they'll need someone to listen to it. If you ever need to share your story, find someone you trust, and be vulnerable. If anyone ever needs to share their story with you, be empathetic and be present. Our futures depend on other people.

ACTIVITY 1.1
START WITH A FUTURE FOCUS

Take some time now to think about what you've learnt in the last chapter.

The series of questions on the following pages will encourage you to think about who you want to be or become, and to apply the lessons you've just learnt in developing a future focus to the process of upgrading your leadership mindset.

I encourage you to answer the questions, but if you find this activity doesn't work for you, consider journalling. It's also a valuable use of time just to sit and write about your values, your goals, and any challenges you need to tackle in your leadership role.

Who do you want to be or become?

Are you prepared to be 'comfortable with discomfort' through the process of working towards who you want to be as a leader?

In what ways could you make upgrading your leadership mindset a priority?

What are your primary values? Do they align with the values of your organisation?

How do you think your leadership makes your team feel? Can you think of ways to improve this?

List some good character traits or behaviours in your team members that you value. Can you think of ways you could show your team that you value them?

Do you leave people 'better than you found them'? If not, can you think of ways to improve this?

Can you think of ways to become more vulnerable, more empathetic, and more present in your leadership?

SKILL II

DEVELOP A POSITIVE PERSPECTIVE

Is the World Really Going to Implode? Or Could You Put Things into Perspective?

Could you put things into perspective, and understand that this pain or situation is temporary? And that emotional control is more important than blowing this situation out of proportion?

Leadership is so lonely at times. You feel like you've shattered a mirror, been cursed by a black cat, or walked under a ladder. Every day. Forever. And it never stops. Right?

Leadership pressure comes in so many forms. From so many directions. How we respond (or react) to that pressure is often about the perspective we've chosen to take.

Perspective taking is not a new topic. Around 500 BC, the Greek Philosopher Heraclitus talked about the difference between appearance and reality, where nothing ever simply 'is' but is 'becoming' something else.

In 2020, we call that perspective taking. What are we experiencing? Could it be interpreted as something else? Something less stressful, something less dramatic? What could it become if we responded differently?

For some leaders, perspective taking comes easier than for others. Why can some leaders stay calm under fire, and others struggle to keep it together? Is it genetics, or our nature? Or is it our experiences, our nurturing? Nature or nurture? Or both?

I say both.

We know that some people are born more pessimistic than others. And some are more optimistic than others. Regardless of how you look at the glass of water, it either has water in it or it doesn't. Look at a 9 upside down and you'll see a 6.

In a previous life, I was a maintenance superintendent, which meant I was responsible for the maintenance in an industrial plant. I would freak out—literally—when the plant broke down. Every time I got a call about a breakdown, I would turn it into a catastrophe of epic proportions.

After about eighteen months of stressing about keep the plant running, I looked to my manager for coaching and advice. He never seemed to get stressed like I did. One day, he explained that he'd been in the Navy. The aircraft carrier that he was on was bombed, and suffered substantial fatalities and casualties. He shared that plant breakdowns are not life and death events. 'When my life was in danger, I got stressed. Nothing much seems to stress me anymore', he said.

We teach perspective taking in our training and coaching. It's about the three elements of turning the problem around, to look at it differently (1). Then, engaging with others (2), to get their perspective. And then, languaging it differently (3), and reframing the problem or the situation.

The next time you're stressed, try those strategies. Don't thank me now!

HOW'S THAT WORKING OUT FOR YOU?

What a great question. And one that I ask my leadership coaching clients all the time. To work out what they're doing that's not serving them. And to work out why they persist with whatever it is that's not working. Especially if the leader is not getting the results that they want.

And don't worry, I have to ask myself the same question sometimes. I usually don't like the answer. Because although doing the same thing and expecting a different result is the definition of insanity, the human species is persistent. We don't give up easily, and we persist even when it's time to take a different approach.

As you read this, make it personal, and think about a behaviour you'd like to change. Something that you're doing, and doing again, that's not getting the results you desire.

Firstly, why do we persist doing things that don't serve us? There are three reasons:

ONE THE SIMPLEST IS BECAUSE NO ONE EVER CALLS US ON IT.

And we don't call ourselves out on it.

Hominins are habitual creatures. And from a neurological perspective, habits are just neurons that have been wired together to form a behavioural pattern that's easy and consistent. Even when we aren't getting the results we expect. Until we can break the neuronal connections. Literally. For this one—get a confidante.

TWO NEXT, WE HAVE A RANGE OF LIMITING BELIEFS.

We'll continue doing the same thing, because 'it's the way it's done', or 'that's the only way to fix this'…all while we continue to live in hope that something will change. We might even think that it's too hard to change, or that we're not good at the thing we're trying to achieve. For this one—get reflective.

THREE BECAUSE THERE'S SOME SORT OF REWARD OR INTRINSIC BENEFIT FROM THE BEHAVIOUR.

As much as we don't want to admit it, there is an upside to every behaviour pattern. Even if it's just a time saver or if it gives us something to complain about, we don't do things that don't serve us in at least some small way. Think addiction. Even addictive behaviour has a pleasure part to it. We're motivated towards pleasure and away from pain (even it if is short term). For this one—get a coach.

SECONDLY, WHAT WILL IT TAKE TO MAKE LASTING CHANGE?

Generally, this question can only be answered with an understanding of your ability to change (knowledge and skills to develop an updated behavioural process) and your willingness to change.

The skills part is an easy one. A leadership coach (or a confidante in your team) can assist with this one. Or do some training. Or just Google it. Skills and knowledge can be learnt. But knowledge is not knowledge without action. You don't know something if you're not applying it.

If someone asks you 'how's that working out for you?' that might be enough for you. Here's a better question to ask if you're not getting the results you want from the behaviour patterns and habits you're running: 'In relation to this issue—are you interested in changing or committed to changing?'

The answer to this question will tell you all you need to know about why you're persisting with a behaviour that isn't supporting you or getting you the results that you're chasing. And it can change not only the behaviour, but the perspective you take from then on—a more positive one.

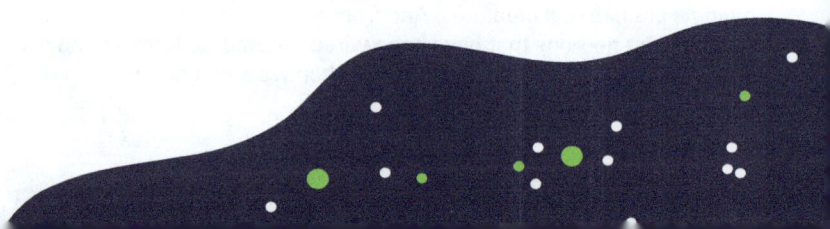

HOW I GOT OUT OF MY DEPTH TOO QUICKLY

BOOM!

You're a leader, and you've just had a catastrophe. The economy has blown up. The plant has blown up. Your life has blown up. What do you do?

Here are the three most common responses from leaders whose existence has gone BOOM at some stage. And a fourth one, where humans are the key concern.

ONE THE FREEZE-AND-FREAK-OUT RESPONSE.

Yes, an extra F word in there (and it's not fight). Some leaders are like the proverbial deer in the headlights. In Australia, it's like driving down that outback country road at sunset and a large kangaroo is sitting in the middle of the road and hasn't got a clue that the lump of metal coming towards isn't a light of truth, but a kangaroo-killing machine. But it freezes anyway, not knowing what to do. There's a fear response too, especially as the car gets closer. But it still can't move—it's frozen in place.

Its stress response keeps it glued to the spot. To its detriment, usually. For humans, when the BOOM is too much, we don't know which way to turn, and what action to take. So, we do what the kangaroo does.

Until someone drags us into a meeting, or needs our support, or needs something else from us. Basically we freeze, until a human shows up, and the human is a reason to get into action.

LEADER ACTION

Pull yourself out of the freeze- or freak-out response, take the lead, step into the BOOM situation, and work through it. With the help of others. And to help others. Because humans are the key concern. Always.

TWO THE FIGHT-AND-FEND-OFF RESPONSE.

Yes, another extra F word in there (and it's not flight). Some leaders get aggressive at the first sign of pressure. They go on the attack. As well as getting aggressive, they can tend to get abrupt and abusive.

They act like what Australians call a bungarra lizard (a 2-metre long prehistoric sand lizard). If you've ever lived in the bush, you get warned about bungarras. Never corner a bungarra, is the warning. Because if you do, they only know one way out, and that's to run straight up and over you. And they need their sharp claws to climb, and apparently—so the warning goes (not sure how true it is, but I don't want to try it)—they climb well. And fast. Straight up your body.

A bit like what some leaders do, under pressure.

Until someone has the courage to call them on their behaviour, and gets them to check themselves, and their response to the BOOM.

LEADER ACTION

Understand that the humans around you are feeling the pressure too, and that they need to be supported and cared for. Create a safe space, and become more compassionate and empathetic. Because humans are the key concern. Always.

THREE THE FLIGHT-AND-!@#K-OFF RESPONSE.

Yes, another extra F word in there (and it's a bit naughty—but every book I pick up these days has it on the cover, so it must be OK). Some leaders become invisible when the pressure is on.

They seem to disappear into the night and reappear when the BOOM is over, or the work is done. A good strategy for their own self-preservation, but not great for their team, who need them more in those moments than most others.

These leaders are a little bit like the Australian wild horses. Who can sleep standing up. This is an evolutionary thing, and like a human flight response, a horse can go from sleeping to galloping in no time flat. Evolutionarily, the horses that could flight (or f-off quickly) survived longer than horses that slept lying down, who were easy prey for carnivores. That strategy is a winner for wild horses, but not great for leaders.

Until someone calls the leader out on their aloofness and asks for support or help, leaders flight off, and for whatever reason, think that's OK. I can remember as a young tradesperson, being alone on a job at night, at the end of shift, with no leadership around, not having a clue what I was doing. It was the leaders that stayed and helped that I respected the most.

FOUR THE CARE AND CONNECT RESPONSE.

Or, as psychologists term it, tend and befriend.

To care and connect is to be a good leader. And a good human. When things go BOOM, you can't do it all on your own. You don't have all the answers. You don't need to. You have a team that know more than you (collectively) in relation to the correct response. They just need to be listened to and heard.

During a BOOM event, care factor is the most important element of any leader response. Leaders who demonstrate care factor keep their emotions in check. They take charge of the situation, and they make sure that their teams have a safe place to work from. They create what is called 'psychological safety', and they create a safe place for others to step up and be part of the response effort.

LEADER ACTION

Take charge, create a safe place for others to offer help, then thank those people for their efforts. Because humans are the key concern. Always.

These responses are the result of your perspective. If you can move towards developing a positive one, you'll be more likely to respond by caring and connecting—which will help to positively influence the person you're responding to, and further improve your own perspective with the positive benefits it brings to both of you.

HOW TO DEVELOP YOUR RELATIONSHIP WITH FAILURE

During 2002, I was in charge of the maintenance of an industrial plant that was part of a smelter in New South Wales. It was 3 p.m. on a Friday afternoon. I'd done some calculations to determine how much bolt tension should be applied to the bolts in the pipework of a critical part of the plant.

So, when one of the team was tightening up the bolt and asked if I was sure that he should tighten it to what I had calculated, I said very confidently, of course. The problem was that I'm not a mechanical engineer. I had an electrical background, so I wasn't really the right person to be doing those calculations in the first place.

When the fitter tightened the bolt (based on my incorrect calculations), it cracked the cast iron pipework. Which meant that the plant couldn't go back into service. The pipework was an odd shape, and it couldn't be weld-repaired. It had to be rebuilt from scratch. Which would take between 24 and 48 hours, due to the manufacturing process required.

In short, the plant was then out of service for the time that it took to obtain a new section of pipe, to repair the damaged one. The material cost of that mistake was hundreds of thousands, if not millions, in lost production. Not a small loss for that business. And not a small failure on my part.

To this day, that decision rates as probably my worst failure in the workplace. The most expensive, at least. And probably the most embarrassing. Because if someone better qualified than me had have done the calculations, they would have allowed for the stress point in the pipework, where there was a spacer (it wasn't flat pipe on pipe, that the bolt was doing up).

And you know the old saying that you don't get remembered for the good things you do, only the one failure? That's what happened in this case. It was tough. In the end, it happened, and I was up all night (which was common at that workplace) working with the supplier to get the pipe rebuilt.

After plenty of thinking and feeling bad about that incident, here's what I learnt about dealing with failure, and how your response to it can shape a more positive perspective into the future.

ONE RESIST RUMINATION.

Rumination, as opposed to reflection, is overthinking what happened. Going over it in your head with a negative perspective on the incident. Talking yourself down and giving yourself a hard time about how silly you were, and how badly you performed. And how badly others are going to think of you. Rumination is negative self-talk, and it keeps you stuck in the past.

Reflection, on the other hand, is more of a positive review of what happened. With a forward focus. Develop the mindset that failure is OK, it's part of life, and it happens. If you're out there trying new things, that is. Reflection is about knowing that you are OK as a human. Knowing that your intent was right, and you didn't mean for this situation to occur. It's about being gentle on yourself and knowing that you'll find a way (with a future focus) to prevent this same thing from happening again. Reflection helps you learn about what went wrong, and why.

In my experience, this is the toughest thing to do. To change your thinking from how bad the situation is, to what you could learn. Reframing is a skill that can help here. It took me months to feel better about the pipework failure. When I got the lesson, though, which was that I should have gotten some support with the technical decisions I was making, I felt better.

From a psychological perspective, reflection is the key skill that will let your subconscious mind know that you're ready to deal with a similar situation in the future. Subconsciously, you'll have a level of fear or anxiety about the situation, and that fear can destroy your confidence. Because your subconscious will keep you from being in a similar situation, because you aren't ready to deal with it. Until you get the learning from the failure, that is!

The questions you should be asking yourself to help you reflect should be around what you can learn from the situation.

TWO OVERT OWNERSHIP.

Dealing with failure is about taking ownership for what happened. Overt ownership is not simply reporting the failure or sharing it with your leader. It's about completely and openly owning it.

By doing what it takes to make the situation right. If it can be made right.

This is the one that I see too often as a coach. People going to their leaders thinking they've taken ownership by admitting or 'owning up to' a failure or a mistake. This is completely not overt ownership. To me, this is covert ownership. That is, thinking you're taking ownership, but really you're just handing the issue over to someone else. Uncool.

Overt ownership means doing everything in your power to remedy the situation. Fixing the issue. Addressing what happened. Not giving it to someone else to fix.

The upshot of overt ownership is that you feel way better about the situation because you're getting into action. And you go to your leader with the action plan, not the failure or the mistake. It makes for a different discussion. A discussion with a more positive spin. I went on the journey with the manufacturer and worked day and night (literally) to make sure that the pipework was repaired as soon as it could be.

The questions you should be asking yourself to help you take overt ownership are around what you can do to address the situation, and to repair any issues that have been created.

THREE FUTURE FOCUS.

Having a future focus is really the outcome of resisting rumination and overtly owning your part in the failure or the issue. Having a future focus is about focusing on what you're going to do differently moving forward, and into the future.

From what you've learnt, and from what you've done to rectify the situation, it's then a matter of where to from here. What are you going to change in your behaviour or your decision making that will ensure that you don't let the same thing happen again?

Having a future focus starts right now. In this very instant. Get into action. Being on purpose. And knowing that into the future you won't make the same mistake because you've changed your thinking or your processes to set yourself up for success.

For me, this was a matter of ensuring that I put processes in place to get the technical support I needed, when I needed it. The questions you should be asking yourself to support a future focus are around what needs to be put in place to prevent recurrence of the issue.

So, how do you develop your relationship with failure? Learn from the situation, do what it takes to rectify it in the moment, and think about what you need to do to prevent the same thing from occurring into the future.

Failure is normal. It doesn't define you. And a positive perspective of it can bring the learning you need to change your future for the better.

HOW TO RETAIN YOUR TOP TALENT

2020 was the year of lockdowns and working from home. 2021 was the year of the great resignation. 2022 was the year of quiet quitting. 2023 was the year of moonlighting (or even career cushioning), or supplementing your income from another source. None of these options are good for your business, or your productivity.

But what can you do to be proactive, and to ensure that your top talent stays on? And stays because they want to—not because they have to, to take a pay cheque—but because you give them a good reason to?

It's all about perspective. If you want to retain your top talent in the 2020s, here are some top tips.

ONE EMBRACE FLEXIBILITY.

Remember again for a moment that it's the 2020s. Old-school organisations and old-school leaders are not going to be successful anymore. Even though 89% of organisations are following Elon Musk's lead and adopting a voluntary separation process (Credit: Spiceworks.com), or voluntary redundancy, as you might know it, the underlying issue is that it's not the under-performers who are leaving, it's the top talent.

Because they can get a better deal elsewhere (rightly or wrongly). Because their expectations have increased (which is OK). Because their leaders aren't adapting and developing a 2020s workplace (which is absolutely happening right now).

I feel like the next 2–3 years will see the landscape of working arrangements settle down and go back to the pre-pandemic office-based practices. Or organisations will shift their thinking to a post-pandemic mindset. One or the other will become the norm, but for the moment, flexibility is key, if you want to retain top talent. If your top talent wants to work from home for some of their working hours, or they want to work different hours, or they want to work compressed hours, have the conversation, and listen to why these are important to your team members. These changes may not all be practical, but they should at least be heard, and considered.

TWO TEAM MEMBERS DON'T LEAVE ORGANISATIONS. THEY LEAVE LEADERS.

Sadly, leadership growth has not moved at the same trajectory as employee flexibility has. Or articles like this would not be a thing.

Some senior leaders are inspired by layoff programs and processes, like the way it was done at Twitter. Cut the dead wood and move on. And this is completely necessary at times, but at the same time, the more poorly handled the layoff process is, the more difficult it is for top talent to feel confident that they're not going to be next in the firing line.

Remember that other global organisations have undertaken mass layoffs, but they haven't been as public. Why? Because they were done in a more people-centred way. And that is too boring to make the news. The more professional the process, the less fanfare.

I feel like leaders are still reeling from the past 2–3 years. I know that they should have embraced and moved on, but the pandemic was such a disruptive force that leaders feel like it should be done and dusted now, and that things should go back to how they were. When they probably never will. Leaders that are unwilling to listen, that aren't embracing psychological safety, that aren't leaning into people over production, will retain their positions. But they won't retain their top talent.

THREE CARE FACTOR.

Teambuilding.com recently listed the top eleven things that organisations can do to address the challenge of quiet quitting.

I feel like this is the best list of things leaders can do, although a list of eleven could be seen as long and arduous. I will list the ten things below, but if you like my summarised version of them, it'll increase your care factor, and help you think about what team members need to feel engaged at work. What they need to feel cared for. What they need to feel valued at work.

If you're a leader, and you feel like your team is quietly quitting, try to keep increases in workload short-term. Properly compensate and remunerate your team members. Make stepping up optional, and be upfront about future role growth. Lean into employee recognition strategies, and at the same time, try to monitor mood and behaviour changes. Encourage breaks, and support employee wellbeing. Build rapport and relationships, while maintaining boundaries to promote a work life balance.

Whatever you call it, the great resignation or quiet quitting, if your top talent is leaving, it's time to intervene. Changing to a more positive perspective with flexibility and care factor will change theirs, too.

FALSE EXPECTATIONS APPEARING REAL

Crapola perspectives lead to crapola feelings, and to crapola behaviour.

Recently, I had an experience that scared the crapola out of me. And there was no real need to experience that fear (aka: false expectations appearing real). I thought my life was in danger, literally.

Here's what happened, and why it's so relevant for us in business, and life.

This year, I'm climbing Mount Larcom as many times as possible. Aiming for fifty, but may not quite make that. I'm working hard on it. I'm up to twelve for the year. It's a 3.3-kilometre climb, and it's far from easy. It takes around 1.15 hours to get up and a little less to come down. And due to my other commitments, I generally start climbing at crazy o'clock. Most starts are between 3 a.m. and 4 a.m.

Recently, I was walking along the trail, and it was pitch black, other than my head lamp. And apart from the toads croaking and the leaves rustling, there wasn't a lot of noise or action. Until, suddenly, and unexpectedly, I looked up and saw a human in front of me. Sitting on a rock, on his phone. No head lamp, pitch black, just sitting there. Scared the heck out of me.

'I don't see people here at this time of the day,' he said. I replied, 'me either.' As I kept walking. Nearly running by this stage.

Just imagine. Pitch black. Out in the middle of the bush, half an hour out of town. And only two of us on the mountain. One of those humans now walking like he was being chased. Which I wasn't. But your mind goes all over the place, seriously. I was wondering where he would bury my body. Every noise I heard, I thought it was him coming up behind me. I kept stopping to look back, straining my eyes to see if I could see him coming. I remembered the stories about backpackers being murdered and tried to remember what the survivors did to get away from their attackers.

I was seriously next-level freaking out. It was a fear I have not experienced probably ever.

And then, when I was coming back down the mountain, I saw this card that was left on a pile of rocks that said, 'You are saved.' I doubled down on the fear levels. I was saved—from what? Being dumped on a mountain, never to be found or heard from again?

And you know what? All I could think of was that I might have even turned about and not gone up the mountain that day if I saw that person earlier.

But here's the thing. I know that the person I saw was just doing his thing. He wasn't there to harm me, or anyone else. He probably didn't even leave that card on the rocks. And when I got home and told my family I was lucky to be alive, and showed them the photo, it turns out the card said, 'You are loved.'

I worked myself into a dither that morning. I was so scared. And all that fear was totally unjustified. There was nothing to fear. It was my imagination. False expectations appearing real. And to think that I might have turned back just because there was another human there early in the morning.

I've thought about this story a lot since it happened. And wondered how much I (we) have let fear stop us acting. How many times have we turned around instead of tackling a challenge head on? How many times have we focused on what might go wrong instead of what might go right? How many times have we created expectations that were imagined?

Too many, would be my answer to the questions above.

And the message is to turn Fears into Pears—positive expectations appearing real. Imagine how good it'll be to get to the top of your next mountain climb! And how much better that will feel?

HOW TO ELEVATE YOUR LMX

The quality of a leader will be determined by the quality of the exchanges that they have with their team members (also known as Leader Member Exchange, or LMX). And this is heavily influenced by perspectives on both sides of the exchange..

LMX as a theory has been researched widely since 1975, but if you haven't heard of it, you're not alone. If that's the case, this bit's for you.

When I say elevate your LMX, what I mean is to increase the quality of the communication and connection that you have with all team members. Not just those who you trust the most, or who you rely on the most.

Let me give you the short version first. LMX is about a reciprocal exchange between leader and team member. Reciprocal being the operative word—meaning here, a two-way exchange, that's about an elevated level of dialogue. Honest. Open. Candid. A two-way dialogue based on a degree of mutual trust, loyalty, support, respect, and obligation. The concept was developed by Fred Dansereau, George Graen, and William Haga.

What is also important about LMX is simply that higher quality LMX leads to a growth- and development-focused relationship (for the team member), and lower LMX is associated with less team member growth (and subsequent growth opportunities). Higher LMXs result in career conversations. They result in idea generation sessions. They result in candid (reciprocal) feedback sessions. They result in a more developed relationship.

Please read this paragraph carefully, as this is the most important, and probably the most honest, element of LMX theory. It says that leaders have a subconscious rating process, where they (we) make a subliminal judgement call about each and every team member.

Team members (unknowingly, and unwittingly) end up in the 'in-group' or the 'out-group'. And yes, leaders (we again) treat these two groups of team members differently. Yes, we are only human, but it's good to know how this works, and what you can do to make sure you're more conscious with your leadership, and that you take an LMX approach to your conversations. With a positive perspective, and not just writing team members in or out.

Here are the three parts of LMX explained.

ONE ROLE TAKING.

No matter how much you read about LMX, there's never much written about this part of the process. The line is generally 'this takes place when a new member joins a team, and their abilities are initially assessed by the leader.' And I get that it's a simple process, but there must be more to it than just that one line.

I think about the Tuckman model, where teams go through forming, storming, norming, and then performing. And every time someone joins a team, the team will go back into forming stage, regardless of the characteristics of the new team member. Some team members fit in, and some don't. Right? So, the storming stage might be longer or shorter, based on the team member. And potentially how well the new team member gets on with the leader.

Yes, a leader does make an initial assessment, but if you're reading this, remember that leaders do change their minds. It's not all bad news if you get put in the out-group from the outset (that's my take on it, at least).

TWO ROLE MAKING.

Role making is what happens after leaders categorise their team members.

Team members who are subconsciously added to the in-group are trusted more. They're given more growth opportunities. In short, these team members experience a better relationship—and, dare I say it—treatment from their leader. Conversely, team members who are subconsciously added to the out-group are not communicated with as openly or honestly as their in-group counterparts.

If you're a team member, here's how to tell if you're in the in-group or the out-group. And this comes straight from the mouth of a CEO who I have a lot of respect for. Their take on it was simply: my in-group get their messages responded to quickly. And in their preferred format. The out-group have to wait longer, and they might get an email when they prefer texting, as an example.

Oh, and if you're in the in-group, you'll most likely be provided with privileges and perks that the out-group isn't. And you'll have more of a voice during decision making. In-group team members are heard more than out-group team members.

Again, this is not all bad, because the goal of the out-group team members should be to get to the in-group. By doing good work, and by becoming a valued team member. And needless to say, it's incumbent upon leaders to be self-aware enough to understand who's in their out-group, and work on developing more trust in those team members. Remember, as much as you think you're hiding your feelings about in- and out-group team members, they already know what group they're in.

THREE ROUTINE SHAPING.

The issue with in- and out-groups is that, in LMX theory, in-groups get more in, and out-groups get more out. It's a self-fulfilling prophecy, as team members respond to the way they're treated, and generally respond in kind. For leaders, this is a challenge, as leaders need to be willing to open their mind and increase the trust that they have in the out-group team members. The issue is that the in-group treatment or the out-group treatment becomes routine for the leader. It becomes habitual. And that is scary.

Because habits are heuristics. They are the path of least resistance, and they are hard to break. Breaking bad habits takes effort, and willingness.

If you're a leader reading this, hang onto your hat, because here's something that you can do. It comes under routine shaping (although it is the positive spin on this part of LMX theory).

Leaders—and we train this regularly—need to use a routine to lean into systems leadership. Systems leadership is about creating habits, not being slave to them. It's about using your calendar and your schedule to create systems that hold you accountable to elevate the way you interact with the out-group team members.

Schedule one-on-ones. Schedule career conversations. Schedule walk-around time. Schedule important conversations, so that every one of your team members knows how important they are. In team meetings, schedule time for each team member to contribute. To have a say. To have an input. When it comes to routine shaping, create routines that serve you, not that sabotage you. Schedule it, and then be present.

Then, ask bigger questions. And trust your team members to do their best work. Including providing the growth opportunities for them to do that.

Approach each person with a positive perspective, and elevate your LMX.

WHAT WE CAN LEARN FROM THE BIGGEST PLANT ON EARTH

There's one plant on Earth that doesn't have a stem. It doesn't have any roots, and doesn't have any flowers. It only opens for six whole days, at the end of its 13-month gestation period. It's a plant that we can learn a lot from.

I did a video on this same topic this week, but I felt like I needed to further explain what we can learn from the Rafflesia plant in this section. Why? Because I got to see the Rafflesia plant, in full bloom. Which is extremely lucky, and rare, because of its short blooming period.

It was such an amazing experience that I couldn't stop thinking about it.

Here's what I think the Rafflesia can teach us about perspective.

ONE THIS PLANT STARTS WITH NOTHING.

The Rafflesia plant starts from basically nothing. It's a pod. Thirteen months before it blooms, from nothing, it starts growing. It continues growing, until it's ready to bloom. And bloom it does. It blooms with the biggest leaves on planet Earth. Then, it dies.

It's a truly amazing plant. Amazing to see. I consider it a privilege to have been lucky enough to see it. If you ever need inspiration to achieve something great in your life, think of the Rafflesia plant. It starts with nothing, but becomes the biggest flowering plant on the planet. If you need confidence, start where you are now. Start, even if you're just a pod. Start, even if you don't have enough resources. Even if you don't have everything you think you need.

Just start. And see what you can achieve in the next thirteen months.

TWO DO WHAT IT TAKES.

Question—is thirteen months a long time? It's the whole life of a Rafflesia. The Rafflesia works hard to get ready to bloom. It'll do what it takes to open its massive leaves, which are at least six feet across (in my estimation).

Here's the thing. In the life of a business owner, thirteen months is not really a long time. Or is it? Here's my experience...

I grossly overestimated what I could achieve in twenty years in business. And I grossly underestimated what I could achieve in thirteen months. t\ Thirteen months is over a year. A year. You can achieve so much in a year.

And you know what? I've never gone hard for thirteen months. At least not as hard as I should have. I've never gone as hard as the Rafflesia and committed everything to a cause. Until now. Watch this space.

THREE BE THE BIGGEST AND THE BEST.

This was the amazing thing about the Rafflesia. You have to be lucky to actually see it in bloom. It's the biggest plant on earth, and it has the most vivid flower colour—red, with white spots. Not only does it grow, but it also grows into something everyone wants to see.

And a fun fact is that the Malaysian family that own the land that contains the Rafflesia plants charges an admission fee for every person to go in and see it. For the six days that the plant is in bloom there. They put a sign up out the front, and people stop. People fall over themselves to get to see this plant in bloom. I would have paid twice as much as they charged.

The message is to be the person that everyone else wants to see. The business that everyone else wants to work with. The content creator that people want to read or watch. The person with the contagiously positive perspective that makes big things happen.

Yes, you can become that. In thirteen months.

WHAT I LEARNT FROM WRITING 100 PIECES OF CONTENT THIS YEAR

I used to suck at writing content. I used to suck at being consistent with it. And I used to suck at being confident to put things out there into the content-verse. Because it's hard to do all of those three things for a long period of time.

This year, my focus was on written content, and the team's content strategy has been built around a Wednesday blog and LinkedIn post, and a Friday LinkedIn newsletter. Recently (because we number them in our filing structure), we hit the 100 mark for written content pieces. We might have missed one or two during the year, but in general terms, we were pretty consistent the whole time.

The process is: I write it, the team posts it. A team effort. There were days though (like today—when I'm hungover and writing this at 6 a.m. on December 23), when the absolute last thing I feel like doing is writing a newsletter story. But then I get started, and I get into it because I love the process of putting thoughts on pages.

Here's what the commitment taught me about the importance of keeping a positive perspective.

ONE WITHOUT A SCHEDULE, NOTHING HAPPENS.

This is the biggest thing for me this year, and it works in every area of my life. My calendar is king. I can safely say that if it's not in my calendar, it won't get done. Period.

Every week, on Tuesday, there is a calendar reminder to write content for

Wednesday (and on Wednesday, in case I miss it on Tuesday—double whammy). Same same on Thursday for Friday.

We also have a content calendar, that has all of the content ideas in it. So, with the calendar, combined with the content headings, the writing gets done. The thinking decreases significantly, and there's no such thing as writer's block.

And I know this one isn't that sexy, and it's not ground-breaking, but sometimes things don't need to be earth shattering to be the tip you need to get into and stay in action. There have been many times, when I see that in my calendar not done, and I get it done last minute. It gets done, though.

TWO NOT EVERYONE READS YOUR STUFF.

Not everyone reads your content, and that's OK.

Of the 13k-ish followers that I have on LinkedIn, each of my written pieces gets between about 400 and 1,000 views on average. Earlier in the year, the Friday newsletters were regularly over 1,000 views, but then LinkedIn changed an algorithm, and all of those views instantly halved (even the previous posts halved). Which is cool.

I work with heaps of influencer types, and for them, that's a tragedy. For me, I've always been OK with a little reach, and not a viral reach. Because I write both for readers, and for me. Obviously, I try and put information out into the universe that helps others, but at the same time, I find writing cathartic. I find it something that I can do, to collect my thoughts and ideas. And the content gets repurposed. It's on blogs. On other social media sites. And in my range of books.

The strange part about it is that our business is always growing. And because we don't do any reach-out marketing (we are going to start that soon—I have a business that has never really been marketed), and we keep expanding. When I ask the team what's happening, and what's changing, they always say they think it's because more people are seeing our content.

I'm not sure about that. I feel it's about old-fashioned service, and turning up for our clients each and every time. I haven't missed a client engagement in eighteen years, in sickness or in health. Regardless of what's driving our growth, the one thing I know is that you don't need to go viral to get traction.

THREE YOU MIGHT NEED TO BE CONTROVERSIAL.

If there's one massive lesson that I've learnt this year, this is it. Be controversial, and say what you think.

I've never really been controversial, but I'm confident and comfortable enough now to actually say what I think. I look back over my content, and it's very vanilla. It's nice. It certainly isn't controversial and doesn't talk about the big topics. Not the big ideas, and not the big news. It's positive.

But a positive perspective doesn't necessarily mean writing positive content. Personally, I am now (after all these years) ready to share personal thoughts, beliefs, and opinions. Having a positive perspective helps you to be brave enough to put the ideas out there, because they're worth sharing.

Recently I've been focused on video, more than written content, and that will give me the platform to share more of myself and who I am. Which may get more or less views—who knows what can happen (refer to point two above).

My message to a first-time content creator would be to be real. Don't try to please everyone, don't try to be too professional and too proper. Just say it how it is, and put it out there with the positive intent that it'll do someone good. Don't try to offend people, but if you're controversial, you will say things that aren't popular. Just ask Dr Jordan B Peterson.

ACTIVITY 1.2
DEVELOP A POSITIVE PERSPECTIVE

Take some time now to think about what you've learnt in the last chapter.

Answering the series of questions on the following pages will help you to develop a positive perspective, so you can upgrade your mindset and perform better in your leadership role.

Alternatively, consider journalling. Sitting and writing about your challenges and how you view and deal with them can help to put them all in perspective, so you can move forward more confidently. With a positive perspective, and with a lot less rumination and worry.

What are some things you persist with doing, even though they don't serve you?

What reward or benefit do some of your limiting beliefs give you?

When you're under pressure, what's your primary response (freeze-and-freak-out, fight-and-fend-off, flight-and-!@#k-off, or care and connect)?

If your primary response isn't a good one, can you think of ways you can change to a more adaptive response?

When you fail, what strategies do you use to work through and overcome it? What strategy could work better for you?

In what ways could you be more flexible in accommodating your team members? In what ways could you operate with more care factor?

Can you think of ways you can elevate your LMX (during role taking, role making, and routine shaping)?

What tasks could you schedule to better manage your time?

SKILL III
THINK ABOUT YOUR
THOUGHTS

I WONDER IF, BEFORE WE ALL GOT SUCKED INTO THE SCREENS AND THE SOUND BITES, WE SPENT MORE TIME INTROSPECTING.

Thinking about how we feel, and why. Even if it's just spending time in quiet, and spending time with ourselves.

Introspection is a concept (and skill) that is attributed to Wilhelm Wundt, one of the earliest Psychologists, in the late 1800s. Probably when we weren't as busy, and things weren't as stressful.

As a leader, especially under pressure, introspection is a key skill. It allows you to stop, slow down, and focus. Focus on something else, other than the event or the situation that you're coping with in the moment.

The best way to think in an introspective way is to ask yourself questions. And not questions that start with why. Why me? Why now? Why this? Those questions don't help. What and how questions are best, and they'll help you unpack what you feel. What emotions you are experiencing? And how will you channel those emotions for good? And how will you do that in a responsive way, not in a reactive way?

It's amazing how a moment of introspection can bring calm to your day. And calm to the moment.

Introspection, or versions of it, are the first part of emotional intelligence. Emotional intelligence starts with a self-awareness of your emotional state and putting a name to the emotion. Then, it's a matter of regulating the emotion. Fun fact: there are humans who struggle to name the emotion. They struggle to answer the question 'what are you feeling?' The name for that is alexithymia. Alexithymia is a Greek word, attributed to Freud, and it translates as 'no name for emotions'. Alexithymia can be treated, but that takes time and effort. It's a condition that impacts how people relate to others, and it can be detrimental to relationships for the nearly 10% of the population that are suspected to have it.

In short, when we don't take the time to introspect, and to work through our emotional state and responses, we are in fact taking an alexithymia-based approach to life. We're choosing to ignore what makes us human.

But how do you be introspective? If you asked Siddhartha Gautama (aka: Buddha), you would have been told to be quiet. To meditate. To search for Nirvana from within.

If you asked your leadership coach, I'd coach you to ask yourself questions. To be mindful (what you can see, hear, and touch right now in the moment), and to focus on your thoughts and not the situation. And then to focus on others, and how they're feeling in the moment. Then you can respond to the situation accordingly.

One word of warning here is that introspection can become overthinking (or rumination) if you start to beat yourself up for feeling or acting the way you are. These states are not helpful, and will cause you to feel worse about yourself than better. You'll become reactive, not responsive. Most literature around introspection comes with a warning label: over-introspection can be detrimental. It's like water—the body needs it, but it can drown in it, too. This is the yin and the yang of life!

The more you can introspect, the more you can be in emotional control, behavioural control and situational control. Introspecting helps you to create conscious control—the thing that'll help you to lead better when you're under pressure.

But thinking about your thoughts isn't just introspecting. It's also about going meta, and thinking about how you think in the first place.

How To Use Metacognition To Be A Better Leader

In the 2020s, when I mention the word meta, you could be forgiven for thinking about Facebook and Mark Zuckerberg. During the second half of 2021, CEO and major shareholder, Zuckerberg, announced the name change, to position the former Facebook as a platform that would be part of the metaverse. Aka, 'a composite universe melding online, virtual, and augmented worlds that people can seamlessly traverse' (Credit: New York Times). In short, meta means the next level up.

Instead of thinking Facebook when you think about meta, think studies. If you spend your time (which I am guessing most of you don't) reading research reports and studies, to try and understand what's going on in the world, you'll know there are meta studies. Meta studies are a study of the studies. Researchers will review any number of studies on the same topic and look for similar correlations or causation in the data. That review, and the consequent detail that it produces, is called a meta-study (generally speaking). It's a study of the studies. The next level up.

So, what is metacognition? As a concept, metacognition has been around since 1976 when the term was coined by the American Psychologist John H Flavell. Flavell was interested in the development of children, and he critically analysed the works of the early developmental psychologists like Jean Piaget. Flavell was most intrigued by the theory of mind, which is the ability for children to understand that there are other people in the world that also have feelings and thoughts, just like they do (but different thoughts and feelings to them). This work gave Flavell the insight into how we learn, and how we perform cognitively as adults. And more specifically, how we apply what we've learnt, through cognitive regulation. Metacognition has therefore been described as 'thinking about thinking.' The next level up.

It's probably more specific than that, though. Metacognition is about how you learn and gain knowledge, and then how you apply that knowledge (and if the learning process has been effective).

So, how can leaders use metacognition to think about their thoughts, to influence them, and to take their leadership to the next level?

ONE KNOWLEDGE AS AN ELEMENT OF METACOGNITION.

A lot of the metacognition research work has been focused on students, and classroom settings. Given that leading is about learning though, it's important for leaders to understand how they learn new skills and knowledge. One great report on metacognition that I came across was penned by Emily Lai,[27] who explained that metacognitive knowledge is the knowledge that you have about your cognitive strengths, as well as your cognitive limitations. In other words, what you learn easily and what you don't learn easily. There are three types of metacognitive knowledge: declarative knowledge, procedural knowledge, and conditional knowledge.

Declarative knowledge is what you know about yourself as a learner. What things you learn and remember well, and what things are harder to learn and remember. Like names, or phone numbers, as an example. Or processes, or procedures. Or general knowledge. Or historical dates. A superpower for leaders is to be able to remember things quickly. Understanding how to improve their declarative knowledge will help the leader be better at cognitive processing and information recall. Declarative knowledge is easy to verbalise.

As a leader, how do you learn best? Is it reading, studying, writing, asking questions, listening to an audiobook, watching TED talks, doing classroom training, or something else? And what makes it easier for you

to learn something new?

Procedural knowledge is about having a cognitive understanding of what you do. Procedural knowledge relates to things like riding a pushbike (as a simple example). Which, if you were asked to explain how to do it, would be difficult to verbalise. You just do it. Metacognition challenges you to think about how you do what you do. And what techniques you apply. To think about what rules of thumb (heuristics), or what methods, you apply to your leadership or to certain situations or circumstances. Imagine for a moment trying to explain to someone how you do leadership.

As a leader, how do you do what you do (and why), and how would you explain your thought processes to someone you were coaching?

Conditional knowledge is simply knowledge relating to when, and how, to apply declarative and procedural knowledge to learning. It allows leaders to allocate their cognitive resources to the learning process in a way that makes them more effective at learning (and listening). This is a key element of metacognition, as self-aware leaders know what conditions (internal and external) they learn best in and retain most from.

As a leader, how, when, where, and what do you need to learn to be more effective in your role?

TWO REGULATION AS AN ELEMENT OF METACOGNITION.

The regulation of thinking and learning is about planning what you're going to do, monitoring if you've been effective, and evaluating if you've achieved your overall goals.

Planning is about the identification and selection of the appropriate strategy for the situation or condition. And planning how to learn or work 'in a strategic manner, to achieve a goal or objective' (Credit: Jennifer Livingston).[31] In other words, in a difficult situation, your planning process (and metacognition) will kick in, and you will think through to determine what the best strategy is to apply and what will work best in a situation. And then you can apply the strategy to your learning or your situation.

Planning: As a leader, what strategies do you have available to you, for when you're under stress or duress (internal or external pressure)? You can do some of that thinking in advance!

Deep reflection (after the event) or introspection (during the event, in the moment) is the key leadership and metacognitive skill—and one that should be practiced as much and as regularly as possible. Reflection is a learnt skill, and it's like keeping a mental (or written) journal of your experiences, and why you will or won't take the same approach into the future.

Monitoring: If you do nothing else after reading this section, please think about how you can add reflection to your leadership and life. And you might think you're doing it well already, and that's great. Make sure that it is reflection, though, and not rumination (big difference: one is positive, and one isn't).

Evaluation is about reflection and looking back on the situation with a critical eye and determining if you made the right decision and if you applied the right strategy. This is about asking metacognitive questions, like 'how well did I do'?, and 'what would I do differently next time?' It's the first and most basic part of reflection, but it's more of a high-level review of your outcome. It's somewhat binary, and is about a yes or a no.

Evaluation: As a leader, think about a situation that you've been through, where you've tried to learn something, or you've had to solve a problem. Unpack what went well and what didn't.

That's metacognition, in a nutshell. It's not complex, and it's completely worth the effort to understand and apply it—because thinking about your thoughts is one of the most effective ways to move them into line with what you want to achieve, and who you want to be as a leader.

How To Be A Conscious Leader, And Why

Thinking about your thoughts is one of the best ways to become a conscious leader—which is a good leader.

As a leader coach, I regularly hear the words 'old-school leader' and 'new-age leader'. I coach a mix of both types of leaders, and if I was to describe the difference between the two, it would be that new-age leaders are more connected to other humans. They're more transformational in their approach. And more importantly, they're more emotionally competent. These leaders take a real 'people' approach to leadership.

Old-school leaders tend to be more transactional in their approach. They're more direct, and they tend to be too busy for all that touchy-feely stuff, like dealing with feelings. These leaders are typically more interested in production than people. They can't understand why people can't just chip in and get the work done.

And it's not up to me to tell leaders that they should be one way or the other. My job is to help leaders create psychologically safe and high-performing teams, whatever that process looks like for each individual. It's different for everyone. The one strategy I share with leaders who want to be more new age is to lean into being a conscious leader. Now, for some, this is a big shift, but worth the effort! And it's well explained in the book of the same name, by **John Mackey, Steve McIntosh, and Carter Phipps.**[34]

Be ready for a shift in mindset, though, as this is a leadership style that uses big words like 'love' and 'care factor' and 'virtues' and 'connection'.

One comment in the book relates to one reader's take on conscious leadership, and they noted that:

> **Rarely does a book move me to tears, yet this one did, by holding up a mirror to the kind of leader I most deeply want to be. Conscious leadership is a powerful invitation to shift our mindset from the win/lose games of war to the community-building virtues of love, authenticity, and integrity. It's a book built on the radical idea that business can be a force for bringing more love into the world. Count me in.**

And:

> **Leaders today are called to a faster pace, sharper strategy, and broader responsibilities, but also to greater awareness, humility, and authenticity. Conscious Leadership will help you summon the courage to open your heart, dig deeper, and keep growing as a conscious leader.**

There are three elements of conscious leadership, which both influence your thoughts, and are the product of them. They include:

ONE VISION AND VIRTUE.

Vision and virtue are about having a strong direction and sharing that with your team in a way that they can connect with it. The vision is about purpose, and the virtue piece is about behaviour (the word virtue is defined as behaviour that's based on a high moral compass).

Vision and virtue are broken down into purpose first, lead with love, and always act with integrity. Putting purpose first means doing the work to make sure that your team is clear on their purpose, and that it aligns with your purpose as the leader. And it's about having a bigger purpose, and one that's worth working for.

Leading with love is about putting people first and knowing that humanity is the key concern when it comes to leadership. There's a ripple effect caused by leaders, where leaders' actions ripple out through the team member, to their families, and to society. Leaders have the rare ability to impact a wide range of people through their leadership and love.

Acting with integrity is about doing what's right, and doing what you say you're going to do. Integrity is perhaps the most respected value in leaders, and leaders that fall out of credibility with their teams generally lack integrity.

LEADER ACTION

Challenge yourself to do a self-assessment on how strongly you lead with vision and virtue, and ask yourself if you put love and people first.

TWO MINDSET AND STRATEGY.

Mindset and strategy relate to thinking differently about business. Not doing business to win, but doing business to make a difference. Not treating business as a war to be waged, but as a value to be added. Not as a short-term pursuit, but as an infinite game (**Simon Sinek-esque**)[52] of building long-term relationships. Then, with a mindset like that, putting strategies in place to deliver on the long-term goal of doing leadership to grow businesses and to grow people to add long-term value.

Mindset and strategy are broken down specifically into finding win-win-win solutions, innovating, creating value, and thinking long term. Conscious leadership is about having a positive-sum world view. As Alexander McCobin, CEO of Conscious Capitalism, puts it, 'A positive-sum worldview is a foundational premise of capitalism, where we seek out mutually beneficial exchanges so that we create more value for everyone than existed before the exchange.'

Having a win-win-win approach highlights that there is an onus on leaders to think about the team, the business, and the society in which we all live and operate.

LEADER ACTION

Think about your leadership strategy for a moment, and about how what you do could have a bigger impact on your team and on society. And if you're in business, how your actions are helping others win, too.

THREE PEOPLE AND CULTURE.

People and culture should be the focus for all leaders. All great leaders are supported by great teams, and those great teams don't get great by accident. The leaders of great (high-performing) teams understand how important culture is, and how important it is to have a growth mindset. The growth of team members is a key driver for conscious leaders.

People and culture are further broken down into constantly evolving the team, regularly revitalising, and continuously learning and growing. For me, this is the cornerstone of leadership, and conscious leaders take people and culture to the next level. By fostering a culture of learning and coaching. By making personal and professional growth a priority. Not just talking about it, but ensuring that team members are challenged to develop their technical and relationship skills.

As part of this section, there is a cool take on revitalisation that I love from the book that talks about leaders being able to unplug and power down, and supporting their teams to do the same.

> **For leaders in any field or area of expertise, the power of rest, repose, relaxation, and rejuvenation should never be underestimated. It might seem counterintuitive to suggest that such passive, quiescent activities can be the fount of dynamism and creativity, but that's exactly the point. Indeed, there may be few things that spur productivity more than those behaviours that allow us to empty our mind of prosaic mental clutter.**

LEADER ACTION

Take some time out of your busy schedule to recharge your batteries and help your team to do the same.

As you reflect on the above, think about your thoughts, and how bringing them into line them with the strategies of conscious leadership could help you and your team to grow and develop into a high-performing team.

THE SUBTLE ART OF THINKING FAST AND TALKING SLOW

Most people struggle to think on their feet. Especially leaders. More especially, leaders under pressure. And that's the most important time to be able to practice the fine art of thinking fast and talking slow. But what does that really mean?

Well, it means multitasking your emotionality and your languaging. And this is the only thing on planet Earth that can effectively be classed as multi-tasking (according to Anton Guinea,[55] of **The Guinea Group**). Most psychology texts will tell you that multitasking isn't a thing; it's called task switching. I'm here to tell you that if you can't multitask what's in your heart and head with what comes out of your mouth, you'll struggle to connect with other hominins. Let me explain.

Just reflect for a moment and think about the best communicators that you know. I'm guessing these people don't talk continuously. My theory is that they do very specific things to engage others in dialogue. Their influence is created by doing things like reading the play, listening to understand, and speaking with leader languaging.

Reading the play is about being able to focus on the person you're speaking to, and understanding what's going on for them, while you're having the conversation with them. Good leaders know what the other person's body is doing. Even where their eyes are going (left means they're recalling, and right means they're constructing—Google NLP Eye Patterns, Images, for more information). Reading the play is about being empathetic and feeling what the other person is feeling while you're conversing. Then, tailoring your communication accordingly.

Listening to understand is perhaps the most important of the thinking fast and talking slow skills. When you're listening to understand, you're present. You're caring enough to make the other person your priority in the moment. Regardless of all the stress or pressure that's going on around you. And if you don't understand, ask more questions. Or ask better questions. Don't comment or make a statement until you're clear on what's being communicated to you. Listen more than you speak (use your ears and mouth in the ratio of how many of them you have—2:1) and let silence do the heavy lifting if you need to. You don't have to fill the gap of quiet with words (most people think you do).

Leader languaging is a key skill. Most people don't choose their words carefully. They don't realise that words have power, and talk straight to the limbic system of the brain—the emotional part. Words can be triggers and can change someone's day. Or life. And if you think this is an exaggeration, think back to the time you were most hurt by someone. You'll remember exactly what they said...even if it was thirty years ago. Leaders who can think fast and talk slow have a strong understanding of the power of language, and they choose their words carefully. They choose words that convey the message, but that do no harm.

In summary, the subtle art of thinking fast and talking slow is about helping you build better relationships, build better communication skills, and build better teams. FYI, this is the skill that the great orators and public speakers use. They can focus on the experience that their audience is having, while tailoring their message accordingly.

Yes, it sounds like hard work. But I can tell you, after practicing these skills for the last twenty years of thinking about thoughts, and learning how to change them to be a better leader, it's worth the effort!

MANAGING YOUR TIME AND CARING FOR YOUR TEAM AT THE SAME TIME

Your thoughts underpin how you behave as a leader. And thinking about how to bring them into line with who you want to be as a leader is a critical step in becoming that leader. But it's hard, when you're under pressure.

The modern leader arrives at the office. They're greeted with a new and long list of unread emails and cannot possibly understand how they all came in overnight. Before they sit down, their phone is starting to buzz with messages and requests for their time. Then the phone rings with another catastrophe to attend to. Or so it seems.

They think that today might be the day that they finally lose their self-control. And they know that they aren't behaving in a way that a great leader would. How can they? They're nervous, worried, anxious...they're under pressure. And there's no letting up.

And then one of their team members knocks on the door, and needs their support, and their undivided attention. Just think about what their teams must be going through if the leader is under so much pressure.

How can leaders take a step back, and pull themselves out of the stress and pressure that they find themselves in? And how can they influence their thinking to bring it into line with good working leadership that gives team members the care and attention that they need?

Here are three hot tips.

ONE BE STILL, BREATHE, AND BE IN CONTROL.

This really is easier said than done, though making the effort is certainly worth it. In resilience speak, this part is called getting composed, and being present. As much as you have a heap of other things to deal with, being still and breathing are the most important things you can do to be present for everyone in your team.

They need you in control. Team members can tell when you're not. We've surveyed team members, and asked them what they want from their leaders, and the responses are care factor and consistency. Consistency of emotional state. Not a roller coaster. Yes, staying in control is a skill. Yes, you can get in control just by breathing into your stomach and oxygenating your brain's frontal lobes. Your team will appreciate it.

TWO BE OPEN, AND STEP INTO CARE FACTOR.

Be open with your body language, and open with your head and heart. Stepping into care factor is about listening to your team, and their challenges, and giving them the support they need in the moment (their issues are major for them right now). Mistake number one that leaders make is to be tapping away on a keyboard when team members are talking, sharing ideas, or asking for support.

And you won't believe this—I've been asked in the past to coach a leader on how to be more ignorant, so that team members can see they're working and stop bothering them. True story (but I didn't, of course). Stepping into care factor is stepping into psychological safety, where leaders are listeners.

THREE BE COURAGEOUS, AND GIVE AWAY SOME RESPONSIBILITY.

This is the process stuff. Be clear on the priority of the issue. Be clear on whose issue it is. Be clear on the solutions. If there are none offered, prompt for them. Be clear on actions moving forward. Decide to support, where you can, and task allocate regardless. Maybe you don't need to take it all on yourself, and you can get the monkey off your back. You can own the issue without owning the action. You can change your thoughts, which can change your actions.

After all that's done, at about 8:10 a.m., or whatever time you've started for the day, go to the coffee machine.

ANTON, I'M NOT A NARCISSIST, AM I?

I got asked that very question in a leadership coaching session recently. By a leader who'd been told that they were a narcissist.

Which isn't that uncommon these days, as more and more leaders (and their teams) learn about psychology, and what drives behaviour. Narcissism is like the buzz word of right now. And, at times, rightly so. Thinking about your thoughts can reveal the ones that are working for you and your team—and the ones that aren't.

Here's how I answered the question—and if you know me well enough, you'll know it was with some questions of my own. Here are the three questions I asked (note that I have taken some poetic license to tell the story in a way that makes sense and talks to the topic of narcissism).

Question: Do you know what narcissism is?
Answer: Well, yeah, sort of? Making it all about me, right? Or being aggressive, maybe.
Discussion: Ish.

There are generally three types of narcissism (and these are all explained differently, depending on the text that you read). Let's look at it, not from a psych perspective, which would talk about it as a diagnosable personality disorder, but from a leadership perspective. The three types of narcissism include exhibitionist, closet, and toxic narcissism.

Exhibitionist narcissists (also called grandiose narcissists) take a 'look at me' approach to life. It's all about them. They want to be in the spotlight, and they think they're better than everyone else. 'They think they're amazing—they think themselves to be smarter, better-looking, more powerful than other people, and they pretty much believe it' (Credit: **Business Insider**). In short, they're over-confident, and they really don't care what others think about them.

As a leader, they're always right. They're doing the best job. They can't be told. And they certainly don't think your idea is better than theirs.

Closet narcissists (also called vulnerable narcissists) take a 'poor me' approach to life. It's all about them, but they play the victim card. It's the behaviour of these narcissists that created the term 'gaslighting' which is about always feeling bad about yourself when you're around a closet narcissist. They're passive aggressive, and nothing is their fault. They want to be grandiose, but don't know how. And they're frustrated by that. They're chameleons and are nice to you one minute (maybe in public) and not so much the next (maybe in private).

As a leader, they're unpredictable. Their team members will never feel good about themselves, but they won't know why. Their team members don't ever feel worthy or valued. Or cared for.

Toxic narcissists (also called chaotic narcissists) take a 'wilful damage' approach to life. They thrive on (and actively cause) chaotic situations. This is the worst type of narcissist, as they go out of their way to be destructive and malevolent. Toxic narcissists 'are perfectly fine destroying the careers of other people, basically fine with just imploding people emotionally, physically, and spiritually' (Credit: **Business Insider**). It's safe to say that you don't want to be in the team of a toxic narcissist.

As a leader, they are very, very harmful. Their team members not only feel hurt, but they're really hurt. Their careers are damaged. Their emotions are damaged. Their resilience is damaged. And all very overtly. Out in public, for all to see.

It's worth noting that narcissism is characterised (generally) by grandiose behaviour and fantasies, arrogance and entitlement, very low levels of empathy, and a need for admiration and attention.

Question: Why did the person think you're a narcissist?
Answer: I'm actually not sure. I didn't ask, I was really taken aback by the conversation, and it hurt a bit to be called that. I've never been called that before. Though there are times when I could have acted like all three of those types.
Discussion: Great. An honest response. And narcissism is considered by some as a spectrum. That is, we're all on the spectrum, and tend to be narcissistic, even if it's only in a very small way.

Here's the big thing, and this is what we work through in our leadership programs. Do you feel like you're helping more than you're hindering? Do you feel like you're healing more than you're harming? What I mean by that is that leadership, by definition, is about lifting people up, not putting them down. It's about being a good human, and leaving people better than you found them, even when you must have robust conversations.

Leadership interactions should be done in a positive and empathetic way, that does no harm. Here are the big three questions to ask yourself, if you feel like you could be considered narcissistic:

- Is my intent good, or is it to harm others? (You need to answer this honestly—a true narcissist doesn't have the right intent.)

- Am I aggressive, abusive, or abrupt in my delivery or interactions? (If so, that's uncool too—because it means that you're happy to keep hurting others.)

- Can I be empathetic, and understand what others are experiencing? (If not, that's very uncool—because it means that you're not only happy to hurt others, but also that you have zero understanding of the impact that both your behaviour and the experiences of others has on their emotional state.)

Question: Where to from here?
Answer: I think we can always continue to do self-development work. So, I'm going to take it on as a challenge to work on how I show up as a leader. If you were me, what would you recommend?

Discussion: Great question. Here are the things that you could consider as an action plan to continue your leadership development. And maybe don't think about this as an 'anti-narcissism' plan; think about it as a 'working on being an even better leader' plan.

- **It's not about you!** Remember that leadership is about the team performance, and the individuals in the team, and their development. The easiest way to be a great leader is to be thinking about how you can support your team to become a better version of itself, and to take your team to higher levels of performance. Where your focus goes, your energy flows—if you think about your team, you'll be more likely to be seen as a caring and connected leader.

- **Empathy can be learnt.** Remember that being able to empathise with other humans is potentially the most important skill you can learn as a leader. And yes, it can be learnt. If you're up for it. Empathy is about being able to think through (cognition) what it might be like for the other person in this situation. Then, feeling (emotions) what it is that they might be feeling. The big part of empathy is compassion (action). Every single human is born compassionate. But it can take effort at times to go out of your way to help another human when they're in need. It is worth it, though.

- **Create conscious control.** This is the big one! Without conscious control (emotional, situational, and behavioural control), you'll never maintain great relationships with your team members. Thinking fast and talking slow is the key skill required to manage your emotions. Which is basically about knowing what your triggers are, and responding, not reacting, to situations, circumstances, or human behaviour. And doing no harm.

Thinking about your thoughts can help you to identify patterns in your thinking that are helping others—and the ones that are hurting them. It's a critical step in changing your thinking to steady yourself on your path to becoming a leader who works with purpose to reach their 'why.'

Simon Sinek Is Onto Something With Finding Your 'Why'

But what is your 'why'? Thinking about how you think will tell you.

Leaders who are part of our coaching or training programs get to work through why they do leadership. My observations are that at least 90% of the leaders we work with haven't done the exercise of clarifying why they lead other humans.

As a leader, your team doesn't buy into what you do or how you do it. They buy into why you do it (thanks Simon Sinek).[52] But if you don't know why you do leadership, how can you share that with others?

It's such an important concept—let's unpack why.

FIRSTLY, THOUGH...

If it's so important understand your why, what's the reason that so many leaders have never thought about it? When I ask leaders why they do leadership, the three most common answer are: 1) Because I was on the spot, and no-one else wanted to fill in; 2) Because I was a good technician; and 3) Because it pays more. And I get it, these three are the main reasons that people end up leading other humans. Cool.

But when you're there, surely the importance of the role kicks in, given that, after parenting, leadership is the second most important role on planet Earth? Surely leaders sit back and think about why they put themselves through the daily hustle of leading?

Apparently, they don't very often. Maybe it's a business thing, or maybe they just never get around to it.

NOT THAT QUICKLY ...

I won't let you off that easily. Sorry in advance. No excuses. Accountability. Take the time, make the effort, and put the thinking into why leadership is your calling (if it is). Then share that with your team. And let it drive your behaviour, and influence theirs.

IT REALLY DOES MAKE A DIFFERENCE

And if you do the exercise properly, you'll be amazed at how much value you get from it. We have hundreds of examples of leaders going from wide eyed to confident in sharing their why. The secret is simple, and thanks again, Simon Sinek.[52]

Grab a pen and paper. Think about your leadership. Start with the two words 'I believe'. Then keep writing. Finish the sentence at least three times, and then not only write it, but feel it. Feel just how important those beliefs (and values) are to you. And when you know that your beliefs drive your behaviour, you can be true to yourself when you're leading. By giving limiting beliefs away, drawing from positive beliefs, and stepping into your why.

This really is a powerful process. Check out Simon Sinek's work for more information on how to do it.

How To Have A Real Conversation With Your Leadership Coach

Recently, I got an email from a coaching client, who expressed how grateful they were that we had had 'a real conversation'. It was my first session with this client, and it was great feedback to get after just one session.

Of course, I asked what they thought made it a real conversation, and the answer was around the topics that we covered. We talked through big issues like their inferiority complex, imposter syndrome, fear of failure, and a range of other topics that most people aren't comfortable to discuss. The heavy stuff, the real stuff! It works, because they're thinking about their thoughts, and figuring out how to change them.

What I shared is that coaching sessions work best when our clients are willing to open up their hearts, and really unpack what's happening for them. What their fears are. What their frustrations are, and what they're focused on right now.

Let's look at these separately.

ONE WHAT ARE YOUR REAL FEARS?

What things are you putting off because you're scared to confront them? Most of the time, this is a conversation, or a range of conversations, that our clients are avoiding. Fear (false expectations appearing real) stops us from taking action. It means that we overthink what could go wrong, instead of focusing on what could go right.

Public speeches or job interviews are the two main things that people bring to sessions for support with. These situations can cause a range of emotions for people, and they can cause our clients a great deal of stress—until we talk through them and work out how they should approach the situation. Usually with heaps of preparation, is the coaching advice I provide.

LEADER ACTION

Yes, some conversations are very difficult to have, and some could even be relationship enders. But most don't end up nearly as bad as you imagine they will. The sooner your deal with worry and anxiety, the sooner you find the confidence to get through the situation, and the better you'll feel!

TWO WHAT ARE YOUR FRUSTRATIONS?

This is the area that we spend most time talking about. Rightly so. Leaders are under pressure. They're stressed, and they're crazy busy. They get frustrated by a range of things, including not getting enough support from their leaders or their teams. Not being able to resolve a dispute. Or not being able to move forward on a project. Among a myriad of other things.

Leading under pressure falls right into that category. Recently, I was discussing this point with a client, and learned that one of the key leadership skills for managing frustration is consistency: of emotional response, and of temperament. In other words, creating conscious control.

LEADER ACTION

Yes, leadership is stressful. There are things that cause frustration. So, it's important to deal with frustrations. And it's important not to over-share with your teams just how frustrated you are. That's your challenge to deal with as a leader.

THREE WHAT'S YOUR FOCUS, RIGHT NOW?

Probably my favourite part of coaching sessions. When a client comes to me and says, 'right, I need a hand to develop this, or build that, or create this.' Great, let's get the presentation built, or the business case mapped out. Or the process developed.

This is good, fun work. I've worked with clients on everything from position descriptions, to five-year plans, and everything in between, giving the leader a different perspective. Fun fact: I was working with a leader on a restructure during one session of two hours, that went for six hours.

LEADER ACTION

Yes, there's always something to do, and yes, sometimes a different perspective is useful. Someone outside the organisation and outside of your team can give good ideas and opinions that you may not have considered yet.

In summary, the next time you're sitting down with your leadership coach (reach out if you'd like to become a client of ours), remember to come prepared with your fears, your frustrations, and your current focus areas.

Then, we can have a real conversation.

ACTIVITY 1.3
THINK ABOUT YOUR THOUGHTS

Take some time now to think about what you've learnt in the last chapter.

The following questions will help you to think about your thoughts, develop a better understanding of how you perform in your leadership role and why, and how to improve your conscious control to be a better leader.

As a leader, how do you learn best? Is it reading, studying, writing, asking questions, listening to an audiobook, classroom training, or something else?

As a leader, how, when, where, and what do you need to learn to be more effective in your role?

How would you explain your thought processes to someone you were coaching?

As a leader, how do you lead with vision and virtue?

What are some ways you could do business not to win, but to make a difference?

What are some ways you could be more courageous, and hand over some responsibility to your team?

Do you believe empathy can be learnt? Can you think of ways to further develop your empathy as a leader?

SKILL IV
LEAD UNDER
PRESSURE

SOME LEADERS JUST SEEM TO HAVE IT ALL TOGETHER.

No matter what happens, they stay calm, they don't react (or appear to), they don't fly off the handle, and they seem to just 'take it in their stride'.

All leaders face pressure. Whether the pressure is about the achievement of budgets or numbers, or if it's about always having the solution and being right. Or the pressure that comes from having to make big decisions. Or even having to engage in robust conversations.

Regardless of where the pressure comes from, there are some fundamental 'laws of leadership' that, when applied, will change the life of the leader and make life easier for their team members.

While there are so many skills you need to develop to upgrade your mindset and your leadership, there are a few key skills that you need to learn in order to be a better leader when you're under pressure. The real skills required to lead under pressure include intrapersonal skills, people skills, and information skills. Without them, the pressure will win.

Let's unpack these separately.

ONE INTRAPERSONAL SKILLS.

A long time ago, in a place far, far away, it was thought that your Intelligence Quotient (IQ) was 80% responsible for the success that you'd achieve during your working life. Actually, the place wasn't that far away, and it wasn't that long ago that this belief existed. With the advent of the IQ in the early 1900s, came what researchers thought was the ability to measure how smart people are. And of course, that must determine how successful they would be, right? Not so much.

If it's not IQ, what is responsible for our success, especially as leaders? It must be EQ (Emotional Intelligence) then...and if EQ is more important than IQ, maybe our success is based on something like 80% EQ and 20% IQ. Cotrus, Stanciu and Bulborea (2012)[15] conducted a study on students, to clarify if their success really was dependent in eight parts out of ten on their intelligence quotient, or their emotional intelligence. They confirmed that for students, that was the case.

But many years before that, in 1995, the person responsible for creating the concept of Emotional Intelligence, Daniel Goleman[22], stated very clearly that he didn't think it was possible to come up with what percentage of your success can be attributed to your emotional intelligence. What he did point out though, was that:

> **Emotional intelligence trumps IQ primarily in those 'soft' domains where intellect is relatively less relevant for success—where, for example, emotional self-regulation and empathy may be more salient skills than purely cognitive abilities.**

That is, in the domain of leadership.

In other words, EQ is more important than IQ when people and their emotions are involved. Aka: Leadership.

The intrapersonal skills are those skills that have to be practiced internally, and that need to connect the limbic system of the brain (emotions) to the smart brain (pre-frontal cortex) in order to create control. Emotional control, behavioural control, and situational control. Emotional control is the basis of emotional intelligence.

And, like all intrapersonal skills, the focus of emotional control is around responding not reacting to stimuli. It's about reflecting and rendering. And it's about being present. These skills are simple, but not easy, especially when you're in a BOOM moment or a BOOM period.

The process of emotional control involves emotional self-awareness, then emotional self-regulation. It then involves emotional social-awareness, then emotional social-regulation (in others). A learnt skill set.

If you do nothing else after reading this, just ask yourself, what emotion am I feeling right now, and why?

TWO INTERPERSONAL SKILLS.

The purists might say that emotional intelligence (as discussed above) is actually an interpersonal skill, not an intrapersonal skill, as it's about how we deal with others. I don't concur with this viewpoint, as interpersonal skills are more than emotional intelligence. They include care factor, connection, and character. These skills align with **John C. Maxwell's irrefutable Law of Leadership** (Law 3) which is the Law of Solid Ground.[36] Leaders who can care, who can connect, and who are strong of character, can engender respect and trust in their team.

When it comes time to lead under pressure, teams must trust their leader. Period. What can happen is that leaders can forget that their teams are feeling the pressure as much as they are. Team members feel the pressure too. But they don't have the information that the leader has, and so are left to make assumptions or presumptions about what's happening.

With some care factor, a level of psychological safety can be achieved, where everyone feels safe to ask questions about the situation or circumstances. Physical safety is a big deal, and keeping people safe during a BOOM event is critical, as is connecting with people on a personal level in order to understand their situation.

Care factor, connection and character can all be demonstrated through empathetic behaviour. Empathy is a key skill of leaders, and one that's being talked about more and more in recent times. But what is it? It's the ability to put ourselves in others' shoes, and understand their position, and their emotional state. For sure. But real empathy (again unpacked by Daniel Goleman[22]) is about compassion.

Compassion is taking action. Compassion is not a feeling. It's taking action to make someone's life better. In psychology, we know that the vast majority of humans (like bonobo monkeys, our closest relatives) are born compassionate. That is, we're wired to care for and help others. Cortes, Barragan, Brooks, and Meltzof (2012)[14] studied at what age children would give up food, even when they were hungry, to help another child. Nineteen months was the age that children would voluntarily share their food—sharing without being told they had to.

So why, when the BOOM moments happen, do we become less compassionate? Why, in the moments when others need us the most, do we focus on ourselves, to the detriment of our teams?

If you do nothing else after reading this, go and see what you can do to help out a team member or even a perfect stranger.

THREE INFORMATIONAL SKILLS.

The informational skills, or process skills, are those skills that are about using information to make decisions. Leaders need courage to 'make decisions under fire.' Yes, there is fear, but yes, there needs to be action. That action includes making decisions, delegating, and disseminating information, no matter the pressure.

Obtaining the right information in the first place is as important as what you do with it. A bad decision made with correct information is much better than a bad decision made with little or wrong information.

The process is face fears, make decisions, and have a future focus. The future focus ensures that the leader is looking to the longer term, as well as fighting the current BOOM fire.

And delegate. This word is somewhat overused in leadership circles, and can sometimes nearly be touted as the panacea for all leadership woes. That's not the case, but what is certain is that when the pressure is on, the more people that are responding to the BOOM event in a controlled way, the better the outcome.

Leading under pressure means not taking on everything yourself. It means drawing on others for support—which helps you, and empowers them.

How To Empower Others Like Larry Page

Lawrence Edward Page was born on 26 March 1973, in Lansing, Michigan, USA. Larry Page had an unusual beginning. His parents were both professors in the field of computing. Dr. Carl Victor Page, Larry's father, taught at Michigan State University as a professor of computer science and artificial intelligence. Gloria Page, Larry's mother, taught computer programming. This might not be remarkable now, but in the early 1970s, computers were a new science, not even grasped by the general public. Larry Page's future might have been set before he was born.

The house where Page grew up was full of early computers and copies of *Popular Science* magazines. This strange environment allowed Page to begin tinkering with computers when he was a child, which is exactly what he did, for the rest of his life.

Following his school years, he studied Computer Engineering at the University of Michigan, before enrolling in graduate studies at Stanford University. Page had begun working on a project related to the World Wide

Web, encouraged by a professor. Page was looking at the ways in which web pages were linked to one another. At first, Page worked on a way to find out how many pages on the web were linked to any other page. Search engines at that time could only determine how many times any particular word appeared on a certain page. Therefore, web searches produced results simply based on particular words and often returned huge lists of irrelevant searches.

Page was interested in ranking pages, or websites, based not purely on the frequency of a word, but also on the number of links that led from a site to any given other site. His friend Sergey Brin had expertise in data mining, having already written over a dozen papers on the subject. Brin was interested because of the project's complexity. At that time, there were an estimated 10 million pages on the web, any of which could potentially be linked to any other. The two went to work on the complex project, and the result was two papers.

The second paper, with the mouthful of a title, **The Anatomy of a Large-Scale Hypertextual Web Search Engine**,[6] made a splash in tech circles. Soon after they wrote it, the paper had been downloaded more frequently than almost any other scientific document on the internet. They had developed their new search engine, describing it in that paper. The program was then called 'BackRub', and it was run on the motley collection of personal computers in Page's dormitory room.

Very quickly, the two boys realised that they were onto something. They renamed the page, and the google.com domain name was registered in 1997. The name was chosen as a derivation of the word 'googol', which is the name of an enormous number that consists of a one followed by 100 zeros. They chose the name to represent the enormous amounts of data that would be coordinated by their search engine.

Fast forward to 2010, when two co-authors and myself released an international best-selling book (**Millionaires and Billionaires—Secrets Revealed**),[23] which included a chapter on Larry Page, and Google employed around 24,400 staff. It now employs over 156,000 staff. Page doesn't simply think in terms of providing a quality service to make Google the best search engine. He thinks big, and puts that thinking into his business. In everything Page and Google do, he has an eye towards improving the world. He set up his company that way: he makes sure that his employees are empowered to work in that way, and he wants to offer users the tools to work that way, too. He says, 'talented people are attracted to Google because we empower them to change the world.'

The above paragraphs are an excerpt from the chapter on Larry Page, but I'm fascinated by one word that Page uses, and that is to 'empower' talented people. So, what does that really mean? Some people that I've asked about empowerment call it enabling, or trusting, or some other derivative of being authorised to make a change, or to make a difference.

So, how can you empower others, even when you're leading under pressure, and how can you do it like Larry Page and Google?

To answer this question, let's first understand what empowerment is. And let's turn to the organisational psychology definition, which is psychological empowerment. Psychological empowerment is defined as an 'intrinsic task motivation reflecting a sense of self-control in relation to one's work and an active engagement with one's work role' (Meng and Sun, 2019).[39]

There are four key concepts of psychological empowerment, which include Meaning, Impact, Competence, and Self-determination.

ONE MEANING.

Meaning is about how much a person's work helps them achieve their personal goals and objectives. It's about how much their work lines up with their self-identity. How much their work is aligned with their personal values, and how much their work can help them express themselves. Meaning is the most personal element of the work experience. It's also perhaps the most important.

TWO IMPACT.

Impact is different to meaning, in that it's how a person's work helps them contribute to their organisation's goals and objectives. And how much their work adds value to something bigger than themself. This is about value proposition, and being involved in work that makes a difference to the output of an organisation.

THREE COMPETENCE.

Competence is simply how able staff feel to do their jobs and perform the functions required of them. Feeling competent is related to feeling confident and capable, and it's developed from skills, knowledge, and experience. People who feel competent feel like they can deal with the demands of their role, and they aren't easily overwhelmed.

FOUR SELF-DETERMINATION.

Self-determination means having a high level of input into how a person performs in their role. It's about a level of autonomy that suits the team member, and that suits the organisation. Having self-determination means having a say in your position description, and your work in general. And it's about having a level of control over your destiny.

Team members who feel like they're high in the four areas of psychological empowerment will say things like 'My work activities are personally meaningful to me' (meaning); 'I have significant influence over what happens in my department' (impact); 'I'm confident about my ability to do my job' (competence); and 'I have significant autonomy in determining how I do my job' (self-determination). (Credit: Li, Wu, Johnson & Wu, 2011).[30]

And what studies have demonstrated is that psychological empowerment increases employee engagement. And it's linked to increased organisational success. It's also linked to a reduction in emotional exhaustion and burnout. So, employee wellbeing levels increase. While absenteeism reduces. Winning.

So how do you do it like Larry Page? Put simply, you focus on it, and you understand how important it is to have a psychologically empowered workforce when you're leading under pressure. And you do what it takes to help your team members find meaning, to have an impact, to build their competence, and to have self-determination in their role.

Hire staff with those things in mind. Do it like Google!

HOW TO BE AN EXPERT IN LEADERSHIP LANGUAGING

Leaders can sometimes forget the importance of their language. Especially when they're under pressure, which is when language is most important. It can be a serious game changer, when it comes to improving or negatively impacting a relationship.

A significant amount of my coaching work is around how to use languaging more effectively. And how to use language to connect more with team members. Recently, I was working with a senior manager, who was worried about having a conversation with one of their leadership team. The manager was worried that it was going to be a 'relationship-ending conversation.'

Only because the manager hadn't worked through (at that stage) how to effectively convey their message, in a way that was not triggering for the other person. Once we were able to talk through it, and talk through the approach, the manager was confident that the conversation could build the relationship, not break it.

The research of a friend of mine revealed that good leaders realise that 'individuals are a complex patchwork of social norms, cognitive conditioning, and personal constructs, which are all powerful in shaping a person's identity'. People's perspectives shape how they receive a message.

This is not to say that you shouldn't deliver bad news. Leaders have to. Regularly. It's so that you can deliver bad news with the right intent and get the right outcome. If you're committed to that. In the book **Fierce Conversations,** Susan Scott[50] explains that relationships are built on conversations. Conversations are the relationship. So, if you want a good relationship with your team, choosing your languaging carefully, and leaning into connection as well as direction, will help you, no end.

These top three things will help change your languaging and your connection—if you can nail them.

ONE HAVE MORE QUESTIONS THAN STATEMENTS.

Having bigger and better questions is the key to connection. When you're asking questions, it shows that you're more interested in the other person, and you're being more interested than interesting. It's very difficult to get to know someone if you're talking at them, not with them.

Asking questions is a skill set. It's simple, but not easy. It takes practice. The better quality the question, the better quality the answer, and the better quality the conversation. The thing about questions is that questions are the main skill of a coach. And leaders are coaches. All good coaches understand that questions are not just open vs closed, or direct vs vague.

Good coaches and leaders understand that the best questions are Socratic questions. The Socratic approach to questioning is based on the practice of disciplined, thoughtful dialogue. Socrates, the early Greek philosopher/ teacher, believed that 'disciplined practice of thoughtful questioning enabled the student to examine ideas logically and to determine the validity of those ideas' (Credit: Wiki).

Thoughtful questions, like what people are experiencing. Why they think that's happening for them, and how they think they can respond not react. Other ways to use thoughtful questions is to start with 'which approach do you think we should take?', 'could we consider other options?', or 'would another option be worth planning out?' Thoughtful questions allow you to linger in the conversation. They allow you to find out more about the person that you're chatting and interacting with—and to get a deeper level of understanding about what's going on in the life of that human.

Even if you're not an expert at thoughtful questions (yet), asking questions is the most important thing in moving you in the right direction.

Develop the art of asking bigger and better questions, and then work on asking Socratic questions—to build a deeper connection.

TWO LISTEN TO UNDERSTAND, NOT TO RESPOND.

I couldn't tell you the number of leaders that I coach in the fine art of listening to understand. This is about not finishing sentences for others. Not looking as though you're just waiting for your turn in the conversation. Not having a pre-recorded script or a default response to ideas or opinions. And definitely not drifting off in the conversation in your head, until the other person has finished talking.

Listening to understand is the one big thing that you can do to value someone. If a team member ever says they don't feel valued, what that means is that they don't feel heard. They don't feel understood. And this is an easy thing to change.

My tips for you are to hang off every word. Literally. Listen with an open heart and an open mind. Be interested in what the person is saying. Find a way to engage your brain in the conversation and focus intently. Look into their left eye and connect. Paraphrase with 'so what you are saying is...' Or even linger in the conversation with silence to show you are processing information. Sometimes it's important to let silence do the heavy lifting.

The language that you want to use is language like 'help me understand', 'so what you mean is', or 'what's an example of that?' These statements (or questions, depending on how they are asked) are clarifiers, and they demonstrate that you're engaged, and that you do want more information before responding.

LEADER ACTION

Develop the skill of listening and clarification, so that you can listen to understand, not to respond—to build a deeper connection.

THREE THINK FAST, TALK SLOW.

One of the most important skills of good leaders, and good communicators, is the skill of being able to think about the emotional experience that someone else is having while you're in conversation with them. This is the skill explained by Daniel Goleman,[22] and it relates to emotional intelligence.

And social emotional awareness, and then social emotional regulation.

What that means is that you can understand what's happening for the other person, and change your tone, your volume, your pitch or even your language to suit the situation. There are times when you need to deliver bad news or challenge a team member. And there are times when you want to deliver good news and recognise a team member.

During potentially high-emotion conversations, your ability to be aware of emotional states and adapt to the situation to create more or less emotion is the highest level of communication skill that you can develop as a leader.

This skill is important because every word has the potential to be a trigger for another human. Triggers are things that cause an emotional response. Common trigger words include 'no', 'I disagree', or 'you're wrong'. The word 'but' (try using 'and') is a major trigger for a lot of people, but it's used frequently in high pressure situations.

Now there might be times when you choose to use words like these, but be aware that when people are triggered, they're not going to be at their best in the conversation. As a leader, try to choose words that are less triggering.

LEADER ACTION

Be acutely aware of the experience of others when they're with you, and change your strategy accordingly—to build a deeper connection.

Leadership languaging, and communication, is about asking questions, listening to understand, and thinking fast and talking slow. It's as much about connection as it is about direction—and it's what you need to be better leader for your team, especially when you're leading under pressure.

THE STORY OF THE KING AND HIS WILD DOGS

Story time. My favourite time, by the way. Love a good yarn, especially when there's a leadership message in there.

Now, you have a job to do, though. As I tell you this story, I want you to think about who you are in it. There are three characters: the King, the Minister, and the Dogs (yes, it's OK to be the dogs...not all the time, but for this story anyway). And you might have heard it before, but let me put the leadership spin on it, and add a psychological safety spin as well.

Once upon a time, there was this King that had ten Wild Dogs. He used them to torture and eat all his Ministers who made mistakes.

On this day, one of the Ministers gave an opinion that was wrong, and that the King disliked, and that appeared to be a mistake. So, the King ordered that the Minister be thrown to the Dogs.

Following the decree of punishment, the Minister said, 'I served you ten years, and you do this?'

And then as their last wish, the Minister begged, 'Please give me ten days before you throw me in with the Wild Dogs!'

The King agreed.

In those ten days the Minister went to the guard that was guarding the Dogs and told him he wanted to serve the Dogs for the next ten days. The guard was baffled. But he agreed to the Minister's request.

The Minister started feeding the Dogs, cleaning for them, washing them, providing all sorts of comfort for them.

When the ten days were up, the King ordered that the Minister be thrown to the Dogs for his punishment.

But when he was thrown in, everyone was amazed at what they saw. They saw the Dogs licking the feet of the Minister!

The King was baffled by what he saw. He asked, 'What happened to the Wild Dogs?'

The Minister then said, 'I served the Dogs for ten days and they didn't forget my service...yet I served you for ten years and you forgot all at the first mistake!'

The King realised his mistake and ordered the Minister to go free.

I know, right? It's a great story, and quite a deep one, if you get into it.

So, who are you in that story? And here's my leadership reflection on each of the parties, including where they started, and maybe where they ended, as a point of reference. You might be at one end or the other, or you might be somewhere in the middle.

THE KING

The King was not a great leader at the start of this story. The King's leadership team lived in fear. They couldn't offer an opinion, let alone make a mistake, or they'd be sacked, or even worse—ostracised from the team. The King was intolerant, lacked empathy, and was unable to listen to the ideas of others. The King hadn't been to one of the TGG Leadership Training programs, and hadn't learnt the skills of creating conscious control or keeping emotions in check, even when team members might not have a great idea that they want to share. There was no emotional intelligence on display from the King, who overreacted.

The King then transformed. Through a lived leadership experience. The King's belief systems and values were challenged (and changed) by being made to have an emotional experience, and one that meant the King couldn't feel anything but remorse for the Minister and a level of guilt or shame for his own behaviour. Let's hope that behaviour change was permanent, and the rest of the Ministers didn't have to live in fear anymore!

At the end of this story, the King was willing to be challenged. And to change his mind. That's Challenger Safety.

THE MINISTER

The Minister was a solid team contributor. Always offering suggestions. Maybe even an over-contributor at times. Maybe making decisions without all the right information. And due to that, the Minister's information maybe couldn't be trusted. And the King, having coached the Minister in the past to make sure they provided the right amount of detail, had made another mistake. Or offered a suggestion that was not grounded in a business case or with good data. In some ways, the King had reached his limit (certainly not a justification for the behaviour), and due to a lack of emotional control, the Minister was sent to the Dogs.

The Minister then transformed. The Minister decided to use his skills to 'manage upwards'. The Minister was thinking quickly and talking slowly. The Minister knew that if he could help the King to understand what it's like to be in the Minister's shoes, the King might just change his behaviour. And it worked. The King stepped into empathy.

But the most important part of this story is that the Minister had a new team to work with. Once the Minister had joined his new team, he worked hard to build relationships with the other team members (the Wild Dogs). The Minister turned up in service (in the right way, with the right intent), and was able to connect with the other team members in a way that meant they became a high-performing team and were able to work well together.

The Minister to was able to apply a new strategy, to learn from his mistake, and contribute to a better outcome for everyone. That's Learner Safety and Contributor Safety.

THE WILD DOGS

The Wild Dogs (aka, new team members) were not very inclusive. They were known as the team that no one wanted to work with. They were aggressive, abusive, and abrupt. They hurt each other at times, and they certainly didn't include new team members very well. They were angry. And it felt like you'd been ripped apart each time you had to deal with them. They had the reputation of being a mean and nasty team, who were hard to work with, and hard to deal with.

That Wild Dogs team then transformed. They went from being an angry team, to being a team that welcomed a new team member. They were willing to change their belief systems and values and be accepting. They were welcoming of new ideas, and they became willing to help each other and to make sure that the new team member felt accepted and valued. After only ten days, the new team was a high-performing team. A team that worked together towards the same goals and objectives.

This new team became friendly and inclusive, and they all worked together and got along a lot better. That's Inclusion Safety.

Who are you in this story? And why? Maybe you were one at one point, and now you're at another point. Keep up the learning—it's how you'll learn to lead better under pressure.

DON'T LET THE PRESSURE WIN

If leaders could only see themselves when they're carrying on like pork chops, and berating their people just because they can. It can look like the 4-year-old having a temper tantrum because mum didn't buy them a chocolate at the shop. Seriously...

But they can't see themselves. And you know what? They can't see the damage that they're doing to other humans, when they let the pressure win.

Letting the pressure win means simply that you've given yourself permission to carry on, to get abusive, aggressive, or abrupt. The three As, and you've given yourself permission to let your emotions control your behaviour, instead of your rational brain.

It's a choice. We all do it at times. The challenge is to demonstrate emotional control more times than you lose it. Don't let the pressure win.

Because when it does, and you react (from the limbic part of your brain—which is hundreds of thousands of years in the making, so it's very primitive), you tend to do and say things that you regret. Or that you need to apologise for later.

And that's the only way you will not let the pressure win. By having emotional control. And care factor for others—who don't deserve to be treated with the three As!

Emotional control is like a muscle. If you use it, it grows bigger and stronger, for the next time you need it. Emotional control is responsible for behavioural control—behaviour follows emotions. And the situational control follows behavioural control.

In short, as a leader, if you want to be in situational control, at all (or most) times, you can't let the pressure win.

In our leader coaching sessions, I ask the question 'are you in eustress, or are you in distress?' Eustress is good stress, and keeps you focused and productive. Distress on the other hand is you letting the pressure win.

Distress comes from the Latin word 'distringere'. Meaning 'anguish; grief; pain or suffering of the body or mind', from c. 1300. Sounds awful.

Treat it like a competition. Me in control: 1. Pressure: 0.

Think for a moment what the 4-year-old looks like. Don't think about your response as an onlooker (as we judge the parent, without knowing what's going on for them). Think about what you would do, or have done, if that was your child. What would work best? Shouting back? Probably not. Smacking? Probably not. Reasoning with them? Probably not.

The thing that I found worked for our boys (that doesn't for girls, I'm told) is to change their focus. 'Grandma's coming over soon, let's get home' or 'your shoelace is undone'. Will that work all the time? Probably not. But if it works even once in that situation, could it work for you? I regularly use the word focus in our programs, and coaching.

FUTURE FOCUS

The first thing to do when the pressure really tries to win is to have a forward focus. 'What are we dealing with?' followed by 'what does a better situation look like?' and 'how will we get there?' Future focused.

PEOPLE FOCUS

Next, consider putting the people around you first, not last. Focus on people, not processes. Engage, and engage some more. Ask for help. Ask for ideas. Rely on connection, not direction.

SELF-FOCUS

Finally, and perhaps the most important thing to focus on is your own ability to deal with stress and pressure. Focus on not letting the pressure win, by having boundaries. Hold yourself accountable for your reactions and commit to responding instead. Commit to keeping yourself in good shape, emotionally and physically, so that you're ready for the distress when it shows up. Focus on your personal psychological safety, and be the leader that people remember because you dealt with stress, not used it as an excuse to lose your !@#t. Because BOOM situations will come.

HOW TO COPE WITH PRESSURE WHEN THINGS GO BOOM

The human species has developed to cope. We have survived millions of years of catastrophic events. We have even survived when other species of hominids didn't. We are resilient, and we are copers. But what does coping really take, as a leader, when things go BOOM? How do you lead under pressure when bad things happen?

Firstly, coping is not about being resilient. During the BOOM event, you're not practicing resilience, you're practicing the skill of 'getting through it.' Dealing with it. Grieving through it. Managing it. Being resilient will set you up with the skills of being able to cope more competently with a BOOM event. In the moment, it'll help you to rethink the way you think about the pressure and the stress of the event.

Here are some tips.

ONE RETHINK PRESSURE.

In her 2013 TED Talk,[38] **Kelly McGonigal** shared some interesting research on the stress response. Kelly shared that it's not the stress itself, but how we think about the stress, that matters. I know right? Confusing. In short, if you think the stress and pressure you're feeling is positive, it'll help you be your best right now, because you'll be more focused and alert. But if you have a negative association with the pressure, you're likely to struggle to cope in the moment, and in the long term.

Rethink pressure by looking at it through a positive lens. Know that as a species, humans are designed to experience pressure. Pressure keeps us sharp, it heightens our senses, and produces cortisol and adrenalin so that we're ready to act (yes, fight-or-flight). Or focus on the task at hand. While we don't have to worry about sabre tooth tigers these days, the pressure can still be thought of as supporting us, rather than sabotaging us.

Rethink pressure to use it to your advantage. And rethink the pressure of the situation, so that you can cope during it, and get through it more quickly.

TWO RESTATE PURPOSE.

When you're in a tough situation that you're trying to cope through, reconnect to purpose. And restate why you're doing what you're doing, and why the current situation is worth the struggle.

Restating your purpose helps you connect with it. Remember that if you're leading a team through a crisis, it's important to help them to know that there's a bigger picture, and that their struggles are being directed towards an outcome that'll be worth the effort. Your purpose might be just to survive the BOOM event, or it might be to build the most successful business in your space, or it might be to choose to take the chances that lead to the change and growth you need.

When you restate your purpose, you start to get a sense of it all being worthwhile, and your emotional brain starts to relax and to understand that the thinking brain is in charge. And when reasoning is in charge, most BOOM events are manageable.

And remember that on the other side of a BOOM event will be a reflection period of what you did well, and what you could do better next time. There will be some learning!

THREE REJECT FEAR.

That's a big call, right? Reject fear! The challenge is, BOOM events create fear. Fear of what's going wrong right now, and the fear of the future. Think of COVID for a moment—the biggest fear that people had was what their future held. How would they earn a living? When would it ever end?

If you've followed any of my work, you'll know that I work with leaders to help them create conscious control. Part of that process is about being courageous. And having the courage to step outside of your comfort zone (which you'll be doing during a BOOM event) and to try things that might not work. To tell your team how you're feeling and what's happening. And to trust yourself and your team to get through this BOOM event.

Rejecting fear takes courage. Leadership under pressure is about control, care factor, and courage—even when dealing with BOOM events.

And especially when you're trying to lead through them with team members who aren't on board with what you're saying.

HOW TO TALK TO PEOPLE THAT DON'T LISTEN

When you're leading under pressure, the one thing you don't want to have to deal with is team members who don't listen. Team members that nod encouragingly, then do something else. Or that just don't seem to hear what the leader is saying, which ends up in miscommunication or quarrels about what was said. It would be so much easier if team members just listened. It can't be that hard, right?

This might be good for team members to read, too. Listening to your leader is important, for both of you. If you'd actually like a harmonious working relationship, that is.

In my experience, for the team member that doesn't listen, there's generally an underlying relationship issue. It's not really a listening issue. It's a trust issue, or it's a respect issue, or it's a care factor issue. If I interviewed the team member who doesn't listen, they'd tell me that they have an issue with their leader. For whatever reason.

The fact remains though, that leaders need to be able to give clear direction (task allocation), and the team member needs to be aware of what's required, so the work can get done.

So, as a leader, how do you talk to a team member who doesn't appear to be listening?

ONE BUILD A BETTER RELATIONSHIP.

As mentioned above, a lack of listening is generally not the obvious issue that it seems to be. And it depends on how it shows up, as to what the likely issues might be. Being a mediator, I sit between leaders and their team members when the issues get too big.

It's the responsibility of the leader to sort out the relationship. And to understand what is happening between the two of them. That takes, firstly, extreme ownership to acknowledge it. Secondly, it takes radical candour (real conversations) to address it.

Read some of the other sections that I've written already for ideas on how to build this relationship. The first thing that you can do as a leader is practice active listening. That's right. Just read that again.

If the team member isn't listening, it can be a sign that the leader isn't. Here's the psychology: humans have a habit of projecting. Projecting means that we blame others for their behaviours, in the same areas that we have a behavioural issue in. We project our issues and faults onto others.

So, if you want to build a relationship with a team member who you think doesn't listen, the first thing to do is to be a good listener.

TWO SET EXPECTATIONS.

The big thing here for the leader is that the leader needs to do task allocation. That's one of a leader's key roles, and team members that don't listen and clarify, or don't listen and follow through, can cause the leader a great deal of angst. And they cause issues for their team, and for their team's performance. For that reason, leader languaging needs to be very clear, and it needs to be quite direct.

The most effective words you can use as a leader are 'my expectation is.' Or some other derivative of that, with the word 'expectation' in the sentence. Setting expectations creates clarity, and it develops deadlines, and it accentuates accountability. When you set expectations, you allocate the task, you clarify the deadline, and you finalise the follow-up plan. Then you get agreement.

Then you follow up. If your directions aren't followed (for a period of time), it might be time for more formal processes or discussions.

THREE PARAPHRASE AND PUNCTUATE.

Providing positive reinforcement when team members do a good job would be the most underutilised leadership tool on planet Earth (or in the Aussie culture, at least). The second most underutilised leadership skill is leadership paraphrasing.

What I mean here is not about the leader paraphrasing something the team member said. This is about asking the team member to paraphrase what they heard. Leadership-driven paraphrasing is an important communication skill that needs to be practiced and needs to be perfected. It can be such an effective tool to ensure that the team member is clear on the task allocation and clear on expectations.

As a leader, punctuate the importance of paraphrasing, by practicing it regularly. Get into the habit of asking your team member what they heard. What they understood. What they commit to. And then watch your communication quality improve.

In summary, if you have a team member who you feel doesn't listen, become a better listener. Hear what they're saying, and understand if they have issues. Then, as part of your conversations, use the word expectation. Finally, use the skill of leadership paraphrasing, which is about asking your team member to repeat back what they heard.

Commit to learning these skills. They'll save you when you're leading under pressure—the most important time for your team members to listen to you.

ACTIVITY 1.4
LEAD UNDER PRESSURE

Take some time now to think about what you've learnt in the last chapter.

Answering the series of questions on the following pages will help you to learn more about how you perform in your leadership role when you're under pressure, and why. Alternatively, think or write about ways you could improve your conscious control and change your focus to be adaptive rather than reactive when you're in a BOOM situation.

Outline some of your emotions, and how you deal with them, when you're under pressure.

Can you think of something you could do right now to help a team member, or respond to them with more compassion?

Can you think of a BOOM event where you used delegation effectively? Or didn't, when you should have?

Can you think of any ways you could help a team member get more meaning from their work?

Can you think of any ways you could help a team member achieve their personal goals and objectives for their work?

Can you think of any ways you could show a team member how their work adds value to the organisation?

Do you think your team members feel confident and capable in their roles under your leadership? Why, or why not?

Do you think you're a good listener when dealing with your team? Why, or why not?

What ways can you think of to improve your future focus when you're under pressure?

What things could you do to stop reacting and start responding thoughtfully when you're under pressure?

SKILL V

KNOW YOUR LEADERSHIP STYLE

ONCE UPON A TIME IN THE WORLD OF LEADERSHIP, A BOOK WAS PUBLISHED.

It defined as succinctly as it could the difference between transformational and transactional leadership.

And what it meant to be a transformational leader. The year was 1978, the book was titled **Leadership**, and the author was James MacGregor Burns.[8]

Are you a transactional or a transformational leader? Or, let's go one step further, and add two other leadership styles to the mix, as there's a leadership style that sits before both transactional leadership and transformational leadership.

So, what's your leadership style? Remembering that transformational leadership is the nirvana of leadership, and that there are times when you might need to demonstrate the other leadership styles. On purpose, not by default. And with the right intent. Also remembering that under pressure, leaders can tend to revert to a 'lower-level' leadership style.

TEPID LEADERSHIP

Tepid leadership (a TGG descriptor) is about hands-off leadership. The leader who is tepid would describe themselves as having an 'autonomous' style. 'My team is self-managing,' they might say. 'They're all good at their jobs, and they don't need me interfering.' Yes, but they do need to you understand what is happening in the team. In a textbook on leadership, this style would be defined as laissez-faire.

TRANSACTIONAL LEADERSHIP

Transactional leadership is based very much on the exchange. Or a contingent reward. This leadership style is conditional, and you'll hear transactional leaders say, 'if only they'd do what they're supposed to, I'd reward them.' These leaders are very focused on process and procedures. They expect strict compliance with business practice and are on the lookout for variance or non-compliance.

TRUST-LESS LEADERSHIP

Trust-less leadership (another TGG descriptor) is about overly hands on leadership. Aka: micromanagement. The trust-less leader might say that 'if you want it done properly, you need to do it yourself,' or 'I have to keep showing people how to do their jobs—when will they ever learn?' Trust-less leaders miss getting the best out of their teams, as they don't allow them to shine and be their best. A textbook definition might call this leadership style an authoritarian one.

TRANSFORMATIONAL LEADERSHIP

This leadership style, in short, is about developing more leaders. Inspiring followers to achieve extraordinary outcomes for themselves and the team. In 2015,[44] **Wendy Quinn** described that transformational leaders focus on individualised consideration of each team member. They create intellectual stimulation, they provide inspirational motivation, and a role model of idealised influence. These leaders engage hearts and minds. Be one.

WHAT LEADERSHIP STYLE AM I?

I'm a good leader...now. But I wasn't, in the early days of my leadership journey, even when I thought I was.

I'm one of the 90% of hoomanz on planet Earth who aren't born leaders. I'm a bred leader. Through and through. The leadership lessons I've learnt—especially the big ones—were learnt in the school of hard knocks.

One of the questions I used to ask myself was, 'what leadership style am I?' Which is a nice question. Not a great question, but a nice question. A better question would be, 'what leadership style do I want to develop?'

Some leaders say to me in coaching that they're stuck with their style, and they can't change it. For them, they're one style, and that's it. Not true, but remember, if you believe it, it's real for you.

Leadership is learnt. If you're happy with your current leadership style, stick with it. But if you think there might be an opportunity to change or improve something, try that and see what happens. Upgrade your mindset, upskill your leadership, and uplift your teams.

But how do you develop your leadership style? Great question.

ONE GET BACK TO BASICS.

Now, at least 50% of my readership will check out after this paragraph. Tell you why. Because every time I use the word transformational leadership, our clients say that it's outdated, it's cliché, it's boring.

And it might be boring for you. But it's not boring for your teams, and your team members, who want you to demonstrate transformational leadership rather than transactional leadership.

Transformation leadership, in its simplest form, is about creating more leaders. Plain and simple. That means seeing the potential in others, being willing to develop them, and making sure they get the opportunity to shine.

As a team member, who doesn't want that? Just because you don't like the word transformational, doesn't mean that's not what's required.

Be transformative. Don't direct your team members (transactions). Be proactive (not reactive) and communicate for connection, not direction.

So what leadership style am I? Heading towards transformational!

TWO FOCUS ON YOUR COMMUNICATION STYLE, NOT YOUR LEADERSHIP STYLE.

Here's a thought for you—instead of trying to work out what style of leader you are, work out what type of communicator you are.

Something as simple as DiSC profiling can tell you a lot about your style. It can tell you if you're Dominant (direct), Influential (connected), Steady (facilitative), or conscientious (detailed).

And if that style is working for you, double down on it. If you think you might like to learn another style, do it.

High Ds or High Cs aren't great communication styles for leaders. There are times when you need to be direct or focus on numbers. Cool. But I can tell you that team members don't respond to leaders who are high D or high C. There's just no connection.

The big thing about focusing on your communication style is that you get to know yours, but you also get to know other people's styles.

Having done DiSC work for so long (and this is a bit of my weirdness), I categorise people when I speak to them into D, I, S, or C, and I try to tailor my style to theirs. Why? Because people don't want to be communicated with in your style. They want to be communicated with in theirs. Simple.

It's not what leadership style am I— it's what communication style am I?

THREE YOU CAN GET ALL THEORETICAL ON IT.

I'm theory-based hooman. I'm studying a PhD in leading under pressure, and how to help leaders stay calm during trying times. I spend my weekends reading research reports—no kidding. And I love it.

Someone asked me in a session the other day, where all of my knowledge retention comes from. And all I could say is that I research a lot.

There are very few leaders that I come across who could really hold a quality conversation about leadership styles. Which is cool. But I just think that if you really want to know what leadership style you are, go deep on the data. Unpack the research and the statistics. The way to do this is to put 'scholarly articles' at the back of your search in Google. Google will give you a list of research that's already been done on the topic. FYI: the words 'what leadership style am I' are some of the most searched on Google, in relation to leadership (see **Answer the Public**).

Most people would do a quick search and move on. But to really answer this question is a full day of research. Pick twenty research articles, and unpack them. Understand the research. If that appeals to you. If not, all good. Again, you do you.

My research has taken me through theories like authentic, conscious, and charismatic leadership. There's the Great Man theory of leadership (not really PC, but hey). There's humanistic leadership, there's trait leadership, contingent leadership, and there's even Machiavellian leadership (definitely Google that one). Even Adolf Hitler wrote a book on leadership. True story. I can't bring myself to read that one, yet, but it's out there.

Again, it's good to know where you are now. But it's even better to be heading for some leadership style that's more aligned with who you want to become as a leader.

So it's not what leadership style am I—it's what leadership styles are there? You'll find one that suits you. Then, go after it. Tell people what you're trying to achieve, and really, really, lean into that style.

One way to find it is with DISC profiling.

WHY YOUR DISC PROFILE IS MORE IMPORTANT THAN YOU MIGHT THINK

Fun fact: the same person who developed the character of Wonder Woman also developed DiSC profiling. I know—how cool! Dr William Moulton Marsten was a psychologist, lawyer, and comic book writer. He was also an outspoken feminist, and he developed Wonder Woman as a model of what's possible for women when they step into their power.

Prior to that, though, Marsten was focused on helping people understand and channel their emotions. It was groundbreaking at the time. And his book included a quadrant to describe the four different personality styles. At the time, they were called Dominance, Inducement, Submission, and Compliance. But these days, we know these four personality styles as Dominant, Influential, Steady, and Conscientious. Aka: DiSC Profiling.

WHAT IS DISC PROFILING, REALLY?

DiSC Profiling is the simplest and most effective way to truly understand how you operate, how you communicate, and why. It's a tool that unpacks your pace and priority at work, and it helps you understand your natural working style, as well as your adapted style (how you're adapting to be successful in your current role).

The process? It's a simple online survey, that doesn't take long to complete. We use DiSC Profiling with our clients, and include it in our two-day intensive leadership workshops, because it produces such an accurate and thorough analysis of their behaviour characteristics, and explains how dominant, influential, steady, or conscientious you are—and why. Our clients tell us they can't believe how bang-on their profiles are!

Let's quickly unpack the meanings of each behaviour characteristic. Dominant people tend to be very direct in their communication. Influencers are the salespeople, or those with high-level people skills. Steadiness indicates a preference to teamworking, and contribution. And conscientious people are the details workers, who like numbers, data, and processes.

BUT WHY IS THAT IMPORTANT?

DiSC profiling is important because self-awareness and self-understanding is the first step in any leader's journey to success. The phrase 'know thyself' has been around for a while now. And because DiSC is psychology-based, it allows you to understand yourself more deeply. When you unpack your profile with someone who's qualified to do so, they can give you an even more detailed explanation of the information provided.

On that note, please don't do your DiSC Profile unless you do unpack it with a DiSC practitioner. It'll create more questions than answers for you.

EVEN MORE IMPORTANTLY...

Not only does DiSC profiling help you understand yourself, it teaches you to understand other humans, and why they do what they do. This is the big winner, and where our groups get the biggest aha! moments.

The most important learning from DiSC Profiling is how to communicate with other people—especially others that aren't the same profile as you. Now that's where the magic happens! The space that it creates for you helps you to break down barriers, to get to know others, and to build better working relationships.

When you understand yourself, and others, your world changes.

HOW TO REALLY USE YOUR DISC PROFILE

We've administered a tonne of DiSC profiles over the last however-many-years, and it's one of my favourite leadership coaching activities to help people understand themselves and to understand others—and to understand why that's important!

But how do you really use that 30-something-page document, that tells you if you're Dominant, Influential, Steady or Conscientious? What makes it more than a report? What makes it the thing, the tool, that changes your life, changes your communication, and changes your team leadership? What you do with it, of course!

So, what can you do with it?

ONE READ IT BY YOURSELF.

I know this sounds straightforward. But most people don't. And this includes me (I am a high Influencer, and I don't have much Conscientious in my profile—aka, I don't do details and data). What I do though, is know the bits of the document that are relevant and that can move the needle for me. I refer to my profile regularly (yes, I use my profile in training programs—I take the attendees through my profile, to help me explain mine, and to help them understand their own profiles).

My profile is always in my computer bag, and it's never too far away when I'm doing one-on-one coaching sessions in case we need to refer to it. Not only do I read it, but I've internalised it, and I understand it. Yes, there are some parts of it that are 'vague', but I value the information, and I make it a priority to stay on top of it, and to keep 'knowing' it. Why? Because it's important that I do, as I not only train it, but I use it daily.

TWO READ IT WITH YOUR LEADER.

This one freaks people out. 'You mean you want me to sit down with my leader and tell them all about my personality and how to communicate with me?!' Ahhh, yep. Especially the page that's got the dos and don'ts on it. Just imagine for a moment if your leader is the type of person that'll take that information on board, and work on their communication style to better connect with you! Winner.

Now, I get that some people's leader might not be that growth mindset-focused and may not be as approachable as others. In general, though, if there's any chance that your leader is willing to take on board that detail and that information, have the conversation with them. If they ask why you're having the chat, just say it's to 'help you help me.' The idea of that conversation, obviously, is to set your leader up for success. To help them understand how to do great communication with you, and that if they step into the don'ts that you might be triggered and not do your best work.

It really is an amazing conversation to have, and one that'll really help you out. Mind you, though, if your leader is a good leader, nothing you tell them will be a surprise. If that's the case, that's outstanding. You're lucky that you're working with a great human.

THREE READ IT WITH YOUR TEAM.

This one REALLY freaks people out. Like above: 'You mean you want me to sit down with my team and tell them all about my personality and how to communicate with me?!' And again...ahhh, yep.

Especially the page that's got the improvement opportunities on it. Let your team know that you've been through your profile, and that you've reflected, and that you're going to actively work on one improvement area. You can pick more if you really want to, though one is enough. You might take your team through them all, but at the end of the day, this is about making a commitment to your team that you're willing to work on your personal development. And that you're willing for your team to hold you accountable to your improvement action. Now, don't say that you are, if you really aren't—that's not great for your credibility.

If you're doing a DiSC profiling process with your team, this is easier. Everyone has their own improvement actions, and if they're willing to share theirs, it creates some openness and better connection between team members, and between them and you.

As a side note: for the above actions, I have presumed (to a degree at least) that you are part of a psychologically safe team. And that your leader and team members are willing to listen, and to work with you on what matters to you in your DiSC profile.

Needless to say, the above actions can be reciprocal. Feel free to ask your leader to share their dos and don'ts, so that you're aware of them. Also, with the right intent, be willing to hold your team members accountable if they share their improvement opportunities.

Use your DiSC profile. Make it count. It's instrumental in discovering and developing your leadership style, and in your learning to be a better leader.

EVERY DAY IS A SCHOOL DAY... OR IS IT?

You learn something new every day, right? Of course you do. You wake up and learn what the weather is doing. You learn what's happening in the news, if you watch the tele. At work, you learn about what your team is struggling with, or what their goals are for the day. But is that really learning? Or is it just living, and passively looking for and listening to new information without internalising it?

Every day is a school day. But only if you're active with your learning strategy. And yes, learning is a strategy, and it's the number one most important thing that leaders can do for their personal development and professional growth. In our training programs, the first morning of our two-day workshops is about the L from the LEAD process (learning), and we follow that up with engagement, articulation, and demonstration.

For me, if you're waking up and learning, that's passive. If you're making your learning and your personal and professional development a priority, you're doing active learning.

So, what are the key elements of a being an active learner?

ONE PICK A TOPIC TO LEARN ABOUT.

Maybe it's just leadership in general, or maybe it's empathetic leadership or adaptive leadership or conscious leadership. Or leading under pressure with created conscious control.

Importantly, though, pick a topic that really lights you up, that you feel is not only important, but that will actually help you as a leader. The more interested in the topic you are, the more likely you are to be invested in the process of learning more.

TWO DEVELOP A PLAN AND A PROCESS.

This part of the process is about finding the process that works for you.

Right now the knowledge on the planet is doubling every 12 hours (crazy, hey?!)—but in 1945, knowledge was only doubling every 25 years. There's no shortage of information out there.

Here are some of the ways you can build an active learning plan (what you'll learn). Start with the topic you chose, then find a book to read. Watch some YouTube videos, read some research reports, or listen to audio books—turn your car into a university. Work out what will be easiest to fit into your life, and it doesn't have to be every day; every week would be a good start. Then, put the process together (when you'll learn). Is it in the mornings, instead of watching the news? Is it at night, before you go to sleep? Is it listening to Audible when you're driving? Commit to the process, and watch your learning go up!

THREE GET COMMITTED, NOT JUST INTERESTED.

Some leaders reading this have already started to think about all the extra time that this will take. *Anton, I am crazy busy already!* I know, I get it. But some of the ideas that I listed are not time stealers. They are actually NET (no extra time—like while you are driving) investments in time. Seriously. You can learn stuff on your drive to work and back. Easy!

Fun fact: we have had 20-year leaders come through our programs, and when I ask them what the last book they read was (on leadership or otherwise), they tell me that they haven't read a book since high school. True story. And that's not wrong, it's OK, they're still in leadership roles. We all have our own strategies, but if you want to understand your leadership style and develop into a better leader, you should be committed in your learning—even when you're crazy busy.

HAVE YOU NOTICED THAT WE'RE NOW CRAZY BUSY, NOT JUST BUSY?

As if being busy isn't enough, we're now CRAZY busy. Which I get, and I know the world is crazy busy. Most of our clients are leading under pressure. Whether it's the pressure of putting people over productivity, or the pressure of pushing performance, leaders are struggling to cope, let alone develop their leadership style.

And their teams are suffering. If the leader is crazy busy, the team members feel that. They'll sense the urgency, and the impact of the pressure on the leader. And more importantly, it's seriously hard to lead, and to create conscious control, if you're crazy busy.

Now this section is not about time management and helping you be less busy. I'm not sure that's the answer. I'm going to come at this section from a psychology perspective, and let you know what you can do to feel less crazy busy, which I think will help you more. In coming sections I'll provide some time management tips, but for now, let's talk about the psychology of being crazy busy (and how to not be...sort of).

ONE CHANGE YOUR LANGUAGING.

Here's your challenge after reading this: to not have 'crazy busy' on repeat every time someone asks you how you are. I know that'll be tough for some, because it really has become a default response.

Now I want you to change your languaging for the sake of others, including your team members. Every time they hear that you're crazy busy, they feel like they either can't approach you right now, or that they're not your priority. That's sad, right? Words have power in them, and they speak to the emotional part of our brain—the limbic system. Hominins are very intuitive creatures, and they pick up signals quickly and easily, especially through your language.

More importantly, change your languaging for you. Even though you're leading under pressure, and you're busy, find another response. One that feels right to you, and that rolls off your tongue. In response to 'how are you?', you could try:

- I'm very productive
- I'm happy
- I'm in control
- I'm all over it
- I'm getting it done

It'll sound strange at the start, but give it a try and see what happens. And let me know, please—I'd like to know how others respond.

TWO CHANGE YOUR FOCUS.

When you're crazy busy, you're focusing on all the things that you don't have. Like when you're lacking time, or some other resources. The universe has a habit of giving you more of what you asked for (aka, the book **The**

Secret),[9] so if you're crazy busy, the universe seems to give you more to do. Regardless of your workload, try focusing on all of the things that you have got: think about how well your team is going, or how much they've achieved recently. Or how much you've gotten done. This one is a bit like me in the pool doing swimming training (which is hard for me, FYI). I always count upwards, instead of down. That is, in my head, I always focus on how far I've come (like 2k of a 3k set), not how far I've got to go (like 1k still to swim). It's such a great mental trick.

For me, the best tip I can give you on changing your focus is to get a gratitude journal, and start writing in it. Every day. If you're looking for some more information on this topic, see my radio interview with **@The Pulse 94.7** recently (Robert Cameron).

THREE CHANGE YOUR PRIORITY.

Remember that this isn't advice on time management, it's advice on your psychology, your personal psychological safety, and your conscious control. Here's the thing: when you're crazy busy (or just saying you are), it's hard to be in control, and in charge of your emotional and psychological state. Being crazy busy elevates (heightens) your emotional state.

Here are the top three things to prioritise to help you be less crazy busy. The first thing is breathing. I know, too boring, right? But I can't tell you how many studies and how much research has been done on the power of breath. We now know that meditation (breathing exercises) changes your brain (read that again if you need to). 50% of the leaders I deal with tell me they either can't or won't meditate. That's cool. But try it. Just breathe deeply. Your brain is the biggest user of oxygen in your body, and without oxygenating your frontal lobes, you just don't think clearly.

The second thing is down time. Take some time to do some self-care. This topic has been talked about a lot, so another eye roll moment for some. But take this one seriously and watch your business change (or how it feels will change, at least). We take this one so seriously that all our coaching clients get some form of self-care as part of their coaching package (like a massage or movie voucher).

The third thing is to get more sleep. Sorry, too boring again. But get more sleep, and watch your emotional state change. I won't bore you with the studies, but some psychologists will tell you we're on the planet to benefit from sleep, not for our waking hours (there's a thought).

And if you make not being crazy busy a priority for you, in general, your mental state and the state of your team will change for the better. The workload might not, but how you process it will—and that's one of the most important things you can do to develop your leadership style.

MY 28TH EXPLOSION ANNIVERSARY

I'll leave off this section on discovering your leadership style with an anecdote about my own leadership style development—and how it transitioned from physical safety to psychological safety.

At this time, 28 years ago, I was lying in the intensive care unit of the Gladstone Hospital, with most of the top layers of my skin blown off my hands and face. I was in the most excruciating pain I've ever experienced, and I was trying to understand what the heck had happened and why I was lying in intensive care looking like a French Fry.

Yes, it was only second-degree burns. Yes, I only spent two days in intensive care, before spending about five weeks in the burns unit in Brisbane. Having my skin forcibly removed every morning. By the most caring and compassionate nurses (burns unit nurses are really the best there is. They see and treat the worst of injuries, and deal with death and debilitation on a regular basis). Burns are a horrible injury. And that is something I hope I never go through again. Ever.

It took me about five weeks to recover and get out of hospital. I like to say that I was doing a five-minute job, trying to save five minutes, and I went home about five weeks later. And that was the crazy part about it. There really was no need to rush it. I had time, and the tradesperson working with me was certainly not pushing or trying to get the job done more quickly.

This was purely a personal or physical safety issue. Make a bad decision—which I did—nearly get killed—which I did. Suffer emotionally for the next ten years, trying to unpack why it happened, and why it happened to me. Which I did. I was angry with the world for a while. Until I took responsibility and ownership for the incident. My decision, my actions, my consequences.

About ten years after the incident, once I'd got my head around it, I decided to talk more about it (I couldn't talk about for ten years, it made me too upset, and brought back painful skin-removal memories). And memories of having someone take care of your hygiene for you (I couldn't use my hands).

Three things happened. Firstly, my wife and boys and I moved back to Gladstone (we worked around Australia for that first ten years) and when I got back, people wanted to know how I was. I couldn't avoid it anymore. Then, I was employed on a site where the induction involved watching the movie Remember Charlie. I was moved. His story touched my heart. Then, I got the chance to run a safety meeting. And to tell my story. Like Charlie did. And it was well received.

So, I quit my job, and became a speaker...much to my lovely wife's disgust. I was not acting like an adult, apparently. I do now, though, which is good. Love you, Mrs G.

After telling my story around the country and overseas, leaders started asking about how to keep their teams safe. My work went from safety to leadership. And safety leadership. And that journey that has helped me to really unpack what drives people to do what they do, and how leaders can lead under pressure, with conscious control.

Leadership training and consulting has seen me finish a business degree in HR and a science degree in psychology. It's seen me author five books, and read more books than I could count. And most importantly, I've worked with leaders and a range of industries, everywhere, to help them create high-performing and connected teams.

And my life has moved from personal and physical safety to psychological safety, the phrase that Amy Edmondson started to make famous in 1999.[19] Then, in 2012–2014, the internal project (Project Aristotle) found that psychological safety was the main reason that Google was able to create such highly effective teams. Since then, several books have been written on the topic, by Timothy Clark, Dan Radecki, and in 2019, Clive Lloyd[32] (titled Next Generation Safety Leadership). In short, psychological safety is about making it OK for people to share their ideas and opinions without the fear or ridicule, resentment, or rejection.

Personally, not only learning about psychology, but learning about psychological safety, has been the most intriguing and enlightening thing I have ever done. To be able to share with leaders what a psychologically safe team looks and feels like has been next level. My work has transitioned from leadership consulting—that was focused on the process of leadership—to work that's focused on the people side of leadership, on a deeper level.

And with a distinct focus on leadership under pressure, because it's during BOOM events (crises) that leaders need conscious control, and to really lean into care factor and courageous leadership. My work is emotion-centred, and people-focused, and helps leaders to understand why people, and psychologically safe teams, should really be their highest priority.

After 28 years, from an electrician getting blown up by a switch board, to working out that physical safety keeps people alive, and that psychological safety keeps teams alive (and helps them thrive), here I am. Hopefully, a transformational leader, who helps other leaders be transformational.

Living the dream.

ACTIVITY 1.5
KNOW YOUR LEADERSHIP STYLE

Take some time now to think about what you've learnt in the last chapter.

Answering the following questions will help you to better understand your leadership style, and ways you could improve it. Alternatively, think about ways to better manage your work schedule and free up more time to spend on learning the things you want to learn.

What does your DiSC profile say about you?

If you knew the DiSC profiles of your team members, how would this change the way you communicate with them?

What things could you do with your work schedule to free up time for more learning? What topics would you like to learn about?

Do you have a tepid, transactional or trust-less leadership style? What changes could you make to change it into a transformational style?

Think of some big mistakes you've made. What would you do differently to avoid them, or to better learn from them?

What things could you do to inspire your followers to achieve extraordinary outcomes for themselves and the team?

Is your languaging negative or maladaptive? What could you change about it?

AFTERWORD

If you're still with me, congratulations on making it this far. And thanks for finding me engaging enough that you decided not to put this book down and never look at it again.

What I hope has kept you connected to my words is the introspection with which I wrote them. I hope you can see how challenging your irrational fears and wrong beliefs helps you to stop procrastinating, to be a conscious leader, and to make time for real conversations with the people in your life you're trying to lead.

I also hope you can see how metacognition, and learning more about why you think and do the things you do—especially the things that aren't serving you in any meaningful way—can help to find your real 'why', and to put away maladaptive behaviours (like procrastinating, and going BOOM when things go BOOM). Looking at your own personality and leadership style is the way to set yourself free to become the better leader you want to be.

This book isn't the answer to all of your leadership woes. But it's the beginning of the process. A process that needs to start from within, by understanding your own thinking, emotions, and behaviour. So you can stop doing what doesn't work, and start doing what does.

If you're an old-school leader, the one that I wrote this book for, congratulations on getting through a book you probably weren't very comfortable reading. See how getting comfortable with discomfort always ends up with growth?

If you're a new-age leader, the one that I wrote this book for, congratulations on getting through a book you probably thought was going to be a lot less work. See how facing the ugly truth you don't want to admit to—like team members who don't listen and don't respect your leadership—is teaching you emotional literacy, and improving your ability to lead under pressure?

There's a lot more to learn. Every day is a school day, remember? Go and get stuck into whatever piques your interest: metacognition; how to think fast and talk slow; how to have real conversations with people you're leading—or your own leader. This book is the beginning, and as long as you're leading, there shouldn't be an end.

Learn more from me. I have a bunch of books and a team of people who can help you become a better leader. Or don't learn more from me. Learn from anyone whose leadership is inspiring to you in any way. Or anyone whose leadership has caused you to not seek help when you needed it, or to feel unempowered, or to decide to never, ever lead your team like they led you. Go learn how to lead through introspection, and under pressure, and to have enough insight and conscious control not to go BOOM when things or people around you go BOOM.

If you don't remember anything I've taught you in this book, remember how it made you feel. If it filled you with hope and optimism, and overwhelmed you with the urge to commit to being a better leader, good. Go do it. If it filled you with dread and shame about how bad your leadership really is, good. Go get better at it.

Either way, you got this far because you're becoming reflective. You're learning how to think differently. You're learning how to react differently. You're learning how to answer the big questions—including why you're a leader, and why you do what you do.

Congratulations on finishing this book. You're upgrading your mindset. Keep going, and you'll be upgrading your leadership, and your team.

THE
LEADERSHIP
TRILOGY

BOOK 2

UPSKILL

YOUR LEADERSHIP

LEADERSHIP LESSONS FROM LEADERSHIP SPECIALIST

ANTON GUINEA

UPSKILL
your LEADERSHIP

WITH THE UPSKILL MODEL

This model was developed as a strategic tool for putting theory into practice to upskill your leadership.

The model draws on various psychological theories relating to attitude, perception, and emotional experience in the workplace, and structures this information into a practical framework to guide leaders through the process of upskilling their leadership to become better leaders.

It was developed over nearly 20 years of theoretical analysis combined with real-world experience, and it underpins the Guinea Group's winning formula for creating effective leaders, high-performing teams, and workplaces that are both physically and psychologically safe for workers.

Refer back to this model while reading this book. It'll help you form a concrete framework in your mind that will, over time, become a natural reference point as you grow and develop in your attitudes and behaviours, and move you closer to being the leader you want to be.

To make the most of this resource, contact us via our website at antonguinea.com.au for a self-diagnostic tool and action plan to review and improve your skills against the model.

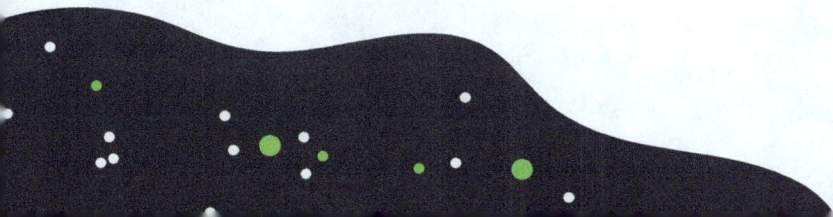

01 CREATE **CONSCIOUS CONTROL**

Skillset: Learn to respond, not react, to BOOM events

02 HAVE HIGH **CARE FACTOR**

Skillset: Learn how to be a good human, and a good leader

03 DEVELOP **YOUR EQ**

Skillset: Lead with emotional intelligence, and social intelligence

04 LEAD **UNDER PRESSURE**

Skillset: Stay in control and lead well even when the pressure rises

05 BE **COURAGEOUS**

Skillset: Take action when it matters, even if it scares you

INTRODUCTION:
UPSKILL YOUR LEADERSHIP

Leadership can be challenging. It can be rewarding. After parenting, it's the most important job on planet Earth (sorry first responders and teachers). And it takes a range of skills and experiences to get it right.

But sitting above the skill sets of leaders are a set of three mandates. The definition of a mandate is an order or being commissioned to do something. The three leadership mandates are the obligations of leaders, from the day that they take on a leadership role. And the mandates are prioritised in this order: a mandate to the organisation, a mandate to the team, and a mandate to the self. Also known as values, transformation, and control (VTC).

Here's how to apply the BIG 3 Leadership Mandates.

ONE VALUES ALIGNMENT.

Here's the background to this mandate, the values-based and organisational-focused mandate.

When leaders (particularly senior leaders) leave organisations, especially when they've had a long tenure with that organisation, the comment that they most often make in my coaching is that: 'My values don't align with the values of the business.'

This is code for: the business has asked me to do something, to say something, to decide something that doesn't feel right, on a very deep level.

Let's slow it down a little at this point. I get that leaders sometimes must support organisational decisions and make those decisions their own. Understood. But there are times when, for the leader, this requirement violates a deep personal value.

129

So, the mandate for a leader is to be firstly very clear on their own set of three values. The most common leadership value is integrity. Yours might be different. Mine personally are energy, engagement, and enterprise thinking. I have a purpose that sits above those values (my 'why') which is to leave humans and businesses better than I found them.

Yours might be respect, teamwork, or any of the multitude of other values that could drive your behaviour. And that's why values are the very first mandate. Research finds that individual values are a driving force behind personal responsibility[40] (Mirvis & Googins, 2010). Again, your values drive your behaviour. They're the first things that you turn to when it comes to making big decisions.

And here's the thing: 90% of leaders (that we train and deal with at least) have never done a values exercise. They've never done the work to understand what their personal values are.

Just Google a values list, and see what words come up, and what resonates for you. Then compare your list to the values of your organisation.

And then, most importantly, understand if your values align with the organisation's values. If they don't, that's cool, you may be able to find a way to reconcile that within yourself. But if you can't, it'll be difficult to stay in your organisation for the long haul.

An understanding and alignment of values is a big thing for leaders. That's why it's mandate number one. When you're being values-driven, you can then step into transformational leadership.

TWO TRANSFORMATIONAL LEADERSHIP.

Here's the background to this mandate, the team- and human-focused mandate for leaders.

In 1978, James Burns published the seminal work on transformational leadership in the book simply titled Leadership. According to Burns, transforming leadership is a process in which leaders and followers help each other to advance to a higher level of morale and motivation.

In short, here's a very quick way to sum up the concept of being a transformational leader: create more leaders. A leader's role is to work with those in their team, to provide them with the coaching, the mentoring, the training and any other opportunity for growth they need to become even better future leaders. Leaders who also understand these three mandates.

And, yes, I hear you, again. Not all our team members want to advance their careers into more senior roles. And some think that they should be progressing faster than they really should. With every mandate comes a quandary. And this is the quandary for leaders: who, and how, to develop more leaders.

There's one way to find out, and that's to have career conversations. Not performance discussions, not mid-year reviews, but career conversations. Conversations that talk through what the team member values (see mandate one), and what they want to do with their working life. For more information on this one, see the book **Radical Candor** by Kim Scott.[49] Some of your team might want to own a hobby farm in the future. And wouldn't it be good if you could equip them with the leadership skills to make that happen? While they're in your team, and while they're growing and producing more for your business, now.

In your team, you have rock stars and super stars (Credit: Kim Scott).[49] Rock stars want to be high performers now, and don't want to progress (so let's not force them to). Super stars want to progress (so let's understand what this progression looks like). And that progression might be quicker than you think it should be, as their leader. Some super stars are just committed to their career growth (but please presume positive intent here—it'll be for the right reasons).

I get the career focus. As a young leader, there was no way I was going to slow down and back off on my goals. I had them in a project Gannt Chart and was totally committed to progressing through the ranks. And I had leaders who supported that. Finally, I got promoted to middle-level management (too young, and too early), and I was working for a human without conscious control and with zero personal control. And that's why I do what I do now, so that leaders are better equipped than that leader was to stay in conscious control.

THREE CREATED CONSCIOUS CONTROL.

Here's the background to this mandate, the self- (and situation-) focused mandate for leaders.

It's long been known—even before we could study the human brain with high-powered technology—that the human has two thinking and behavioural pathways. One could be called the primitive, or the instinctive, or the emotional pathway. The other would be called the thinking, the reasoning, or the rational pathway.

In other words, we have instinctive and reasoning pathways for making decisions, and they both drive our behaviour. The instinctive pathway is routed through the amygdala, in the limbic system, which controls our emotional responses and our fight-or-flight response. The reasoning pathway is routed through our frontal lobes, the parts of our brain which make us uniquely human, and which allow us to plan and make rational decisions, even if the rest of our brain is trying to lose it.

Daniel Kahneman[25] called these system one and two processes, in his book **Thinking Fast and Slow**. In 1924, Frederick Mathias Alexander[1] published what was at the time a very progressive book, **Constructed Conscious Control of the Individual**. My favourite quote from that book is:

> **I do not know of any person who doubts that if people are to evolve in the right direction, the gap between the instinctive and conscious control of the self must be bridged.**

Stop for a moment and reread that quote. That was written in 1924. In other words, the human must have control of self. And yes, it's still as relevant now as it was nearly one hundred years ago. Here at TGG, we call it 'created conscious control.' And conscious leadership (a more contemporary term).

Created conscious control is about emotional control, behavioural control, and situational control. And for every leader on planet Earth, this is a key mandate. To remain in control, regardless of what's happening.

Is that possible? Of course not.

But is it an obligation of leadership? Absolutely.

There are only three things that drive our behaviour, and they are our beliefs (subconsciously), our values (consciously—see mandate one), and our emotional state. And if you don't think our emotions drive our behaviour, just watch an angry person. See what damage people do to other humans, and to their own reputation, when they act on emotion rather than on reasoning.

This mandate is the self-mandate because it's incumbent upon leaders to have conscious control. Without conscious control, leaders don't have behavioural control, and without behavioural control, leaders have zero chance of having situational control. And with leaders being under so much pressure, they need to be able to manage high-pressure situations and high-stress encounters. That's the job at times.

When leaders let their emotions drive their behaviours, and when those emotions are out of control, they hurt other humans. And if they're not on the **The Dark Triad**,[42] they will apologise for their behaviour, and make the excuse that it was just because of their emotional state (uncool).

This is what some leaders don't understand. The hurt that leaders cause humans will be remembered for decades. How do I know? Because I ask people in our coaching and training programs for the leader conversation or conversations that hurt their hearts. Some can remember those conversations from ten, twenty, or even thirty years ago.

Knowing this, why not be the leader who's remembered for being in conscious control, and not as the leader who didn't have that control?

Creating conscious control can be learnt—it's a skill. It's a set of behaviours, habits, and patterns that a leader runs to keep their frontal lobes oxygenated and in charge of the situation. See Daniel Goleman's[22] work on **Emotional Intelligence** for more information on staying in emotional control.

So, there you have it. The BIG THREE leadership mandates, and why they're important.

Yes, these are simple to say. Not as easy to implement. But worth it, if you're serious about upskilling your leadership.

SKILL 1
CREATE CONSCIOUS
CONTROL

IF I WAS TO ASK YOU WHAT'S THE MOST IMPORTANT CHARACTER TRAIT IN YOUR LEADER, WHAT WOULD YOUR ANSWER BE?

And more importantly, if I was to ask your team what they think are the most important character traits in a leader, what would they say?

Well, at the end of last year, we asked. We reached out to my LinkedIn tribe to find out what they thought it was, and we gave people the options of clarity, consistency, charisma, and care factor.

Of the 52 respondents, the results were:

- Clarity – 14%
- Consistency – 40%
- Charisma – 2%
- Care factor – 44%

Yes, there were only a few options provided. Granted, it's only 52 responses. Also yes, consistency and care factor rated the highest. Forget charisma (a trait associated with psychopathy—as we know from the negative leadership styles in Paulhus & Williams' **The Dark Triad**).[42]

When I reached out and asked some of the respondents (that I knew), they were able to talk through what consistency meant for them. Put simply, it was 'consistency of emotional state'. The care factor was self-explanatory. We all know that team members don't care how much you know until they know how much you care.

So, what does this little survey tell us? That leaders who are consistent in their emotional states will connect more with their teams. And emotional control is easy when things are good. But when everything goes BOOM— well, that's a different story.

Leaders need to stay in control. By creating conscious control.

BECAUSE RESPONDING IS MORE IMPORTANT THAN REACTING

My old boss would go red, his veins would pop out of his head, and he would literally explode with rage. And venom. And aggression. Don't be like my old boss. It's not a cool look. And it hurts people!

I think the challenge for him, looking back on it, was that he just didn't have the ability to take half a second and reflect before reacting. It wasn't responding. It was all reaction.

Emotional control is a learnt skill. It really is. We have this primitive brain that reacts to stimulus in a fraction of a second, and our emotions go crazy. Unless we can turn our smart brain on and make it override that reaction, with self-talk, and by being rational, not irrational. And then respond to the stimulus, in a more controlled way.

Deepak Chopra[11] stated it best in his book The Soul of Leadership where he wrote that:

> Emotions are closely tied to belief, ego, and past conditioning. When you get angry at someone, you're also saying 'I'm right.' Defuse this self-centred tendency by asking for as many viewpoints as possible. Finding out what others think won't make you wrong; it will broaden your vistas.

Broaden your vistas it will. But there are times when emotional control comes easier than others, right?

Part of leading under pressure is staying in emotional control. If you're in emotional control, you can create behavioural control. With behavioural control comes situational control.

Yes, it all starts with emotional control, and not going nuts in the moment, only to be sorry later for what you said or did. Your team needs you to keep it together. They're relying on you for the example of how to behave. And they need to know that you'll remain calm under fire, and that you have the ability to take charge of the situation or circumstance with control, care factor, and courage.

And, from our training and coaching programs, what we know works is:

BREATHE THROUGH IT.

You'll be amazed at how powerful your breath is for helping you stay in control. Yogis have known it for centuries, and we've finally cottoned on. Control your breathing, control your response.

BE STILL AND BE UNSPOKEN.

Don't feel like you have to say something in the moment. Take a second or ten (and even better, count backwards) to help you collect your thoughts and your emotions before you do anything.

BECOME SELF-AWARE AND PREPARED.

Know what your triggers are, and prepare for how you'll respond when you're triggered emotionally. If you're unprepared, and you're trigged anyway, revert to the two points above.

Your ability to create conscious control influences everything you do as a leader—and it can become an enduring trait or state that can help you to consistently lead well into the future, come what may.

THE 7 TRAITS AND STATES

In the last section, I unpacked the concept of leadership mandates (values alignment, transformational leadership, and created conscious control). These are critical elements of leadership, and they aren't skills as much as they're a way of being. A way of leading.

Specific leadership skills are either traits or states. Traits are characteristic patterns of thinking, feeling, and behaving that are adopted by leaders in general terms, in most situations; they differ between individuals and remain rather stable across time. States are characteristic patterns of thinking, feeling, and behaving in a specific situation at a particular moment in time. Traits are longer-term, and consistent. States (like moods) are more shorter-term and can vary.

Understanding the seven traits and states, and doing an inventory check on both, helps to develop an action plan based on the specific areas the leader wishes to work on—and to develop conscious control.

The 7 traits and states include:

ONE LEARNING.

Leaders are learners. The best leaders are constantly updating their knowledge base. They're learning about themselves and others. And they're learning about leadership. They're watching TED talks, they're reading books, they're listening to Podcasts or audiobooks, or they're studying a degree or similar.

Learning (growth) is a key human requirement. A human need. It's hard to continue to develop your leadership and your conscious control if you aren't learning new skills and knowledge on a regular basis. There's so much great information out there; it's just a matter of finding it.

TWO ENGAGING.

Engagement is a key leadership skill. Being engaging, and being interested, not interesting. Engaging others in conversations: caring conversations, robust conversations, career conversations. Communicating with others, in their style (DiSC), not your own.

Engaging leaders can hold the space when others need them to. They're emotionally intelligent, and they can think fast and talk slow. They understand what other people are feeling and experiencing. Engagement is about caring and connection, and it's underpinned by conscious control.

THREE ARTICULATING.

Leaders need to be able to give clear direction. Being able to articulate things like why you're a leader, what your leadership values are, and how they drive your behaviour, is a key leadership skill. To articulate what the vision, mission and values of the team are, and what the leader's expectations are. What the consequences of not meeting expectations will be, and why. You can't articulate properly without conscious control.

FOUR DEMONSTRATION.

Demonstration is about leading by example, and leading with integrity. Leading by example is not the most important thing about leadership: it's the ONLY thing that really matters.

Your team don't listen to you as much as they watch you, so remember that your behaviour is always on show. And be cognisant of what it's saying about you. It's important to have conscious control, because others follow your lead. If you ever wonder why your team is behaving in a certain way, always reflect on what you did or didn't do to encourage that behaviour, either consciously or subconsciously.

FIVE EMPATHY.

Empathy sits somewhere between apathy and sympathy. And it's really neither of these emotional states. Apathy is not caring, and sympathy is over-caring. Empathy is understanding, it's not about caring. Empathising is about walking in another person's shoes and understanding from a cognitive perspective what that situation must be like for the other person. It's about having the conscious control to take time to understand the other person's feelings, and being compassionate (which is about taking action of some sort to support the other person, if they need it).

SIX RESILIENCE.

There are six elements of resilience (the PR6, as developed by Jurie Rossouw),[46] and they include vision, collaboration, composure, health, tenacity, and reasoning.

Resilience is not about being able to cope with a tough situation. It's about advancing despite adversity. And you don't build resilience during a tough situation, you develop it before the situation. Or following it. Learning resilience before you need it is about personal development. Learning it following a tough situation can be part of post-traumatic growth (PTG). That way, when the same situation happens again, you'll be ready and better prepared to deal with it.

SEVEN SAFETY.

Your team members need to feel safe. Team members who feel safe will share their ideas, opinions, and views, and they don't have to worry about ridicule, rejection or resentment. Safety is a value, and it's about both feeling safe and working safely. Putting something else (like production, schedule, cost, or even your own feelings) above it could lead to dire consequences.

You're dealing with humans. That's why you need to have conscious control. You're not just dealing with your feelings; you're dealing with other people's—and some of them aren't dealing with theirs the way they should.

DEALING WITH BULLIES IN BUSINESS SUITS

Corporate bullying is an issue in Australia. HRM Solutions (and Safe Work Australia—SWA) has found that Australia has the sixth-highest rate of workplace bullying when compared with thirty-four European countries. According to SWA,[48] the national average rate of workplace bullying has increased by 40%. This is supported by independent research conducted by the mental health charity, Beyond Blue, who suggest that almost 50% of all working Australians will experience bullying at some time in their work life.

Recently, and given my work as a leadership coach, I have done some radio interviews on bullies in business suits (see **my post here**). Yes, my focus is on working with leaders, those that do bully, and those that don't (depending on the situation). It's to help leaders refine their leadership skills and their ability to have a positive influence on their teams and their businesses. My purpose is to help leaders become better humans, and to create high-performing teams.

We do a lot of work in a coaching environment on leading organisations that don't tolerate bullying, and on helping bullying leaders to understand the impact they have on others. Unsurprisingly, it involves conscious control.

We also teach these skills in how to deal with a leader who's a bully.

ONE ORGANISATIONS NEED TO TAKE THE LEAD & MAKE CHANGE.

And they are.

Bullies in business suits usually promote or create what are known as 'toxic cultures.' Recently, an **MIT Sloan Management Review study**[54] detailed that the main reason that staff are leaving organisations, as part of the great resignation, is due to a toxic culture. The study explains that the leading elements contributing to toxic cultures include failure to promote diversity, equity, and inclusion; workers feeling disrespected; and unethical behaviour.

Some organisations (and industries) still appear to accept these cultures as normal or OK. Recently, **Hello Care** reported on the thirty-five staff who were suspended, resigned, or were on stress leave amid bullying at an Adelaide aged care home, and the current and former employees told *The Advertiser* that a 'toxic' work culture was to blame.

The impact of toxic cultures (and bullying) is significant, but that's a topic for another book.

On the other side of the ledger, people-centred organisations like James Hardie (2022) and Cleanaway (2020) are looking at their senior leader behaviour and addressing the cultures in their businesses with programs like executive leadership mentoring, enhanced reporting, and monitoring of the leader's conduct. Yes, corporate Australia is taking a stand, and it's refreshing to see corporate culture turnarounds like these.

My prediction is that there will be more of these examples moving forward.

TWO TEAM MEMBERS AND STAFF NEED TO TAKE A STAND.

And they are.

Working for a bully is crippling. I've witnessed firsthand how much damage workplace bullying can do to team members. And I've been bullied in the workplace myself—which is one of the origin stories that drives the work that I do now.

The sad part is that it's hard to stand up to bullies. In my experience, they get louder, and more aggressive, more abusive, or more abrupt. But you must say something. You need to take a stand. You need to put your emotional and psychological safety first.

There are some very specific ways that you can have robust conversations with bullies in business suits, and create behavioural boundaries with a shared understanding of what you'll accept and tolerate as a team member. Be strong. Your mental health depends on it. Do this by calling attention to their values (or the organisational values) and share that bullying hurts people, and that if they value being a good human, bullying doesn't fit into that value system. Explain exactly how the bullying makes you feel, and the impact that it's having on you and/or your team. Finally, make it personal, by using the person's name a lot in the conversation. Try 'Jane, I get that you're under pressure, but Jane, I need you to stop (be specific here) because the impact is (be specific here). I treat you with respect, Jane, and I really need you to respect me too.'

THREE IF YOU'RE A BYSTANDER, IT'S YOUR TIME TO SHINE.

This paragraph is perhaps the most important part of this section.

One of the main reasons that bullying continues (unchecked) in organisations is due to what organisational psychologists call the 'Bystander Effect'. Britannica defines the Bystander Effect as 'the inhibiting influence of the presence of others on a person's willingness to help someone in need'. Research has shown that, even in an emergency, a bystander is less likely to extend help when he or she is in the real or imagined presence of others than when he or she is alone. In other words, humans are afraid to take a stand to help others in need—when other people are around and watching.

But we also know that bystanders are in the perfect position from which to act. They're witness to the poor behaviour, and they're not impacted personally, which means they can remain unbiased in the situation. They can generally keep their emotions in check, and they can be objective.

Bystanders, we need you! And I'm hoping as you read this that you don't need to help someone in your organisation or team who's being bullied. But if you do, don't miss the opportunity to call out the bullying. You might just be part of the solution, and help change a toxic work culture.

If your business has a toxic culture, or you're witnessing or experiencing workplace bullying, you can refer to the Safe Work Australia Guide to Preventing and Responding to Workplace Bullying.[48] You can also work with us at the Guinea Group[55] to learn conscious control—one of the major safeguards against bullying behaviour.

DOES LEADERSHIP TRAINING REALLY WORK?

It sure does. And we've received too many positive testimonials and thank you messages following our programs to think any differently. And it's probably not even a matter of if leadership training works—it's a matter of what makes it work.

Let's unpack that.

ONE THE SETUP IS IMPORTANT.

The most important thing that a business can do prior to sending people to our programs is to let the attendees know what they're coming to, and why. Set them up for success. Too many times, in my last seventeen years of doing this, have I seen people turn up because there was an event in their calendar, but they had no idea what they were coming along to. Uncool.

We work with out clients, now, to make sure that never happens.

And it worked for one of our attendees. A few days before the program, we got a call to ask if he really need to come along. We mentioned that it could help his leadership. 'I've been a leader for thirty years,' he said, 'And I didn't even know leadership training was a thing.' He had a great time and learnt a lot, which his team now benefits from.

TWO THE TRAINER IS IMPORTANT.

We have a lot of trainees come through our programs, who have a very good 'BS-Meter.' In other words, they're cynical, they're potentially a little closed off, and they don't know if they'll get value from the time they invest into their own personal development.

This is where the quality of the trainer is vital. The trainer needs to be able to work with different learning styles, different communication styles, and different leadership styles. The trainer needs a high level of understanding in psychology and personality traits, and needs to be able to read a room, read humans, and read energy levels. They also need to be able to read a DiSC profile, to help leaders understand themselves and others.

THREE THE TRAINING IS IMPORTANT.

If you remember nothing else from this message, please remember that leadership training needs to be tailored to the audience, and to the attendees. Please don't book an off the shelf (vanilla) program for your team, then wonder why it didn't hit the mark.

When you're organising leadership training—please, please, please—tailor the training. So that you get feedback like this:

> **I would like to express a personal thank you for the training you delivered. It was not only interesting and valid, but I now have a better insight into the emotional side of the way we cope differently under pressure. This will assist me with the way I approach a situation and respond to gain the desired result with all stakeholders.**

So does leadership training work? If it's done right, and with the right approach—which entails a great deal of personal development, in creating the conscious control you need to lead your team in the right direction.

SO YOU WANT TO LOOK MORE PROFESSIONAL AS A LEADER

So you want to be able to lead your team in the right direction. But if you sometimes feel like you appear to be less professional than you could or should, this section is for you.

But what does it mean to look more professional? How do you do that, and why is it important?

This is an easy one. Looking professional means looking like you're in control. Did I say that? Yes. Being professional is another word for appearing to 'have it together', and to be leading on purpose. And with conscious control. So how do you look more professional?

Here are my three top tips, for looking like a professional in control.

ONE BE PREPARED FOR PRESENTATIONS OR MEETINGS.

Too many leaders think it's OK to 'wing it' or turn up without having done the pre-reading or the pre-thinking. And a little tip here: as leaders we expect our teams (and even our leaders) to do the prep prior to meetings, but there are times when we're found wanting on this one. This is seriously low-hanging fruit, and it can help you look professional with very little effort.

TWO THINK ABOUT FIRST IMPRESSIONS.

Think about what your office space says about you. And think about the messaging it sends to your team, or your clients. Especially when they visit to chat about high-value proposals. Paint the walls, put pictures up, buy some new chairs, make your space inviting. If you build it, they will come... and you'll look professional.

THREE FOCUS ON YOUR PERSONAL PRESENTATION.

And if you think this one isn't absolutely mission critical, think again. How you dress and how you present to your team daily tells people all they need to know about you. If you want to look professional, either dress professionally, or groom professionally (preferably both).

But WHY do you want to look more professional? Put simply, if you look more professional, you'll feel more professional. And if you feel more professional, you'll most likely act more professionally. Even deeper than that, looking more professional is a symbol. It says that you care. You care about yourself, you care about how you're perceived (yes, this matters), and you care about your team.

In a nutshell, if you want to look and be professional, you have to create conscious control. It's how you're going to deal with whatever comes your way, without harming anyone, even when you're still learning.

HOW TO FACE IT (NOT FAKE IT) UNTIL YOU MAKE IT

I'm just not a big fan of faking it. I've had to in the past, for sure, but I would much rather do the prep. Do the work. Do the thinking. And then, I'll get up, dress up, and show up. And yes, sometimes fail. And other times shine. It'll be a lesson or a blessing. The challenge for me with faking it is that impostor syndrome eventually shows up (thanks for that research, Carl

Jung), and it impacts my belief system about what I'm capable of.

Conversely, if I face up to what's happening, and get it done, even if it scares the you-know-what out of me, I'll give myself every chance to succeed.

But what does that take? It takes conscious control, and courage. Leadership courage is a central theme of our leading under pressure model, and we teach leaders the skills of having the courage to try, trust, and tell.

Did you know, though, that there are actually four types of courage? They were first unpacked by two researchers **Pury and Lopez** in 2010,[43] and since then, their model has been refined by authors like **Cathy J Lassiter** (in 2017).[26] The four types of courage include moral, disciplined, intellectual, and empathetic courage.

Let's look at these, and at how you, as a leader, can step into action by adopting one of these types of courage.

ONE MORAL COURAGE.

This is the courage that you need to stand up to injustice. To stand up when things are done that are immoral, unethical, or illegal. Think bullying. Think about being a bystander, and think about what it would take for you to say something. Standing up to things that aren't right does take courage—and getting over the fear of the outcome or the reaction of the human whose behaviour you're challenging. This is the courage that organisations are now legally obliged to support, some with a formal whistle-blower policy, to make it easier to speak up against inappropriate behaviour or poor treatment of others.

LEADER ACTION

As a leader, it's your responsibility to have this courage, and to take a stand again behaviour that violates the concept of being a good human. Regardless of the consequences. Regardless of whether the behaviour is being perpetrated at higher or lower levels of the organisation than you currently work at. To have this courage, think about the person who's being hurt, and how much they need your help and support.

TWO DISCIPLINED COURAGE.

This is the courage that you need to stand up for your position. To stand up when things are going badly. When you're losing faith. Or when others are losing faith in you.

And it would be easier to quit, right now, and give it all away. To leave the business, or to take another course of action that means you don't have to follow through on what you committed to, or that you know will be good for you or the business. This is the idea you had, or the project that you started on. Or the team that you took on, that isn't performing. Discipline and the courage to persevere will get you over a lot of hurdles. Note that this courage is akin to being resilient.

LEADER ACTION

As a leader, it's your responsibility to have this courage, and to take a stand for what you commit to doing. And to not giving in easily. Yes, that's easier said than done, but it's the tenacity that you started the project with that you'll need to call on when the challenges show up. Which they will. Have a vision. Know your end goal, and know that challenges are only temporary, and they're there to test your resolve.

THREE INTELLECTUAL COURAGE.

This is the courage that you need to turn your knowledge into action. To go out and learn something, and then apply that knowledge. It's the courage to contribute at a higher level. It's the courage to take a research report, or a blog, and value the information enough to apply it to your leadership style. It's the courage to train others in it, because this new knowledge is important, and worthwhile. And it's about learning from your experience and applying those learnings to get better outcomes into the future.

LEADER ACTION

As a leader, it's your responsibility to have this courage, and to learn new things. Yes, leaders are learners. And without the commitment to learning new knowledge and skills, it's hard to apply anything new or to try something different. Secondly, intelligently courageous leaders challenge the norms. They're willing to back themselves to get a different result, through a new approach and a new strategy, as much as others might push back at the time. Which will happen. Leaders that get good at rejection, get good at resilience.

FOUR EMPATHETIC COURAGE.

My favourite form of courage. Love this one. We train leaders in this type of courage more than anything else. Empathy is an important leadership skill, but yes, it takes courage to implement.

Empathetic courage is about being aware enough of your personal biases and challenging them, so that you're better placed to vicariously experience what others are going through and to understand why. It's about being the person that can understand the trials and tribulations of others, without being exclusive or judgemental. Empathy is a cognitive, emotional, and compassionate process (Credit: Daniel Goleman[22]), where we look to think about and feel what others are experiencing, so that we can be there to include, support, or to care for them, as required.

LEADER ACTION

As a leader, it's your responsibility to have this courage, and to know that another person's experience is their experience, is their reality, and is important or even life-changing for them. Just because you 'judge' it to be less than important or relevant, leaders need to step into their empathetic selves (fun fact: we were all born with compassion, we just forget it sometimes). And they need to hold the space so that the impacted person can talk and share in a safe space that is free from ridicule, resentment, or rejection. This is deep courage, and courage that has the potential to change lives. It's that important.

As a leader, you should adopt the four types of courage, and face up to the things that cause you to be fearful. Drawing on courage, and applying the principles of conscious control, will help you not only face up but to deal with problems in a way that helps, not hurts, your team.

ACTIVITY 2.1
CREATE CONSCIOUS CONTROL

Take some time now to think about what you've learnt in the last chapter.

The series of questions on the following pages will encourage you to think about ways you can improve your conscious control, and how you can apply the lessons you've just learnt in the process of upskilling your leadership.

If you find this activity doesn't work for you, consider journalling. It's also a valuable use of time just to sit and write about your values, your goals, and any challenges you need to tackle in your leadership role.

What could you do to create conscious control, to avoid reacting and start responding in effective ways?

In what ways could you take a stand against bullying in your workplace?

List ways you could more effectively support team members who are taking a stand against bullying in your workplace.

Are you confident in your ability to stand up to injustice?

What personal presentation issues could you improve to present better as a competent but approachable leader?

What tasks or projects have you not followed through on? And what can you do to be more disciplined in the future?

What could you start learning now to gain more knowledge and be a more confident leader in your field?

What personal biases do you need to confront and challenge to be a better leader?

SKILL 11

HAVE HIGH

CARE

FACTOR

THE CARE FACTOR STRATEGY FOR LEADERS

In 2020, John Mackey[34] wrote the book **Conscious Leadership**. In that book (one of my faves), Mackey talked about how to use love, compassion, and human qualities to build the business *Whole Foods Market Service*. He also unpacked the nine elements of conscious leadership.

One review of the book reads:

> **Rarely does a book move me to tears, yet this one did, by holding up a mirror to the kind of leader I most deeply want to be. Conscious Leadership is a powerful invitation to shift our mindset from the win/lose games of war to the community-building virtues of love, authenticity, and integrity. It's a book built on the radical idea that business can be a force for bringing more love into the world. Count me in.**

For me, this book was next level. It talked about the power of love, and how a care factor approach to leadership can change a business and make a difference in society. Yes, it talked about vision and goals, and purpose and process, but the theme of the book was around how to be a great leader by leaning into being a great human.

Mackey unpacks how you can do this, using the three elements of Conscious Leadership (Vision and Virtue, Mindset and Strategy, People and Culture). Each one of these can be broken down into three key strategies.

Number one under vision and virtue is simply to 'Put People First.' It's a simple message. But how do you do that? You can read the book, or you can read on and get my take on it, and (like I always do) find the short cut or the simple way to explain and implement an important message.

ONE CARE FACTOR IS ABOUT TIME.

One of the things that leaders don't want to hear is that their team members feel that the leader doesn't care about them. It's not uncommon to hear this, and our coaching clients present with this challenge at times. Especially when the leader is busy, under pressure, or trying to juggle a lot of balls.

What it means when a team member says they don't feel cared for is that the leader doesn't give the team member (or the team) the time that they deserve. The leader is absent. The leader is preoccupied with everything other than their team.

The solution for this one is to find time in your calendar to be with your team members, and your team, whether that's 1:1 meetings or team meetings. Leaders who take the time to be present demonstrate a level of care factor for their team, and they're respected for it.

Giving time is about making a statement about what's important. When your team is important enough to get your time, your team members feel valued and cared for.

TWO CARE FACTOR IS ABOUT CONVERSATION.

And I don't mean one-way conversation. I mean conversing. And when a leader is conversing, what they should be doing is asking questions, and keeping the discussion moving. Learning about the team member.

The word converse comes from Middle English (in the sense 'live among, be familiar with'); from Old French, 'converser'; from Latin, 'conversari' ('keep company with'. Its meaning is also evident in its components: 'con-' means 'with', and 'versare', a frequentative of 'vertere', means 'to turn'. The current sense of the verb dates from the early seventeenth century (Credit: Oxford Languages Definitions).

Conversation is about connection. And as per the definition, it means to be familiar with team members. To turn towards team members. To keep company with them, with the right level of connection and direction.

But that's not enough practical information. Here's the conversation strategy you need:

- **Ask Psychological Safety questions.** Ask whether it's safe to share ideas, opinions, and views. Ask if it's safe to contribute at high levels, and ask if your team member feels safe to challenge the norms.

- **Ask Psychological Empowerment questions.** Ask whether your team members feel like they're having an impact. Are they getting meaning from their work? Do they feel like they have a sense of self-determination (ownership of their work choices), and do they feel competent to fulfill the duties of their role?

- **Ask Psychological Connection questions**. These questions are about career direction. This is where you learn not 'where' your team members want to be in five years, but 'what' they want to be doing. The 'what' is a better type of question, because when you know that you can look for the right opportunities to help the team member get there. All the while remembering that there are some team members who never want to do anything other than what they are doing now—which is important to understand. When you can converse in a way that is focused on connecting with your team members (and understanding their needs), your team members feel cared for.

THREE CARE FACTOR IS ABOUT COURAGE.

When it comes time to have a robust conversation, if the first two points have been addressed, this third point should take care of itself.

I couldn't tell you how many leaders avoid the courageous conversations. They don't want to hurt the team member by delivering bad news. What they don't realise is that avoidance is ruinous. Avoiding courageous conversations does not help your team members, it harms them. And most of the time, the team member either knows it's being avoided, or would rather know than be kept in the dark.

Yes, these conversations take preparation. They take planning, and they take precision. They need to be handled correctly. When you can have courageous conversations with your team members to support their growth and development, your team members feel cared for.

What could you do today, to give time, to get connected, or to be courageous with your team?

HOW TO BE A GOOD HUMAN AND A GOOD LEADER

If you read the first book in this series, you'll have already read this story. But it's so important that it bears repeating, because you can learn a lot from the person I'm not proud to have once been.

I was not a nice human when I was younger. I was angry, had a log (not a chip) on both shoulders, and was very quick to escalate a conversation. From controlled to crazy out-of-control. Highly emotional. I had zero emotional intelligence, and I didn't care. At that time, anyway.

I was a tradie, so it didn't seem like a big deal that I was angry AF. Everyone was like that. Or were they? There weren't too many on my crew that had the lack of emotional control that I did.

But I made it OK. Until one day it just got out of control. I had a massive stand up blue in the workshop, with the boilermaker on our shift. It was so uncool! Let's just say that the language we used towards each other was pretty colourful.

My lovely wife remembers the conversation that evening, and it was about my baring my soul and being brutally honest about my lack of people skills. I don't remember the exact words I used, but Mrs G remembers me saying that I was sick of not being able to get on with people, and that I was totally committed to changing my approach. And to learning new skills. I just didn't have great communication skills.

And it meant that I wasn't a high-quality human. Why? Because my behaviour hurt others. It literally caused hurt.

So, I wanted to change. But where to start, in the elusive quest for better communication and connection with others, and to be a better human?

It started with study at Monash University, doing management, and then a HR degree and a post graduate diploma at CQU. That'll fix it, I thought. The study was useful, and so was the work that I was doing on trying to understand humans. Understanding others was about watching and listening. Looking and learning. What made people tick? And more importantly, what made them crack?

The journey has never stopped (and I feel like it's an ongoing mission). Recently, I completed a psychology degree. In saying that, the one qualification that was the best thing I ever studied was NLP (Neuro-Linguistic Programming), and love it or loathe it, that program was an eye opener into the human species and how we all connect. Having studied people for nearly thirty years (and now doing a PhD in behavioural science),

I share with leaders some of the simple techniques that they can use to improve their leadership and their connection. Especially when they're under pressure, which is the hardest time to connect. And the hardest time to be a good human.

Here's my take on what it takes to be a good human, and how care factor relates to leading under pressure. I'm still learning these skills, but here are some of the important things I've learnt to date

ONE DO NO HARM.

This is such a simple rule, but one that can easily be overlooked. Now, I get that most people will not go through their life without hurting someone. But it's still rule number one of being a good human.

What no harm means is subjective. In my words, it's simply: don't deliberately make someone feel bad. Don't deliberately denigrate. Don't communicate in a way that is aggressive, abusive, or abrupt. Which can happen when you're under emotional strain. You might lash out. Or you might not take the time to think about your impact on others. No one likes people that make them feel bad about themselves.

For leaders, what doing no harm means is being committed to doing leadership work in a way that's respectful. Regardless of whether you like a team member, whether or not they're in your in-group or out-group (yes, you categorise your team members), every team member deserves respect. Even when you're busy, or under pressure.

Yes, it takes time to be respectful. But yes, you can do no harm even when you're having robust conversations or delivering bad news. That is, if you plan the conversation and the information being delivered. Like being a good human, if you can remove aggression, abruptness, and abuse from your communication style, you'll do no harm. How do I know that? Because at least 75% of the DiSC profiles that I read say that the person will get put out if you're abrupt with them.

You really can do no harm if you're intentional about being respectful. It takes work, but it feels a lot better than ruminating about hurting others, if that ever happens. Do no harm!

TWO LEAVE PEOPLE BETTER THAN YOU FOUND THEM.

If you've ever been to one of our training programs, you'll have heard me say these words. Because it's my absolute purpose in life, and because it's the biggest learning to do that actually helps people have a better emotional experience, just by being around you. You can positively impact another human, even in the workplace.

Now, if you're willing to get a bit cosmic with me, you'll know that I believe every single human carries around an aura. An aura is emotionally charged. And your aura is contagious. Yes, contagious. So, in short, the happier you are, the happier those around you will be. Just by you being in their space. How big a space? The largest distance I've read is nine metres—that means that you have a nine-metre radius of energy that's impacting others (I did say it would be a bit cosmic).

So, now that you know you're influencing others with your emotional state, would it make sense to try and feel good so that others do in your presence? You know the old saying, 'they light up the room when they walk in.' That's because those people walk into the room happy. Plain and simple.

Let's go one step further and say that if you're going to influence others anyway, you might as well be intentional about it. You can, by managing your emotional state.

For leaders, what this means is to be positive. Or at least, more positive than you're negative. This is not about positive thinking, or sunshine or rainbows, but it's about things like using language that's uplifting, not putting down. The good thing about leadership is that you get to work on this over time, because you get to see your team members every day, and you can keep improving on this one.

When you're under pressure, that's the time when you're most likely to be direct. Negative. And angry. And that's the time that you will not leave people better than you found them. Try to be positive in your emotions and your language. Leave people better than you found them!

THREE LEARN MORE SO YOU CAN SHARE MORE.

This is such an underestimated skill for being a good human.

Some theory first (from the Tony Robbins playbook, at least) in relation to learning and growth. Tony Robbins's theory[45] is that the human species has two major human needs: to grow and to contribute. In theory, the more we grow and contribute, the happier we are in life. Great!

Let's take this a step further and consider how this theory could make you a good human. Because the more that you grow, the more you can contribute, right? If you stop learning, you stagnate, and your level of contribution remains the same. Until you start learning again.

To me, being a good human means working on yourself so that you can add more value to the planet, and you can share more with others. Share more knowledge, share deeper conversations, and even share more wealth (the more you learn, the more you earn). You see, the old adage of you can't help others until you can help yourself, and you need to fill your own cup first, is true. To a point. If you're filling your cup with knowledge of some sort. Even self-knowledge.

Some people say we're like trees. We're either green or brown, growing or dying. And there's some truth to this simple analogy.

For leaders, you'll experience learning during the first day of our programs (LEAD: learn, engage, articulate, demonstrate). Learn about yourself, learn about others, and learn about leadership. Learn more. Even just learn about why you do leadership. Most of the leaders that come through our programs can't explain why they do leadership. If the leader doesn't know why they do leadership, how will their teams know?

Learn more so you can share more.

Being a good human is an achievable goal. It takes effort, and care factor, and the best way to do it is to make it a priority. Make humans your priority, and watch your life and your leadership improve. Even when there are new challenges coming.

THE TOP 3 LEADERSHIP CHALLENGES IN THE 2020s AND BEYOND

These next years are going to be tough for leaders. They'll be fraught with challenges in the IT space, in the employee wellbeing space, and in the diversity and flexibility space. Leaders need to be ready to face these challenges and be equipped with the skills need to lead teams in the 2020s and beyond—primarily, the skill of care factor.

Here's how care factor looks different to what it looked like in the past.

ONE THE CHANGING IT LANDSCAPE.

The list of challenges in the IT space is long and difficult. From what software applications you should be using, to the implications of AI and VR for your business, to the risk of a cyberattack on your systems, IT's impact on your business needs to be considered.

But it also offers a lot for your growth as a leader. Applications like Noom or Calm will help you with your health and relaxation. You could also turn to AI, and Chat GPT, for advice on how to deal with certain situations.

Chat GPT is taking the world by storm right now, and rightly so. Some pundits are saying it'll challenge Google into the future. Or you could turn to VR and simulation to train your team members. But all of these take time, and take effort to learn them, right?

With new technology, it's generally a case of short-term pain for long-term gain. Apps are designed to save us time, but it just never feels like that, especially in the early days of adoption.

If you're running a consulting business, video marketing is king right now. Instagram feeds and TikTok videos are hot to reach the younger demographic. And Gary Vee[58] predicted that Facebook reels will be the best way to connect with Gen X in the 2020s.

But even if you don't do any of the above, the one thing that you should be focused on is cyber security. With cyber crime becoming an accepted business model in the 2020s, it's important to care enough to protect your information, and your company's, so you don't end up paying a criminal to get access to your data.

TWO EMPLOYEE WELLBEING SHOULD BE A MAJOR FOCUS.

Last year, the Australian Government released the work-related psychological health and safety Systematic Approach to Meeting Your Duties.[47] The introduction to that document states that:

> This Guide describes a systematic practical approach to managing work-related psychological health and safety. Most elements of this systematic approach are required under work health and safety (WHS) or workers' compensation laws in all Australian jurisdictions. This Guide recognises poor psychological work health and safety can lead to both psychological and physical injuries.[47]

Yes, the psychological safety of our teams has always been important, but now it's moved from being a moral obligation to a legal one. Regulators will now be very interested in compliance with this guidance material, particularly if team members need leave to deal with mental health issues—if they're deemed to be caused by their workplace.

And rightly so. Good leaders understand the importance of psychological safety, and they'll already be doing a lot of what's in that guide. But if you're not adopting the requirements of that guide, you'll be leaving your organisation and team members exposed.

THREE DIVERSITY AND INCLUSION ARE NOW DIVERSITY AND FLEXIBILITY.

Diversity and inclusion have been front and centre for leaders for a long time now, but the last two years have seen a global change in how team members want to work. The workplace has moved from being accepting and inclusive (regardless of beliefs or sexual orientation, etc.) to having to balance a hybrid workforce.

Yes, diversity in decision making has always been seen as the best way to foster innovation and creativity. In the 2020s, though, leaders now need to try and maintain that flexibility, and maintain either a four-day work week, or a workforce that only comes into the office for one or two days a week.

There's data and reports detailing the best work rosters and the most flexible arrangements that promote productivity in work teams. But at the end of the day, leaders need to be all over not just that information, but also the administration and the rostering that flexibility requires. Because every team member is different, and what suits one team member may not necessarily suit another.

Leaders everywhere are in for a tough time in the 2020s, where they'll be challenged on all fronts. It might be time to consider getting a leadership coach, to support you in your commitment to being a leader who's remembered for the right reason—their care factor.

HOW TO BE THE LEADER THAT PEOPLE REMEMBER (FOR THE RIGHT REASONS)

I had some average leaders as I was climbing the ladder of corporate success. They're now called 'old-school leaders.' And I can remember them clearly, and what they said, and how they said it. I went into leadership coaching to see if I could help leaders like them to be better at leading humans—by leading them with care factor. So that teams everywhere didn't have the have the same experience that I had.

Sometimes, though, I have to reflect and remember that there have been some great leaders along the way, too. And I've learnt a heap from them. Particularly, if you've seen my origin story video, where I talk through an incident that occurred on a power station on May 21, 2021 where the leaders stepped up and stepped into leadership under pressure. In a way that was all about control, care factor and courage.

As well as that experience, at the start of our leadership training sessions, I used to take our attendees on a journey of thinking about their worst ever leader. The purpose of that session is to remember what it feels like when we're exposed to poor leadership, so we don't be a leader who's remembered for that reason.

We've changed that up now, because such a negative session (and it was negative) took the emotions in the wrong direction and I had to spend the next two days turning it around. Now, we talk about our favourite leaders of all time, and what they did that made them our favourite leaders. We put all those notes on a whiteboard, and essentially write the playbook for what great leadership looks like from a very personal experience. A much more positive session, sure.

Eventually, the focus turns to me, and the group asks me who my favourite leader has been, and why. So, I share my experience, and I'm very specific about why this person was my favourite leader.

Here's my contribution to that session.

ONE   MY FAVOURITE LEADER WAS PATIENT, AND TOOK A COACHING APPROACH.

I worked for a year on a major commissioning project. A major plant expansion had been completed by a major construction company, and I was working with the owner's team on the commissioning element of the construction project. I was in a tough role (project controls), and it was detail, detail, detail. Schedules and numbers. Facts and figures. Progress and process. Not skills that I necessarily had at the time (I am high (I) influence on my DiSC profile, and very low (C) conscientious). I'm not a details person.

Within a year, I'd turned that around. For that year, I learnt to do data. I learnt to do numbers. With my leader's help.

I needed a significant amount of support and coaching. Once I got the hang of it, things got better. And at the end of the year, we started doing planning workshops that I could facilitate. Winner. Being in front of humans. Way more fun.

But I will never forget that leader, and I'll be forever grateful for the patience that he showed when he knew that detail was not a strong point of mine. I'm sure it was, but nothing ever seemed to be too much trouble for him; he always had time for me, and always spoke in a way that was encouraging and not demeaning. I appreciated that.

One thing I remember clearly was the day that that leader asked for a rewrite of the commissioning plan...in an hour...with a heap of changes. I freaked out. He was patient. He said something like: 'I know what I've asked for is one or more days' work. But I have to present something to my leader in an hour, so I need your best effort for an hour, with complete focus. I gave you an hour, and I need a great hour. Then we can finish it off.' So, I went nuts for an hour, and nailed as much as I could. Which wasn't much, but it was enough.

After that, the coaching started, and he helped me through the document rewrite, in a coaching way. It was like that leader really knew how to work under pressure. It seemed to come naturally, though I feel like this might actually have been learnt behaviour. Regardless, it was an amazing skill. Patience and coaching.

TWO MY FAVOURITE LEADER WAS AN INTROVERT, IN AN EXTROVERT'S ROLE.

This was a revelation for me at that time. There was a period in my life where I was convinced that only extroverts made good leaders. How wrong I was.

Because this leader was such a coach for me, I was able to get an insight into his personality. And I was able to see the quiet times, not just the times that he was in front other others. As an example, that leader would go from being in front of his team, looking like an extrovert, to his office, slouched in his chair recovering from all the people interactions.

He explained that he was highly introverted, and that doing people work was a huge energy drainer for him. He needed time alone to get his energy back, and recharge, before going an doing it all again, for the rest of the day.

It was like that leader had this complete understanding of self, and was totally aware of his strengths and weaknesses. He knew when and how to step up and step into people interactions, even when he didn't feel like it was his skill set. Interestingly, if you asked people about him, they would have thought he was very extroverted. But he wasn't. He was an introvert, in an extrovert's role.

THREE MY FAVOURITE LEADER ACTUALLY CARED ABOUT PEOPLE.

This is an interesting point, because there are leaders who try to care, but struggle to. There are leaders who are very clear on the fact that they don't care as much about people as they do about the process or the output.

One day, I got a call to say my son had been rushed to hospital after falling off his skateboard and bashing his head on the bitumen. He was wearing a helmet, thankfully, but I didn't know that until I got to the hospital.

This leader could not do enough to support and look after me that day, and that week. Time off was not an issue, leaving quickly was fine, and he gave me a lift around town to pick up my car from site and get my son from hospital to home. It was next level care. And I appreciated it.

It was like that leader knew how to care. And it didn't seem like any effort at all. It seemed to be important to that leader, to care for people.

FYI, it's a much better way to start a session, asking about people's favourite leader, and not their worst. And it's nice to be able to share the above reflections with my attendees. Fun fact: I remember that leader for all the right reasons—which were all care factor. You can't lead well without it.

YOU AREN'T LEADING IF YOU AREN'T DOING THIS ONE THING

The biggest challenge leaders have is that they need to give so much of themselves to others. Leaders need to constantly show up, with purpose, with passion, and with persistence. They need to be there to coach, to counsel, and to collaborate. With care factor.

Which can be difficult at times, especially when there are people in your team that are having struggles that affect their work and their focus. And the leader may not be able to understand why those issues are such a big deal. But they are, for that person.

When your team members are struggling, your leadership skills will be on show. And they'll be tested. Because you need to step into their shoes and demonstrate care factor. And compassion.

I'm going to make a big call in this section and say that if you don't know how to be compassionate, or you're choosing not to be compassionate, you're not being the best leader you can be.

Here's why.

ONE COMPASSION IS MISUNDERSTOOD.

Compassion literally means 'to suffer together.' Among emotions researchers, it's defined as the feeling that arises when you're confronted with another's suffering, and feel motivated to relieve that suffering. Compassion is not the same as empathy or altruism, though the concepts are related. (Credit: Greatergood.com)

Compassion is a two-stage process, firstly involving understanding, then secondly acting. There is no compassion without action. You must take an action if you're being compassionate. That action might be as simple as listening. It might be providing compassionate leave, if someone is dealing with loss or grief. It might be making someone a coffee, or it might be driving them to a psychologist.

Our cat died recently, and for some non-cat lovers, that wouldn't mean much. My wife Julie, though, was shattered. More than shattered. And nearly didn't go to work for the day (my son took the day off—our cat was beloved). Most people would not be able to understand that. One of Julie's friends found a photo of our cat (with Julie) and got it put on a key ring as a reminder. Julie didn't know about it, and it made her day. That's compassion—action that matters.

LEADER ACTION

Don't assume you know what the person needs you to do, as compassionate action. There are times when you'll just have to follow your instincts.

TWO MOST PEOPLE ARE BORN COMPASSIONATE.

In baby studies, compassion shows up at about the eight-month mark. Research with eight-month-old babies showed that when one of them was in distress, the others took action so their mate got help more quickly.

Babies have also been found to cry in response to another newborn baby's cry, which psychologists agree are early signs of the development of compassion. Studies have shown that when a baby hears another baby crying, their sucking motion and heart rate slow in response to the sound. They have a physical reaction to the distress that they're hearing. This is a natural response. And here's the kicker: studies have found that a small percentage of newborns don't react like that—which might predict a lack of compassion as the child grows.

It's generally thought that compassion proper begins to show itself in the second year of life. But it could be there a lot earlier. In other words, the vast majority of humans are born compassionate.

LEADER ACTION

If you're a leader struggling with compassion, that's a nurture thing,

not a nature thing. You've either forgotten or not chosen compassion. If you're struggling with it, know it's a skill that you most likely possess, and it just takes some willingness and time to get better at it.

THREE COMPASSION IS NOT SYMPATHY.

Compassion is an element of empathy, says Daniel Goleman[22] in his literature around emotional intelligence. And sadly, most people think empathy is sympathy, which is feeling sorry for someone and crying or hurting for them.

Think of a scale for a minute, with sympathy at one end, and apathy at the other. Both of these are natural emotional states. If someone is in pain, you either feel for them, or you're apathetic (you don't care at all)—there is very little in between. Either high care factor or low care factor.

The challenge with compassion (or substitute that with empathy for this section), you need to understand which natural response you've just experienced, and then move from that to understanding (cognitively and emotionally) so that you can be empathetic. Empathy is an action (as above), not a feeling.

If you're not compassionate and empathetic right now, the good news is that it's a learnt skill. It's something that you can practice.

LEADER ACTION

Prepare for conversations that you might need to have with team members who are hurting. And use words or phrases like 'talk me through it', or 'help me understand', or 'that must be tough'. Please don't start with 'I understand', especially if you don't.

You're not leading (and certainly not leading well), if you're not being compassionate when it matters. Care factor matters. It's how you lead well, in the face of pressure and new industry challenges.

HOW TO NAVIGATE THE CHALLENGES OF LEADERSHIP IN HEAVY INDUSTRY

Leadership can be tough at the best of times. But when you add in an old-school culture, changing technology, and a diverse workforce, leadership gets even harder. This is what leaders in heavy industry are faced with. The last five to ten years has seen unprecedented change in heavy industrial organisations and teams.

The question is, how do you navigate these challenges, and continue to develop your leadership skills, amid the change?

Having a mix of corporate and heavy industry clients, I can see what happens in both worlds and how they differ. For our heavy industry leaders, these are the clients I see having to learn the most and adapt the most.

OLD SCHOOL CULTURE AND BOYS' CLUBS ARE ON THEIR WAY OUT

This is the big one. The new-age leadership style is here, and it's here to stay. We're not going back to the shouting or swearing at each other. Or back to telling inappropriate jokes, or to having naked posters in crib rooms, or to being offensive to other humans.

Yes, there is an expectation of leaders (and workers) in the 2020s, that they'll adapt to the new normal of the new workplace. Where it's easy to be offensive, and leaders need to understand that. They need to change their languaging and their behaviour. They need to develop emotional intelligence. For some, with forty or fifty years of heavy industry experience, this is proving difficult. Rightly so. It's a massive change.

Some people might term this section 'political correctness', and they might even follow that up with 'has gone mad'. I'm OK with political correctness, because it makes us all learn how to be better humans, and not offend others (intentionally or unintentionally).

My experience is that some leaders are holding on to the old school, but most are trying to adapt. And congratulations to them, as their teams and organisations are the beneficiaries of their growth and upgraded skills.

If you're reading this, and you want to make some changes, reach out to us, or do some work on your conversational skills and emotional intelligence. They're great places to start.

TECHNOLOGY IS NOT GOING ANYWHERE

This is perhaps the biggest challenge for heavy industry. It appears to be being embraced well. Or at least to the point where leaders know what technology they need to utilise, and they go and get some training or some instruction on how to do it.

One thing about technology is that it's getting easier to use. Whether it's remote equipment operating technology or messaging apps on a phone, the interaction element of technology has taken massive leaps forward in recent years, to the benefit of workplaces across every industry. For senior leaders, the biggest challenge remains in the cyber security space, with hacker attacks being a very real risk.

For me, technology is such a big part of our lives that I feel like it shouldn't rate as a key challenge for heavy industry leaders. But I still hear some of the challenges that leaders face during coaching sessions.

I only ever have one piece of coaching advice for leaders struggling with technology, and that's to get through the fear of learning something new, and jump in. Do what it takes to learn the technology or software as quickly as you can, and move onto the next one.

WORKFORCES ARE BECOMING MORE AND MORE DIVERSE

Heavy industry is becoming more diverse by the day. Which is great, as people shouldn't be discriminated against because of something about them that doesn't affect how well they can perform their work.

Referring to point one, where a lot of leaders (and workers) are old school, having an Indigenous person, a transgender person, or anyone from the LGBTIQA+ community for that matter, can be a challenge. But why? Why do some people struggle with people who are different from the majority?

It's a challenge because it's so different to how a lot of people in heavy industry were raised (me included). But if you can reframe the situation, and realise that everyone is just another human—someone to engage with and learn from—it really can be that simple. No need to complicate it.

Having said that, there are a range of peripheral challenges that come with diverse workforces, including toileting access. But none of these challenges are insurmountable. If you're engaging with and learning from your people with human-centred acceptance, you can be a better leader in leading diverse workforces.

Old school is out. And technology and diversity are in. And these changes need care factor, which is challenging for some leaders in heavy industry.

As a closing comment, I was part of a conversation recently, where I was advocating for more progressive leadership thinking. The person I was talking about was an ally (and worked on a heavy industrial site with about a thousand people). The conversation ended with the statement from that person to the effect of 'the best thing that could happen to our outdated workforce is for us to hire a transgender or other minority group person, so that everyone has to learn to be accepting.' Well said, I thought.

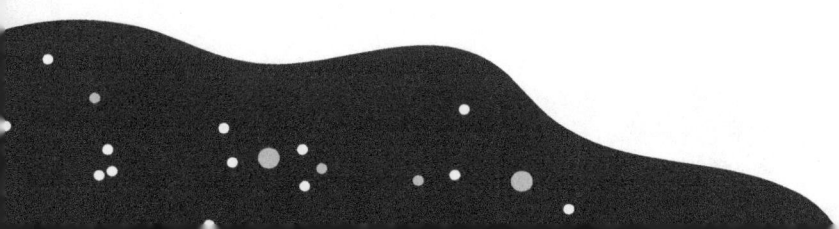

ACTIVITY 2.2
HAVE HIGH CARE FACTOR

Take some time now to think about what you've learnt in the last chapter.

The series of questions on the following pages will encourage you to think about what you can do to have high care factor, and how you can apply the lessons you've just learnt in the process of upskilling your leadership.

Alternatively, consider journalling. It's also an effective way to learn more about being a good human as well as a good leader, and to develop strategies to become the leader that people remember for the right reasons—for your care factor, even when you're under pressure.

What are some of the biggest challenges in your workplace as it moves into a more inclusive future?

What could you do to create more time in your calendar to support your team members?

Do you think your team members feel safe to share their ideas, opinions, and views? Why, or why not?

Do you think your team members feel like their work has an impact in the organisation? Why, or why not?

What opportunities could you provide for your team members who want to upgrade their skill sets or progress their careers?

Answer honestly. Are you 'doing no harm' to your team members?

Are you engaged in learning to share knowledge? If not, what could you learn that you could share?

What could you do to improve your focus on your employees' wellbeing?

What changes could you make in your workplace to create an environment to make it more supportive of diversity and inclusion?

Note some characteristics of leaders you admire the most, and how you could emulate them.

SKILL III
DEVELOP YOUR
EMOTIONAL
QUOTIENT

WHY EI MATTERS

In the 2020s, your Emotional Intelligence (EI or EQ) matters. Daniel Goleman[22] argues that in leadership positions, 85% of the competencies for success lie in the EI domain, rather than in technical or intellectual abilities.

With that in mind, what is it that you can do to develop your emotional intelligence? The answer: a lot.

There really are a range of tools that you can add to your toolbox that will allow you to stay in emotional control while building rapport with other humans. And although we've been doing training in the EI domain for many years, we're finally able to give you an accurate read on your level of EI. As part of our DiSC profiling work, we now have a profiling tool that not only helps you unpack your EI, but helps you to improve it.

And why is that important? Because without EI, the quality of your own emotional experience, and the emotional experiences of those around you, won't be as good as they could, and the relationships you have with yourself and others will suffer. Better EI means better emotional state, and better connections with other humans.

What I love about the profiling tool is that it follows the Daniel Goleman[22] model of self-recognition and self-management, and social-recognition and social-management. For most people that I speak to, it's the social-management element of the EI model that is important.

Let me add as much value as I can by sharing the top five skills of those that are high EI, and that are great at social management (relationships). These these are taken from the EI profiling tool.

EMPATHY, SENSITIVITY, APPRECIATION.

This skill is about understanding others—accurately picking up emotional cues from communication (including words, tone, and nonverbal signals);

managing direct and indirect feedback effectively; and being attentive, sensitive, aware, and appreciative of the emotional signals of others.

SERVICE, COMPASSION, BENEVOLENCE.

This skill is about operating with a sense of contribution. Aiding, helping, coaching, and developing others; operating constructively to contribute to the emotional states and benefits of others; recognising needs, wants and desires; and relating to alternative thoughts, perceptions, and perspectives.

HOLISTIC COMMUNICATION.

This skill is about having the ability to effectively send and receive information including emotional content. It involves listening; engaging and connecting with others; and sending and receiving verbal and nonverbal signals constructively.

SITUATIONAL PERCEPTUAL AWARENESS.

This skill is about recognising and processing dynamic, shifting emotional data. Communicating attention, focus, awareness, and connection; adapting to situational variables and changes; understanding which factors count, and how much; and responding with reasonable behaviour.

INTERPERSONAL DEVELOPMENT.

This skill is about growing and nurturing constructive connections. It's about setting the tone for long-term depth and breadth in relationships; working with quality in personal and professional relations; and having resonance and rapport with others.

Looking at the list, it's clear how these skills can help you be more successful, not only at work, but also out of work. These are life skills that increase the quality of your life, by increasing your emotional quotient, for higher quality interactions with others that are consistent across time.

EMOTIONAL CONSISTENCY IS NOT EMOTIONAL SUPPRESSION

If I was to do a straw poll of our coaching clients, and I asked them the one thing that they value in their leader, one common answer would be (and yes, we have asked) emotional consistency. Or a derivation of such.

And what I interpret this as meaning is not only emotional consistency, but also behavioural consistency. In short, and from your team's perspective, all they want is that the same leader shows up every day (or at least most days). Leaders that are all over the place create teams that are all over the place. A client told me recently that they didn't know which version of their leader they were getting each day. And that is seriously uncool from a leadership perspective.

BUT WHAT IS EMOTIONAL CONSISTENCY?

Great question, and I think it's important to acknowledge that leadership is emotional work, and it challenges us daily to stay consistent and in control. Given that, emotional control isn't about avoiding the crappy emotions. It's about not lashing out with venom and hurting others because you've just gotten bad news or because your world has gone BOOM.

From a psychological perspective, humans can't know what light is without dark. We can't know happiness without sadness. Humans can only have an experience, or an emotion, if we have a contrast or something to compare it to. So, positive emotions are only possible because we have the not-so-positive emotions. In the moments of not-so-positive, don't suppress your emotions. Reframe them, and channel them for good.

Find that way inside yourself to switch your thinking and feeling so that your emotional state, whatever it is, helps others. Not hurts them. Heals others, not harms them. If you need some support or tips on this, please reach out to me **at The Guinea Group**.

In short, great leadership is about predictable leadership. Consistent leadership. That's the easiest way to say it, really. Don't be a tornado or a hurricane. Be a gentle breeze that has a cooling effect, instead of a catastrophic natural disaster effect.

To unpack emotional control differently—and just off topic for a paragraph—I read a lot of books, and I reach out to the authors when I finish them. One author, Sky Nelson-Isaacs[41] (author of the book **Living in Flow**) explained it beautifully in a LinkedIn message reply, where he shared:

> **I'm very keen on the journey of controlling emotions. Not silencing them, mind you, but channelling them to the right output, so that we can stay in flow. When we suppress emotions, our equilibrium starts to shift, so eventually we need to blow off steam. Good leaders under pressure can transmute those difficult emotions into caring and loving emotions and stay top of their game.**

And I think that sums up emotional control. And why it's not emotional suppression. It's about emotional channelling, to use our emotions—regardless of what we're experiencing as leaders—for good. With emotional control comes behavioural control, and comes situational control. And with that comes a high-performing team, who aren't freaking out about how their leader will respond if they share bad news or new ideas.

Crappy leaders are like that. And that's not you. You're a leader with a high emotional quotient—not a leader who lets their amygdala hijack them.

How Princess Elsa managed her 'amygdala hijack' in Frozen

Princess Elsa understands leadership, and how to control her emotions. And how to control her ice-making superpower, especially when she gets out of control. Or at least now she does.

The movie Frozen (or the musical—which Mrs G and I went to see recently in Brisvegas) is an amazing lesson in leadership. Yes, we love musicals. And yes, we were among the only couples there without kids (i.e., the big kids).

For those of you with children, I'm guessing you'll be familiar with the plot. If you haven't seen the movie (which I haven't), the plot is about a princess who is to become queen. Princess Elsa can turn things, like hearts, to ice—if she doesn't control her emotions, that is. Because of that, Elsa is separated from other humans. Including her little sister Anna, who is shattered to lose contact with her big sis. A sad part of the story.

In psychology, the loss of emotional control is called an amygdala hijack. In short, being triggered causes an emotional reaction. That reaction causes us to 'fly off the handle' for want of a better description. We say and do things that are uncool. Then feel sorry, and maybe even say sorry, afterwards. When we've calmed down.

Overcoming an amygdala hijack is about responding, not reacting. Reacting is not the preferred option, as Princess Elsa finally worked out.

So, what can we learn about EQ from Princess Elsa?

ONE   PRINCESS ELSA KNEW THAT SHE WAS RESPONSIBLE FOR HER IMPACT ON OTHERS.

Princess Elsa was very caring. She knew that her behaviour impacted on others, and that her amygdala hijacks could be dangerous. Very dangerous. As a leader, Elsa knew that she could have a serious long-term impact on others if she couldn't control her emotions.

LEADER ACTION

Most leaders don't understand that you can heal or harm, help or hurt. Choose your language, and behaviour, to choose the former of each.

TWO   PRINCESS ELSA KNEW SHE HAD AN ISSUE, AND SHE ADDRESSED IT.

Princess Elsa took an extreme action. She removed herself from other humans until she could be sure she could stay in control. She even got some gloves to cover her hands, to make sure no ice came out of them and froze people. In short, she did what it took to learn how to behave differently.

LEADER ACTION

Being in control is a learnt behaviour. If you give yourself permission to react, instead of responding appropriately, it might be time to think about new strategies for emotional control.

THREE   PRINCESS ELSA NEVER STOPPED CARING.

Princess Elsa saved her little sister Anna, with 'an act of true love.' Elsa was able to undo the hurt she'd caused: she thawed Anna's heart. She never stopped caring and looking out for Anna (while the theatre was shedding a tear—a beautiful moment in the musical!).

LEADER ACTION

Leadership is about Extreme Ownership and taking responsibility for your 'emotional wake' (Credit Susan Scott[50] in Fierce Conversations). Keep caring and try to undo any hurt. ASAP.

Developing your EQ isn't a quick process, especially if you've been operating in amygdala hijack most of your life. But it's more than worth it, to become a transformational leader—and a stoic one.

HOW TO BE A STOIC LEADER

One of the words that I hear more and more often now is the word 'stoic.' And that people are trying to be more stoic. Or be like the stoics, the great stoic philosophers (Epictetus, Seneca, and Marcus Aurelius).

Marcus Aurelius is my favourite stoic philosopher, and he left us with some great quotes and some great ways to live and to lead.

Marcus Aurelius Antoninus (26 April 121 CE–17 March 180 CE) was Rome's emperor from 161 to 180 CE (and a Stoic philosopher). He was the last of the rulers known as the Five Good Emperors (a term coined some thirteen centuries later by Niccolò Machiavelli), and the last emperor of the Pax Romana, an age of relative peace and stability for the Roman Empire, lasting from 27 BCE to 180 CE. He also served as a Roman consul in 140, 145, and 161 (Credit: Wiki).

In his book on Stoicism, John Bowman[5] explains that Stoicism is a 2,300-year-old Greek and Roman philosophy that addresses human happiness. As examples, on escape Seneca wrote, 'whatever your destination, you will be followed by your failings'; on death, Marcus Aurelius advised to 'be content with your allocation of time'; and on suicide, Epictetus suggested to 'quit the game when it no longer pleases you, and depart'.

For me, the thing that gets me about Marcus Aurelius, and the stoic philosophers in general, is how well they articulated the trials, the tribulations, and the tumultuousness of their time in quotes and questions. And how relevant, real, and relatable those quotes and questions still are for our lives and our leadership in the 2020s.

Let's unpack three Marcus Aurelius quotes and see how they pertain to leadership in the 2020s and beyond. And remember, as you read these quotes, they were written in the 2nd Century CE! (And if this section piques your interest, Google more information on the great stoic philosophers and see what else you can apply.)

> If you're distressed by anything external, the pain is not due to the thing itself, but to your estimate of it; and this you have the power to revoke at any moment.

This is my favourite stoic quote. The quote talks to the fact that we have the power to choose our story, to choose our state, and to choose our strategy. The situation, event, or circumstance does not own us; we own how we respond to it, and we can choose to respond well.

In short, we can rephrase, reframe, and refocus any situation, to find a more positive or more pragmatic way to tell the story of what's happened. And things don't happen to us, they happen for us, so they can work through us.

Yes, leadership can be stressful, and it can be filled with challenges and curve balls. It can be filled with BOOM events that throw your day, month, or even your year off kilter. The great leaders realise that it's not the event that matters, but how we respond to it.

The same event will also have a different meaning for different people.

Which is the great thing about being human: we all have a different tale to tell (even of the same event).

The message is to be aware of how you're internalising things. You're in control, and it's not what happens to you, but how you respond, that matters. (Incidentally, I thought I came up with those words, but it's another famous stoic quote—go figure).

> **Every hour, focus your mind attentively on the performance of the task in hand, with dignity, human sympathy, benevolence, and freedom, and leave aside all other thoughts. You will achieve this if you perform each action as if it were your last.**

As a leader, are you interested, or are you totally committed? I mean, is leadership something that you show up for, or is it something that you show up with?

A lot of leaders have been promoted into the role. They've fallen into it. Or they've landed there. Because no one else was available at the time. That's showing up for leadership. For the pay cheque, or for the job title.

When you show up with leadership, you show up with a commitment to your team, your organisation, and your visions and values. You're showing up with the right intent, and with a clear why. You're showing up with a presence that communicates your commitment and your dedication to being the leader your team needs and deserves.

When you show up with leadership, you show up with presence and with congruence (your words match your actions). And you show up with attention to the task at hand. With the virtues of dignity, sympathy, benevolence, and freedom. And then, so does your team! The message is to be present, and to be focused on your tasks, and your team members (not at the same time).

> **In a sense, people are our proper occupation. Our job is to do them good and put up with them. But when they obstruct our proper tasks, they become irrelevant to us—like sun, wind, and animals. Our actions may be impeded by them, but there can be no impeding our intentions or our dispositions. Because we can accommodate and adapt. The mind adapts and converts to its own purposes the obstacle to our acting. The impediment to action advances action. What stands in the way becomes the way.**

This quote really resonates with me. I love it. Because my mission is to leave people better than I found them. While being firm when required, fair when required, and friendly when required. But always with a focus on feelings and factors that matter.

The second part of this quote talks about our intent, and our disposition. With the right intent, as I tell leaders everywhere, nothing can go wrong. You may offend, but you can apologise. You may upset, but you can reverse that. You may hurt, but you can heal that, with the right intent.

Intent is why you're doing something, whereas disposition is how you're doing it. If you can line both of these up in the right direction, watch your influence improve.

The message is to be very clear on your intent and know that humans are your key concern. At one end, leave people better than you found them. At the other end, at least aim for doing no harm. Help, not hurt. Heal not harm.

The great stoic quotes are quotes to live by. They contain so much wisdom that we can lean into now, and in the future, to develop our EQs and our ability to lead others purposefully and meaningfully.

As a footnote, my favourite Marcus Aurelius story is about how he tried to stay grounded. The story goes that Marcus Aurelius hired an assistant to follow him as he walked through the Roman towns square. The assistant's only role was to, whenever Marcus Aurelius was praised, whisper in his ear, 'You're just a man. You're just a man.' (Credit: Medium.com).

WHAT LEADERSHIP MEANS TO ME

I'm feeling reflective. I'm feeling like answering some big questions. For myself, as much as for my audience. This is part of developing EQ as a leader—unpacking what leadership means to you, and why.

I encourage you to do the same. As you read this section, be thinking about what leadership means to you, and how you came to believe those things about leadership and about teams.

For me, leadership is about influence, inspiration, and being impactful. Here's why.

ONE INFLUENCE.

For me, the key skill of leadership is the skill of influence. Being able to influence behaviour is crucial. Being able to influence thinking is also important, if you want to get people on board.

If I reflect on the best leaders that I've had, I feel like they were able to move my heart and mind in a direction that was towards what needed to be done. And towards understanding why things needed to be done.

My reflection here is that influence could be used for both good and for bad, but good leaders have the right intent, and that intent is to help their teams live into the values of the team and the values of the business. And that is at the heart of influence: helping team members mobilise their energy and to point it in the right direction—in the direction of the team's and organisation's values, goals, and objectives.

Influence starts with setting the direction. Then sharing it. Then influencing others to buy in.

To me, influence is about leadership languaging more than anything. Using words to engage and encourage others.

I think about great leaders on the planet, and I think about Barrack Obama, and how his speaking work was extremely engaging. And memorable. Obama was a leader who is remembered for his articulation and his charisma. Key elements of influence.

TWO INSPIRATION.

This is the biggie. The thing. The king. Inspiring others to follow you.

Inspiration is different to motivation. For me, motivation is very much an internal thing. It's generally something that people have or would like to have. 'I want to be more motivated,' you'll hear people saying. Inspiration is giving people something to work towards.

Because they can see you, as their leader, demonstrating the behaviour needed to deliver on not only what's required, but what's possible. Inspiration is about helping people understand their own potential, and then leaning into that potential because they can see you as their leader doing it.

Inspirational leadership is leading from the front. It's leading through action. It's leading from impossible to its possible. It's about demonstrating what could happen if your team follow your lead.

I think about great leaders on the planet, and I think about someone like Elon Musk, who can inspire massive workforces to accomplish massive goals and objectives. Even if those goals and objectives seem crazy at the start, Elon can inspire action.

THREE IMPACT.

My reflection is that leadership is the second most important job on planet Earth, behind parenting. Just think about being in the workforce for forty years of your life and having poor leaders for even some of that time.

Leaders are hugely important humans. And the sad part is that some of them don't know or believe that. A lot of leaders are in their roles because they were the next in line. Or because it pays more. Or because the manager was on leave. Not because they were right for it. And it's certainly not always because they really want to have an impact on other humans.

When I say impact, I mean being life changing. I mean being memorable, for the right reasons. I mean making a difference.

Having an impact means being present when needed. It means being purposeful with your intent. And it means being pumped about people. And understanding why they need to be your focus.

Fun fact: leaders that come through our leadership training programs can remember conversations with their leaders from decades ago. And they remember the crappy conversations more than the positive ones. They can remember the leaders that impacted them negatively.

To me, leadership is about having a positive impact on other humans.

I think about great leaders on the planet, and I think about Oprah Winfrey or Jacinda Ardern, who appear to care for others, and that comes through in their languaging and in their behaviour.

It's about influence, inspiration, and impact for me. Develop your EQ by thinking about what it means to you, and what you can learn about being an influential and transformative leader from other leaders.

WHAT CAN WE LEARN FROM OUR LEADERS?

One of my takes on leadership is that we don't spend enough time reflecting on the leaders we've had in the past (or present) and trying to learn from them. We've all had some outstanding leaders, and some not so great. But they can all teach us something about EQ, whether it's what to do more of, or what to do less of, to perform well in a leadership role.

There's a great stoic quote that says: 'As long as you live, keep learning how to live' (Credit: Seneca). In the 2020s, this quote could read: 'As long as you lead, keep learning how to lead'. One of the ways that we can keep learning is to reflect, recognise, and replace. Reflect on what good leaders do. Recognise what you would not do as a leader. Replace any strategies with new ones, and try new things.

Here are three questions to help you with this process.

ONE — WHAT HAVE MY FAVOURITE LEADERS DONE WELL? (THROUGH REFLECTION.)

This is a question that I ask at the start of our leadership programs. We fill the whiteboard with the best traits of our favourite leaders. We even use first names, to make it personal. Some of the time, mums and dads or grandparents make the list, which is beautiful, too.

In that half-hour session, we get such a great vibe going, and we reflect on why our favourite leaders had such an impact on us, and how they did that. Then more specifically, how we felt and how we responded to those leaders. Integrity always comes up, as do a range of other positive values and behaviour-based adjectives. That session is such a positive way to start two days of training.

That exercise is designed to provide an overview of the traits of the best leaders we have all experienced. At times, it's a sports star, or a movie star, whose name is mentioned; but at the end of that discussion, we have a list of traits that we can lean into. And maybe one day when we do that exercise, your name will make the list, because of how you lead others.

LEADER ACTION

Spend a moment or two, now, reflecting on the best leaders you've experienced, and what made them so outstanding. Also consider what you could do differently.

TWO — WHAT HAVE MY FAVOURITE LEADERS DONE POORLY? (THROUGH RECOGNITION.)

Would you believe that we used to ask this question at the start of our leadership programs (before I changed it to the one above)? I changed it up when I recognised what a negative spin it put on the program and on the workshop, which was hard to come back from.

Yes, everyone has a story of a poor leader. Yes, some of these stories are decades old. And yes, this is what not to do, and the message is that if you want to be a good leader, don't do these things. But it still put the attendees in a negative emotional state.

And that's what happens when we experience poor leadership. Instead of just saying that we feel crappy, or hurt, or not valued, we need to recognise what the behaviour was that made us feel that way, so that we can make sure we don't repeat it in our own leadership.

Specifically, recognise what it was that the leader did when they had the worst impact on your emotional state. It's generally because they were under pressure, they had no people skills, or they were only worried about themselves and not the team (or some variation of these three).

LEADER ACTION

Spend a moment or two, now, reflecting on the worst leaders you've experienced, and what made them so memorable. Recognise what you'd never do as a leader, based on these experiences.

THREE WHAT WOULD (INSERT NAME HERE) DO IN THIS SITUATION? (THROUGH REPLACEMENT.)

Whether it's your favourite leader, someone you aspire to be like, or even your leadership coach, pick someone that does well in the tough situations that you might encounter, whether it's leading under pressure or building rapport with people skills. Then, when you're faced with the same difficult situation, ask yourself the question: what would that person do now?

This is one of the best tools I've learnt over time. I have names like Tony Robbins for my speaking work. Or Richard Branson as a leader. And of course, people closer to home and people I know well. With this question, I find I can replace limiting beliefs and limiting behaviours very quickly. It helps me take a new approach to the situation I'm facing. It makes me think differently, and think about what someone else would do in this situation—someone who's getting better results that I am in that area!

LEADER ACTION

Spend a moment or two, now, thinking about what types of thinking or behaviour you might like to replace in order to get a better result in a specific area of your life or leadership.

When you reflect on what leaders have done well or poorly, you'll be able to see the corresponding EQ involved. It's a good way to develop your own, and to identify maladaptive emotional responses that you can steer away from or replace with effective ones. It's a long-term commitment, but well worth the effort to become a good leader—as good a leader as the ones you admire the most—even when you're under pressure.

THE STRESS VERSUS DURESS QUANDARY

So, you're feeling under pressure right now. My coaching clients are talking about the COVID-19 'crisis' that they're dealing with. Including how do they keep their workplaces safe? How do they ask for proof of vaccinations, and the myriad of things that come with a pandemic? Things we haven't seen before, and hopefully won't again.

With the crisis comes the requirement to stay in control, to have care factor for their teams, and be courageous enough to make the tough decisions that need to be made. It all feels like more pressure. But is the pressure a form of stress, or is it a type of duress? And does it matter?

IS IT STRESS?

The Merriam-Webster dictionary shares that the phrase 'under duress' should not be confused with 'under stress'. Stress is concerned with strain or pressure, while duress refers to wrongful or unlawful coercion.

Stress is very much an internal response. It's an emotional reaction. It's akin to anxiety or panic, and it affects different people differently. But it's very much the bodily reaction to either external or internal stimuli, which might come from applied duress, from worrying about the economy, from worrying about your team, or from having to write a COVID-19 response plan when you have no idea where to start. That's stress. That's you sitting at your desk staring at your blank screen, trying to unpack what they heck is going on around you, and why you can't think clearly, and why you can't find a way to get into action.

Prolonged, or chronic, stress leads to a wide range of mental and physical and complications, including death. Ask anyone in Japan about Karoshi (working themselves to death). That's the perfect example of how you can put enough stress on your body that eventually it will shut down. Maybe even at your desk.

Typically, when you're stressed, you'll be berating yourself for not getting something in on time, or pushing yourself to meet the deadline, or cursing yourself for not being able to do a specific task and being worried about asking for help. Or it might be the fear that you experience when you need to do a public speech.

LEADER ACTION

If you're feeling stressed, there are techniques that you can lean into to help you clear your mind and clear your emotional slate. They include breathing, affirmations, meditation, and mindfulness (BAMM).

IS IT DURESS?

Duress is a totally different kettle of fish (a very technical-ish idiom for a muddle). The reason that duress is such a muddle is that it's externally applied. It's applied by another human. Generally, your leader. Yes, duress is a big deal, because it is, as defined above, a form of coercion. The politically correct leader who is applying duress would call it persuasion; the person under duress would call it manipulation at best, threatening at worst. Basically, duress is bad. Really bad.

Duress (in my mind) is just another word for 'poor leadership' and 'not being able to lead under pressure.' Herein lies the most important point of this section, as it talks straight to one of the first reactions that leaders have when they're under stress. The s@#$ flows downhill, right? If I'm stressed, I need to make it yours (my team members). Then I'll feel better. And they won't. Uncool. But I still hear it.

The duress might not just come from a leader who's stressed. It can come from a leader at any time, when they don't realise, like Spiderman, that leadership comes with great responsibility. Harvard Business Review explains[10] that leaders can stress out (or duress) their team members, even unintentionally, by using negative language, through erratic actions, emotional volatility, excessive pessimism, or by ignoring people's emotions. It's really uncool working for a leader like that. Especially over the long term or over a prolonged period.

A 2003 study[35] by Charlie Marsh proposed that posttraumatic stress disorder (PTSD) and so-called 'prolonged duress stress disorder' (PDSD) have similar symptom profiles, and differ only with regard to the presence or absence of a 'traumatic event.' What this study found was that enough duress-enforced stress can have the same impact on a human as a traumatic event. That is big.

LEADER ACTION

If you're a leader and you're reflecting on the above stressors that you may inflict on your team, never fear: there is an answer. The answer is learning how to lead under pressure (LUP). Take steps to build your LUP skills, and take ownership of your emotional state, your own stress levels, and how you treat others when you're stressed.

DOES IT MATTER?

If you're struggling with pressure, yes, it does matter if it's stress or duress, because there are two very different action plans depending on what you're experiencing. For stress, it's about emotional control. For duress, it's a robust conversation with the person applying the duress, in relation to how you're feeling and how it's affecting you (simple to say, not as easy to do). A hard conversation, but an important one.

For leaders who are constantly in fight-or-flight mode, or who feel like the COVID-19 crisis is getting the better of you, my coaching would include to stay in emotional control (whatever that takes), have care factor for your team (they are struggling too) and be courageous in your decision making (ensuring the decisions are legal, moral and ethical, of course). **Email me** to unpack your Leadership Resilience Review (a 15-minute diagnostic that will talk you through pressure relief opportunities).

Let's close this chapter out with why, as a leader, having sufficient EQ to manage your stress and not apply duress is important to your team. One of the best research papers I've read on the topic of employee job satisfaction was produced by **Prakash Singh** in 2013.[53] The study unpacked the importance of emotional intelligence (and emotional control) for leaders, explaining that employees prefer to be led by leaders who are confident in their leadership role, who send out clear, unambiguous messages, who maintain self-control, who are adaptable and flexible, who face the future with optimism, and who help build a collegial working environment.

Just imagine for a moment if we, as leaders, used all of those skills, and imagine how satisfied and productive our teams would be.

ACTIVITY 2.3
DEVELOP YOUR EMOTIONAL QUOTIENT

Take some time now to think about what you've learnt in the last chapter.

The series of questions on the following pages will encourage you to think about what you can do to develop your emotional quotient, and how you can apply the lessons you've just learnt in upskilling your leadership.

Otherwise, think about how manage your emotions in the workplace, and ways you could upskill your leadership with improved emotional consistency and better resilience.

What could you work on so your communication is more holistic?

What activities could you engage in to create better emotional control?

What impact has your emotional intelligence, or lack of it, had on your team members or employees?

What does leadership mean to you? Influence? Inspiration? Impact? Or something else?

Think about some of your past leaders. What did they do well, or not so well?

Imagine a favourite leader dealing with a leadership issue you're dealing with right now. What would they do?

Can you think of constructive ways to manage your stress?

Answer honestly. Do you think your team members or employees experience duress, either from you, or another leader?

SKILL IV
LEAD UNDER PRESSURE

WHEN WE LOOK AT SOME LEADERS, WE KNOW THAT THEY DON'T HAVE SELF-CONTROL, AND THEY DON'T HAVE CREDIBILITY.

Their catch line is to 'do as I say, not as I do' and you never quite know if they're really going to follow through on what they said they'll do.

Don't be like those leaders.

Why? Because those leaders can't be trusted to follow through, to follow processes, or to follow their own mandate of putting people first. And not only can't we trust them. They can't trust themselves. But what does it mean to have self-trust, when you're leading under pressure?

No discussion on trust will be complete without a reference to Stephen M. R. Covey,[16] who authored the book **The Speed of Trust**. In that book, the first and most critical element of trust is self-trust. Following through on the commitments you make, firstly to yourself, and then to your team.

Let me explain.

ONE SELF-TRUST IS ABOUT COMMITMENT.

To be the leader that you know you can be is about making personal and life commitments and sticking to those commitments. For example, get the simple things sorted. Get up with the alarm, or before it, not snooze it five times. Go to the gym on the days you say you will. Set goals, and work towards them. Read the book that you committed to reading.

Some of these might feel or seem like simple things, but they're not. They're confidence builders. If you increase your self-confidence, you'll make better decisions. You'll feel better about yourself, and your ability to follow through outside of work. Keeping your commitments to yourself is a big deal.

TWO SELF-TRUST IS ABOUT CREDIBILITY.

To be a leader that people want to follow, you need to be credible. Aka: being believable. Convincing. Persuasive. To be credible, leaders need to have the two core attributes: competence and character. Competence to know what's happening in their team, and why. And character, to have the courage to make the calls that need to be made, with integrity, with the right intent, and with the right delivery.

Sometimes the right decisions are not the easiest or the most straight forward. But they're the decisions that are the most legal, moral, and ethical. When you're operating in the legal, moral, and ethical space, your team will see how you demonstrate character (and courage). And you'll trust yourself to do what's right, not what's easy.

THREE SELF-TRUST IS ABOUT CONSISTENCY.

Consistency of emotional state, consistency of response (not reaction), and consistency of behaviour. This is about self-awareness as much as self-trust. Knowing how your physical and emotional state changes under pressure and being prepared to advance through adversity when the challenge or the pressure arrives is about being self-aware and consistent.

And of course, there's no time when self-trust is more important than when you're under stress or pressure. Leadership under pressure requires trusting yourself to be in conscious control, and operating with care factor, to make the tough decisions.

Sometimes, off the bat, and in public.

THE CHRIS ROCK REACTION WAS A LESSON IN SELF-CONTROL

Recently I got asked by a leader to unpack the saga that was played out between Chris Rock and Will Smith at the Oscars. (Which will go down in history as the slapping event that occurred following a Chris Rock joke that wasn't part of the script.)

It was obviously too personal, and not well thought through, in the moment.

So, here's my take on what it means for leading under pressure (noting that my take won't be what you expect. And won't be as direct as the opinions of people like Jim Carrey, who publicly asked for an assault charge to be laid).

Will Smith first though, only briefly, even though it was his action that we're really talking about. In his apology on Twitter the following day (which appeared to be sincere, and heartfelt), Smith used the words: 'I reacted emotionally.' Yes, he did. He gave himself permission in the moment to not process information, and not to respond, but to react.

But the big picture first.

ONE WHAT'S THE REAL CULTURE OF THE OSCARS?

'Where are you going with this one?', you might think. Well, what I go straight to when it comes to episodes like this is what was it about the culture that contributed to it? There's a thought. What encouraged it?

There's been a lot of commentary about the fact that (paraphrasing here) the presenters are going to make jokes from the stage, and the actors need to suck it up. Seriously, the stars presenting the awards would have had months to come up with material to use on stage. Surely we don't have to make it normal to make jokes about people? Surely Chris Rock (who I love, BTW, as I do Will Smith) can do better than that. He's a funny human. He doesn't need to take the mickey out of people.

Or is it just me that feels that you can be funny without being insulting? Why risk hurting other humans when you don't need to, just to be funny? Help me out—what am I missing here?

FYI, there have been actors come out and say that what occurred on stage after a personal joke was their greatest fear. It kept them up at night. Here's a thought—change the joke. You might even get more sleep.

The excuse will be that Chris Rock didn't know about the health condition of Jada Pinkett Smith. Not good enough, in my view. I hope the Oscars read my post on the subject, and address this.

TWO CHRIS ROCK'S RESPONSE WAS NEAR PERFECT.

'Will Smith just smacked the shit out of me,' Chris Rock said, while Smith walked off stage after slapping him. 'Wow, dude,' Rock continued, 'It was a G.I. Jane joke.'

Watch the video closely, and you'll see Chris Rock respond (NOT react) to being publicly slapped. Most viewers (I guess) would have expected him to respond like that.

But here's the alternative. Imagine this: Chris Rock hits back. There's a fight on stage. They roll off the stage together wrestling. Other actors have to rush in to stop the melee. It can't be stopped, and security are called, and on it goes. I believe that could have happened.

The poise and presence that Chris Rock displayed in the immediate moments after the incident says so much about his emotional intelligence and emotional control. His facial expression was disbelief first, then questioning—what just happened? He was processing. Deciding how to respond. Putting the incident through his frontal lobes, not through his limbic system (the emotional brain). You can nearly see his brain working through his body language (which was actually very open, and not aggressive in any way).

Chris Rock saved the night. Saved the event. And I hope he gets credit for that, instead of just the internet bashing of Will Smith. That self-control is a key skill in leading under pressure, equal in importance to empathy.

THE KEY SKILL FOR LEADING UNDER PRESSURE

The key skill for leading under pressure is empathy. And for those who've heard that before, read on, because not a lot of people really understand what empathy is.

In a blog post (What Empathy Really Takes), I unpacked the fact that empathy takes action, and it's neither an emotion nor an automatic reaction. It's not sympathy, and it's not just about trying to understand what someone is going through.

Empathy is about action (that is the compassion piece: there is no compassion without action). Empathy starts with a cognitive understanding of what someone is going through, then having an emotional connection to their struggle, and finally doing something (where possible) to support them—although this is not always possible. This methodology was developed by Daniel Goleman,[22] and it provides a great framework for what empathy is and how to put it into practice. Which is what leaders need to do when they're under pressure. And the pressure might be to deal with a team member who's struggling.

It's in these moments that empathy is critical. Brene Brown defined empathy as 'holding the space.' Being present when someone is sharing their toughest times with you.

In our leadership programs, we train the topic of empathy. And the best way to train it is to use a story from a coaching client who applied it beautifully.

Our client (the leader) was struggling with the absenteeism of a team member. We put a plan together to have the discussion, with empathy being at the heart of the conversation. We suspected that there was an issue outside of work, and it turned out there was. And it was a deeply personal issue that the team member shared, one that the leader had never experienced. The concern for the team member (whose performance had also dropped due to the challenges they were facing), translated into more time off to deal with it.

The leader put themselves in the shoes of the team member, and could then think and feel what it would be like for the team member. Once the leader understood both the issue, and how to support their team member, it was time to actually support the team member. Following the conversation, the leader consulted the HR team (the action piece: compassion), and it turned out that there was a specific type of leave to cover just such a situation. The leader was able to help the team member to get the time off that they needed to deal with the issue; the team member was then able to work through it, and to come back to work with a better mindset. The team member was also grateful for the support.

The key thing in this case study is the leader taking action. The understanding is the first part of empathy, but the compassion is the most important part. While leaders can't always take action like this to support their team members during these periods, they should certainly try.

Some tips to help leaders to be more empathetic include:

- Asking great questions to learn more about the person and their lives
- Then, listening to understand, not to respond
- Being attentive to body language and other types of nonverbal communication (behaviour includes emotions)
- Not necessarily agreeing, but understanding the situation and the position of the other person
- Putting yourself in the other person's shoes

And the most important thing: going out of your way to do something that supports your team member. Yes, I know you're busy, and you've got so much to do, and people take up so much time, and it's like 90% of your job, and you don't get time to yourself (all said with love—I just hear this a lot).

We're all born compassionate. I got asked at a recent program 'well, if we're all born compassionate, why don't some leaders act like that?' I'll leave you with that one.

You can't lead well under pressure without empathy, compassion, and self-control. All of those elements are about the people you're leading and responding to. But what about what you need, as a leader, to be able to keep on track in your leadership journey, when you're putting out fires every day? That's where resilience comes in.

HOW TO BE RESILIENT WHEN LEADING UNDER PRESSURE

Resilience is not just about coping. Resilience is about being ready to cope when you need to. There is a great definition of resilience, from **@JurieRossow**, who defines it as 'advancing despite adversity'.

I love this take.

So, if resilience is about both preparing for a BOOM event, and then advancing through it, what are the skills required at each end of the process? And how do you learn them?

For me, and from my lived experience, resilience is about turning life's lessons into life's blessings. And working out what you could take from the BOOM event that would set you up for success into the future—aka, if the same thing happened again, how would you deal with it a second time, or even a third time? And deal with it better?

In short, we go from living to learning, through a five-stage process that starts with living a life of blessing, living through the BOOM event, to living a life of learning. And the quicker we can get to the learning stage after the event, the sooner we stop ruminating (or thinking negatively) about what happened and what else we should have done.

Let's unpack what you can do before and after the BOOM event, to help you advance despite adversity.

ONE UNDERSTAND YOUR PR6.

As a certified Resilience Coach (though **Hello Driven**), I've been able to learn about both the neurological and the behavioural elements of resilience building. From a skill set perspective, your Personal Resilience 6 are the six life skills that will help you to be prepared for a BOOM event. They include:

- **Vision:** Having meaning, purpose, congruence, and goals for your life
- **Composure:** Being calm and in control, with emotional regulation, self-awareness, and stress management
- **Reasoning:** Adaptability, problem solving, resourcefulness, anticipation, and planning
- **Health:** Getting quality sleep, eating well, and exercising regularly
- **Tenacity:** Being persistent, bouncing back, being realistically

optimistic, and staying motivated

- **Collaboration:** Through strong relationships, support networks, and teamwork

Note that we can send you a link through Hello Driven to complete your resilience profile, and learn ways to improve your resilience. The more you understand the PR6, you better prepared you'll be for any BOOM event.

TWO LEARN THE SKILL OF REFRAMING.

Of the PR6 skills that you can develop, prior to a BOOM event, the one that you'll rely on following a BOOM is the skill of reframing. Or rephrasing. Or reprogramming.

For me personally, the ability to reframe is the best and most useful life skill I've learnt in all my years on planet Earth. By far. This is not the first time that I've said that, and it won't be the last. But what is reframing?

Glad you asked. Reframing is quite a simple skill (simple, but not easy at times), that helps you put a positive spin on any situation or event. It's like finding the silver lining in the dark cloud. It's about focusing on what went right, not what went wrong, and it's about learning from the BOOM event, so that when you talk about it, you talk about it in a positive sense.

You talk about it from a philosopher perspective, not a victim perspective. And you get to the point where you can even share those learnings with others, so that they might be better prepared if they were ever to encounter a similar situation.

Reframing is as much about rephrasing as anything else: about the language that you use, both with your inside voice, and with your outside voice. If you check yourself, you'll notice that you're using either negative words to explain the event, or you're more positive about it. When you get to that stage, you'll know that reframing work is paying off, and that you're starting to look at the event with a different perspective—which, in turn, will help you to stop ruminating about it. Winner!

As a side note, people that have been through traumatic BOOM events, and can take the lessons from the event, have been said to demonstrate PTG (post traumatic growth). And of course, there are people who struggle to get through those events, and sadly the result can be PTSD.

THREE KNOW THAT COPING IS A NECESSARY PART OF LIFE.

Yes, there will be times that you'll have to cope. You'll have to suffer through some tough times. If you haven't yet, go you, congrats. But they are coming. One in two people in Australia will suffer through a mental health challenge sometime in their lives.

Coping is a crucial skill. The more resilient you are, the easier it will be to cope with whatever life throws at you. That's never more true when you're leading under pressure, and the wellbeing of all the people in your team, organisation, and its market are depending on you.

Always look for ways to improve your resilience. One of the best ways I've found is through the practice of gratitude.

BEING GRATEFUL IS PART OF BUILDING YOUR RESILIENCE

There are people on the planet that would love your life. They'd love the freedom that you have, the health that you have, the relationship that you have, and even the struggles that you have. There are people on the planet that would be grateful to be in your position.

And I will, for the sake of this section, presume that you're happy to be in the position you're in, too. But I will also presume, that like most people, you don't spend too much time thinking about how grateful you are, and even less time physically writing down or journalling about the things or people you're grateful for.

The wellbeing benefits of being grateful have been well studied, researched, and documented. And like all good theories, gratitude is not new: it's been espoused by some of the great philosophers, going back as far as the second century. One Marcus Aurelius quote says that 'All you need are these: certainty of judgment in the present moment; action for the common good in the present moment; and an attitude of gratitude in the present moment for anything that comes your way.' So, if gratitude can help the last of the great rulers known as the Five Good Roman Emperors, maybe it can work for us too.

But like everything in our lives that makes a difference, it takes work, and it takes effort. The effort is worth it, though, as gratitude is linked to increased levels of happiness, resilience, and relationships. That means you benefit, and so do the people you're leading.

If you're looking for things to be grateful for, here's a few.

ONE GRATITUDE FOR HAPPINESS & OTHER POSITIVE EMOTIONS.

Sheldon and Lyubomirsky (2006) studied whether or not gratitude could have an impact on our emotional state. Sonja Lyubomirsky[51] herself appears to study happiness more than gratitude. But in an attempt to understand what can change our mood (and make us happy), her work inevitably led to gratitude. Lyubomirsky called it 'counting our blessings.' The study reported that expressing gratitude (being thankful and appreciative) elevates our positive emotions. Why? Because it 'fosters the savouring of positive life experiences and situations, so that people can extract the maximum possible satisfaction and enjoyment from their circumstances.' Gratitude prevents people from taking good things for granted. The expression of gratitude is thought to also increase stimulate moral behaviour (like paying it forward), which in turn also increases happiness. Being happy, and feeling good about ourselves, and about our situation, helps us to enjoy life more.

The caveat, though, is that it only has that effect if we practice gratitude on a regular basis, preferably daily.

TWO GRATITUDE FOR RESILIENCE.

In his groundbreaking and 'unputdownable' book, **The Resilience Project**, Hugh van Cuylenburg[56] talked through the GEM process, which is gratitude, empathy, and mindfulness. In that book, van Cuylenburg unpacked the power of gratitude and the amazing benefits it brings in relation to how resilient we are in our everyday lives. Feeling grateful changes our brain chemistry in a way that makes rumination more difficult.

Rumination is 'getting stuck' and not being able to get past a situation or a conversation or an event that troubled you or that you didn't handle well in the moment. Rumination can be debilitating it not addressed with improved self-talk (and even Cognitive Behavioural Therapy, or CBT). Gratitude helps you to stop ruminating, to cope with what has happened, and move through it to 'advance through adversity' (the definition of resilience). In short, gratitude increases your resilience by reducing your rumination, and helping you to bounce back quicker. Who wouldn't love to be a able to do that?

THREE GRATITUDE FOR RELATIONSHIPS.

Just imagine for a moment all of the amazing humans that you've been fortunate enough to be exposed to during your life, and how many of them have helped shape you into the great human you are today. So, how grateful as you for all of their support? And would you be the human you are without all of their input, guidance, coaching, support, nurturing and care? Possibly not (and, yes, for anyone reading this that is thinking about all of the people that have wronged you—believe it or not, they've helped you too, by helping you learn a lesson in life).

The message is that our relationships shape our life. The great business philosopher (aka motivational speaker) Tony Robbins famously states that 'the quality of your life is in direct proportion to the quality of your relationships.' And this is so true. Higher-quality relationships equate to a higher-quality life. And then there's the find-remind-and-bind theory. The theory posits that the positive emotion of gratitude serves the evolutionary function of strengthening a relationship with a responsive interaction partner (Algoe, Haidt, & Gable, 2008).[2] In short, the more grateful we are, the better we are at connecting with others, and building relationships through interactions and conversation. Remember that we are both a primitive species living a modern existence, as well as a social creature craving connecting. Being grateful helps us connect.

BUT HOW DO I START?

Being grateful is a very easy process. Take a minute now to think about what you're grateful for. Preferably, write it down: writing connects thoughts to the world around us, and once written, it can never be unwritten.

Just give thanks. Say aloud thank you for what ever it is you're thankful for. If you want to start practicing gratitude, please email me for a free electronic copy of your NOW Gratitude Journal, that you can use to get started.

Once you're in a gratitude mindset, it's easier to do the thinking work. Keep your eyes open, and you can learn from all kinds of people who are good under pressure—including triathletes, like yours truly.

WHAT LEADERS CAN LEARN FROM IRON WAR

An Ironman triathlon is arguably the toughest one-day endurance event on planet Earth. Ironman started in 1979, with three athletes arguing (over a beer, of course) about who the fittest athlete was. The 3.8 km swimmer. The 180 km cyclist. Or the 42.2 km runner.

There was only one solution. To put all three together and do them at the same time. And since that first event in 1979, the sport has become an institution for triathletes everywhere, with the pinnacle being the Hawaii Ironman World Championships, held every October in Kona.

The 1989 Ironman World Championship was perhaps the greatest Ironman race ever. In a spectacular duel that became known as the Iron War, the world's two strongest athletes raced side by side at world-record pace for a gruelling 139 miles.

Mark Allen, the calm, controlled, and composed athlete, was trying to win his first Ironman World Championship. Allen used technology, like heart rate monitoring and specific training programs. Dave Scott was the opposite. He was hardcore. His philosophy was to go out and bust yourself up, every session. No science.

Allen had never beaten Scott in Hawaii. Some people thought he never would. Allen finished second in 1986 and 1987, behind Scott.

So, Allen came up with a strategy. His plan was to race on Scott's shoulder for the whole race. For the whole eight hours. Mark Allen and Dave Scott raced shoulder to shoulder through Ironman's 3.8 km swim, 180 km bike race, and 42.2 km marathon. After eight punishing hours, both men would demolish the previous record—and cross the finish line a mere 58 seconds apart (See Matt Fitzgerald's[21] book, Iron War if you love this sport, or you just love the human species). The strategy worked.

Mark Allen won that race, to grab his first world title. He won it with a burst of energy, through an aid station in the final stages of the race.

What can we learn, as leaders, from this commitment to a cause?

ONE CHANGE THE STRATEGY, NOT THE GOAL.

For Mark Allen, he needed a strategy that worked. He and Scott had raced each other plenty of times, with Allen always coming in after Scott.

The goal to win the world championship never changed. The strategy changed. Until it worked, and the goal was achieved. Never change the goal—adapt the strategy.

For leaders, and for leadership teams, this is an important point, as there will be hurdles. There will be obstacles. There will be challenges. That doesn't mean you give up on your goal. It means that you're building resilience along the way. And that you're getting closer with every attempt.

TWO TUNE OUT THE NOISE.

There will be detractors. There will be dissenters. There will be disapproval.

But if your why is strong enough, you'll be able to tune out these voices, even when some of them are your own. As a leader or leadership team, you will be exposed to negativity. Noise. Nonsense.

Set yourself up for success and have a positive mindset. One that doesn't get distracted. For Mark Allen, there was a single-minded focus that drove his behaviour, and that got him to the finish line first during the Iron War.

Imagine for a moment how many people would have thought that, after he tried so many times previously that it seemed implausible that he would ever beat Dave Scott.

But Allen didn't listen to that noise. He didn't listen to the noise that would have distracted him from the mission.

THREE RINSE, REPEAT, AND REPRODUCE.

Fun fact: Mark Allen won that event in 1989, then again in 1990, then again in 1991, then again in 1992, and then again in 1993. Before 1989, Allen couldn't beat Scott. He then won five world championships in a row. He certainly rinsed, repeated, and reproduced what worked.

In relation to rinsing and repeating, the message is to find out what works, and do more of that. And find out what doesn't, and do less of that. Once you have the winning formula for your team, or your business, leverage it. Build on it and ingrain it in your organisational culture. So that you keep getting great results. Like Mark Allen did.

This section has focused on Mark Allen's strategy during Iron War, and what we can learn from that. But it wouldn't be right not to congratulate Dave Scott, too, who's one of the greatest athletes to ever do Ironman racing. Scott is a six-time world champion. A legend of the sport. And I was lucky enough to meet him at a race in Sydney some years ago. Fun fact again: an amazing Aussie Greg Welch won the event in 1994! Go Welchy!

Learn how to lead under pressure from people with grit. They never give up on a goal. They change the strategy, and keep cranking until they find the magic sauce. To do that, they tune out the noise. And once they've worked out the strategy for success, they rinse and repeat, and can reproduce the results they're committed to achieving.

You can do it, too. Here's some more pearls of leadership wisdom from the sport, about the endurance you need to upskill your leadership.

WHY DOING A TRIATHLON IS LIKE LEADING UNDER PRESSURE

Learning how to do something hard is worth the effort. Like a triathlon, and more specifically an endurance triathlon. A sporting event that takes between five and seventeen hours to complete, depending on how much training you've done. But even the short triathlons will be tough, especially when you're first starting out. A little bit like leadership.

And for anyone that doesn't know, a triathlon is a swim, ride, run event, where the bike leg is generally the longest leg of the event, compared to the swim and run. I've been doing triathlons since 2008, and I've learnt a lot about the sport, about myself, and about leadership during that time. Here's how triathlon and leading under pressure are similar, and how we can take lessons from one for the other.

No matter how many times you've lined up on the start line, the swim leg is a challenge. There is never a time in my life when I am surrounded by more people, but feel so alone. We're shoulder to shoulder on this line. Emotions are high, and energy levels are higher. I know that I'm about to be in the water, I'll be struggling for breath, and getting kicked and bumped (the swim is a contact sport) by other swimmers.

For the vast majority of first timers, or even experienced triathletes, the swim leg is not their strongest, so it takes courage and effort to 'toe the water' and to just dive straight in, when the buzzer goes off.

IT FEELS LIKE IT GOES ON FOREVER.

Jump into the challenge, catch your breath, take the bumps, and keep moving forward toward the buoys (goals).

Then it's time to jump on your bike and go for a little ride. The ride leg is good for thinking time and collecting yourself. I make sure I get my heart rate down, get into a rhythm, and focus on hydration and nutrition. The biggest challenge on the bike is overcooking it and going too hard. Remember, you still have a run to do at the end of the bike leg. Most triathletes have had the experience of pushing too hard on the bike and burning their legs for the run.

And of course, follow all the rules on the bike. Don't draft, don't litter, and don't obstruct other riders. Even when there are no technical officials watching. This is the big thing for the fast bikers. They like riding behind other fast bikers. Which is uncool.

AND THERE'S STILL MORE TO GO.

Remember that you have a long day ahead. Don't go too quickly too early, and always do the right thing, even when no one is watching (that's integrity).

Now it's time to run home. The age-old issue for triathletes who get off the bike: they hope their legs still work, and that they can control them. I've felt the jelly-leg effect on numerous occasions, and it's not pleasant. You want your legs to work, but they don't. It's a matter of getting composed and knowing that the feeling will come back soon.

But you get through that weird feeling and run (or walk) whatever distance is required. Until you cross that finish line and get the finish line feeling, that's like nothing else on planet Earth (big statement). I've completed a range of triathlon distances and have run a marathon at the end of a 180 km ride. Which was tough. Regardless of the distance, most triathletes manage to find some energy to finish strong.

AND IT HURTS THE WHOLE TIME, BUT IT'S A GOOD HURT.

Remain composed, know that you're getting closer to your goals (even if you're wobbly right now). And the most important part of leadership: celebrate success when you achieve what you set out to do.

Learn more about the sport of triathlon—it's a great way to learn about the journey of leadership, especially when you're leading under pressure.

ACTIVITY 2.4
LEAD UNDER PRESSURE

Answering the following questions will encourage you to think about what you can do to develop your ability to stay in control under pressure— and to strength yourself as a caring and impactful leader for your team. Alternatively, spend some time journalling about what you're grateful for, and how you could be more resilient.

Do you think your team members or employees see you as credible, and as having good character? Why, or why not?

In what ways could you support a team member who's struggling in their professional life? What about in their personal life?

Are you resilient when leading under pressure? Why, or why not?

Answer honestly. Do you follow through with your commitments? If not, how could you do this better?

How could you work on your emotional control so that you can 'tune out the noise' when you're under pressure?

SKILL V
BE COURAGEOUS

COURAGE: THE ABILITY TO ACT WHEN YOU DON'T WANT TO.

Courage. Without it, fear will stop you from ever moving forward with purpose. Full stop.

If there's one thing we know about leadership, it's that it takes a huge amount of courage. Courage to get started. Courage to keep moving. If you asked the great stoic philosopher, Seneca the Younger, he would have told you that 'sometimes, even to live is an act of courage'. And he's right. Living takes courage, and so does leadership.

Courage is about action. The right action. Even when you're scared. Even when you might not have all the information. But when you know something is the right thing to do.

This section isn't one of those motivational ones where I share with you the story of some great adventurer who was scared, but who got over the fear, and slayed the dragon and saved the fair maiden. (Wasn't Shrek a great movie?)

This section is specifically about when leaders need to display courage, and how they can do that. It's about courageous leadership, and the buckets of courage that it takes to be a courageous leader (Credit: **wework.com**)

ONE TRY COURAGE.

Fun fact. You might fail. You might fall. You might falter. But without the courage to try, you'll never even get started. You won't try new things. In his book **The Courage to Start**, John Bingham[4] talks about going from an overweight couch potato to running marathons, and how he would never have completed all of those runs if he didn't have the courage to start.

If you ask Will Smith, he'll say fail often and fail forward. I'm a big fan of those words, and I can say hand on heart, most of the things I've ever tried in business haven't worked. But they were lessons, in the end, not failures.

Here's the process. Have an idea. Tell the team. Get buy in (hopefully). Get started. You've got this—it just takes some try courage.

TWO TRUST COURAGE.

In my many years as a leadership coach, one of the things that I've heard the most is that 'if you need it done properly, you need to do it yourself'. Oh no, I think, this'll be a hard mindset to change. But it can be changed. If the leader is willing to give up control.

And if the leader is willing to see the qualities and the value that their team possesses. The infinite ability of the collective. Their power to be autonomous and to do their jobs better than their leader can. That's called transformational leadership, which is the leader having trust courage, and the team members having try courage. Winner.

Without trust, leaders will never create more leaders. They'll just create more work for themselves. And arrive at our next session being too busy.

You've got this—it just takes some trust courage.

THREE TELL COURAGE.

Tell them. In a way that's based on your conviction, your commitment, and your care factor. The better you can articulate your vision, the better your team can buy in and get working towards it.

Recently, we ran a two-day leadership workshop for leaders who want to make a difference, are willing to do what it takes, and are willing to stand up for something. That's the key. Part of that program will be for the leaders to unpack the first question of why they do leadership. The vast majority of our trainees have never thought about that question—why do I do what I do? It's the first thing that a leader should be able to tell others. And then, they can articulate it and tell it to engage people in the goals and objectives of the business or team. Winner.

You've got this—it just takes some tell courage.

LEADERS, HOW COURAGEOUS ARE YOU?

Courageous leaders can create a culture of trust and respect, which makes those around them be prepared to follow them. This all creates a recipe for success, development, and evolution within an organisation.

As a young leader, I was scared (petrified, really) of things like making big decisions. Having robust discussions. Trusting others to do important work. And the advice I got was quite broad: just get over your fears. Act in spite of fear. Courage is not the absence of fear; it's acting anyway.

All great ideas (and cliches), and I get them. For sure. But what do they really mean?

Do they mean 'stop procrastinating'? Do they mean 'you're afraid of public speaking; join Toastmasters'? Do they mean 'stop overthinking it and get into action'? I feel like those quotes are quite broad, even for a broad topic like courage. I feel that leaders need better advice, they need better guidance, and they need clearer actions. Why? Because leadership is not broad, it's one discussion, one conversation at a time.

Courageous leaders are very deliberate in their actions. They're not acting despite fear. They're acting on purpose. They're demonstrating courage every day, by trying, telling, and trusting.

Let's apply the principles in the last section to the leadership situation.

ONE THE COURAGE TO TRY.

The only constant in life is change! And with change comes big decisions. Big decisions have to be made, to improve, to update, to progress, and to move forward. And yes, your decisions and changes might be wrong. And you'll get a lesson or a blessing from the outcome.

But make the decision, implement the change and back yourself. Make it with the right information, with the right intent, and with the right foresight, and take your team forward.

LEADER ACTION

The old pros and cons strategy works every time (an oldie, but a goodie). Then, give yourself a timeframe in which to make the decision, and to try something new.

TWO THE COURAGE TO TRUST.

Leaders, please tune in. It's not quicker and better to do it yourself. Seriously, it's not. Trust people to do their jobs, with your support, as required—don't do it for them—and watch them shine. Trust is king if you want to develop a high performing team. Set expectations, set standards, and help your teams exceed them. And watch them transform during the process.

LEADER ACTION

Catch yourself every time you know you're doing the work of your team. Hold yourself accountable for delegating, and for asking the right person to do the right work.

THREE THE COURAGE TO TELL.

There are so many things that you need to tell your team or team members. Whether it's about your vision, or about their performance. If you're saying it in your head (or to your leadership coach), it must be said aloud. Yes, my advice is always if you can tell me, you can tell them. Even if it might not be popular. Robust conversations need to be had. You owe it to the team or the person to have them. In a way that builds the relationship, not breaks it.

LEADER ACTION

Prepare, prepare, and prepare. Do a conversation planner, and make sure you know what you're going to say, and how, and why. Schedule it and communicate your message with care factor.

Yes, courageous leadership is about acting in spite of fear. But it's also about deliberate action. With an outcome in mind, and with a clear purpose.

Courage is a feeling piece. Once you have it, you can turn it into action—and into new ways of thinking. Have the courage now to think about how you think, and whether your coping style is affected by your courage—or your lack of it—when it comes time to deal with problems.

HOW TO ADOPT A PROBLEM-FOCUSED COPING STYLE TO DEAL WITH STRESS

We all cope with stressful situations differently, depending on the level and the nature of the stressful situation or event.

Over the past several decades researchers have identified the main coping styles of individuals, and it turns out that a problem-focused coping style is the best way to deal with stressors.

Stressors might include what psychologists call a 'stressful life event' (like moving house or losing a job), or it might include a major catastrophe at work (like a serious safety incident), or a flood, or an economic crisis.

As well as a problem-focused approach, there are two other coping styles identified in the research that we choose when coping with such events. These include emotional-focused and avoidant coping styles.

Here's an overview of each style.

ONE PROBLEM-FOCUSED COPING.

If you're someone who adopts a problem-focused approach to coping with stressors, you're someone gets into action. You're someone who addresses a problem head on, with a focus on taking action to address the issue or the challenge causing it.

Being problem focused is about taking ownership and responsibility for either solving or minimising the problem, with whatever resources are available to you at the time. This coping style is about doing a root-cause analysis and addressing what it is that's causing the stressor. And potentially having the additional focus to prevent reoccurrence.

Problem-focused coping is believed to be the most effective way to cope with stress, as it's action oriented. It means that the stressed person can take their focus off what they're feeling and focus on what they're doing, or on what others are doing. It's about collecting information, making decisions about the situation, and responding to the challenges of the situation with the clearest thinking possible.

TWO EMOTION-FOCUSED COPING.

The next best way to cope through a stressful life event is to take an emotion-focused approach. Emotion-focused coping is a type of stress management that attempts to reduce negative emotional responses associated with stress. Negative emotions such as embarrassment, fear, anxiety, depression, excitement, and frustration are reduced or removed by the individual by various methods of coping (Credit: **Simply Psychology**).

There are times when this coping strategy might be the most effective. Think about those times when the stressor is out of your control. Like an economic crash, or the death of a loved one. Or something else that can't be addressed through problem solving. This is actually the toughest coping strategy, as it takes a massive effort, and a commitment to emotional control. Things like mediation, breathing, focus change, or even medication are some of the tools you can use to adopt this coping strategy.

In saying that, this strategy is still a winner at any stage, and for me personally, the one that I go to. And most specifically, the tool that I pull out of the toolbox is the skill of reframing the situation. That is, putting a different spin on the stressor, and somehow, as hard as it can be, finding the positive. Turning the lesson (stressor) into a blessing (silver lining). Life gives us two types of emotional experiences—lessons or blessings. The sooner we can turn a lesson into a blessing, the quicker we can use emotional focus to help us get through stressful events.

THREE AVOIDANT-FOCUSED COPING.

As the name implies, an avoidant coping style in one where you pretend the event or the stressor doesn't exist, and you avoid dealing with it. Physically, and emotionally. This is easy for some people, but the vast majority of humans are not able to avoid a situation that causes them stress.

Generally, avoidance is only a short-term measure. At best. It does nothing to help you cope, really. In some cases, avoidance has been related to very negative outcomes for victims of cancer, say, where instead of addressing it, the victim avoided it. Pretended it didn't exist, and passed away.

For me, I feel like short-term avoidance could potentially lead to long-term issues. But I'd have to read some more research reports to validate that thought process.

When you're confronted by a stressor, get into action and do what you can to address the issue. Then, deal with the negative emotions that it causes, and try to reduce the impact of those negative emotions. Avoid the issue, as a last resort, remembering that you might eventually have to deal with it.

Be courageous in your coping style. There's a lot riding on your bravery—you need to be like Spiderman.

WHY BEING A LEADER IS LIKE BEING SPIDERMAN

Once upon a time there was a young man named Peter.

Peter had some tragedy in his life. He lost his parents, aged four, in a plane crash, and was raised by his Aunty May and Uncle Ben. More tragedy showed up in Peter's life, when he was bitten by a spider, and he was changed irreversibly. Then, a robber broke into their house, and Uncle Ben was fatally injured. Uncle Ben left a lasting legacy on Peter's life, when, in his dying moments, he shared with Peter the amazing wisdom that 'with great power, comes great responsibility.'

A great message, and a great story, about Peter Parker. Aka, Spiderman.

Peter (and anyone who watches the movies or follows the story) can learn from those words and remember them. Always. That's what leadership is about. Leaving a legacy that sets your team members up for success, with great advice. Not the opposite.

What does great responsibility mean, as a leader? It means to encourage transformation. It means to do no harm. It means to 'leave people better than you found them' (my personal mantra).

In our two-day leadership programs, we do an exercise where I ask the group if they can remember a time when a leader said something that was hurtful or harmful. And every hand goes up. 'Absolutely I can', is the response from the group members. 'Tell me more', I say...and the story generally starts like this: 'Well, it was twenty years ago, and I had a leader that was abusive/aggressive/abrupt...' 'And you still remember that?' I say. 'Of course, I'll never forget it', is the response. 'How could I? It was hurtful. And by the way', they say, 'that leader had no idea about how to treat humans...' 'Thanks for the story', I finish with, as I work my way around the room and close this little exercise about an hour later.

Then, we flip the script. 'So, team', I say. 'If a leader can have such an impact on you that you remember the stuff that they said twenty or more (often longer) years later, what might be the lesson?' The response is generally 'Don't be like that.' 'Great call', I say. 'Top job. Don't be the leader that's remembered for being crapola at human interaction' (or narcissistic, which is a common word I hear to describe poor leaders).

'Any other ideas?' I say then. Someone in the group will finally have an aha! moment and say (generally very excitedly): 'If leaders can have such a negative impact on people with what they say, why don't we focus on being a great leader, so that our legacy is one that people remember as being really positive, instead of the negative?' 'Absolutely, that's the key message', I affirm. Generally, just as excitedly!

Leadership, in my humble opinion, is the most important job on the planet after parenting (teachers are right up there, as are doctors and nurses and emergency services, of course). Leaders and teachers leave a lasting impact, one way or the other. To learn more from my favourite teacher, go to a recent newsletter here.

Back to leaders. With great power, comes great responsibility. But what does that really mean?

Here's a three-step process to keep that message front of mind.

ONE REMEMBER THAT YOUR TEAM IS WATCHING YOU.

As a leader, you're always on show. The age-old adage will apply in a hundred years just as it does now: what you walk past, you condone. And how you lead (and behave) will be reflected and be mirrored by your team. Yes, teams become a reflection of their leaders. Some leaders don't get this point. And the leader will say 'do as I say, not as I do', but your team watches more than they listen, which is human.

That's why leading by example is so important. And the most important thing is that your team are watching how you treat others. Are you firm, fair and friendly? Or are you playing favourites?

The time when you'll really need to be on your game is during a crisis event, or when you're under pressure. Pressure brings out worst in leaders, and they give themselves permission to default to react, rather than respond. Just ask Will Smith.

LEADER ACTION

With leadership comes the great responsibility to be the role model. Be how (the leader that you wish you had) was. Be the example of how to treat people the way they deserve to be treated. Be self-aware even when you're stressed out. Be aware of how you behave as a leader. Especially towards others.

TWO REMEMBER THAT YOUR TEAM IS LISTENING TO YOU.

As a leader, you'll face real challenges around leading and language. People hear what they want to hear. You think you say one thing, but they hear another. Do some research about confirmation bias and see what happens. And have an aha! moment about why our language connects with some of our team members and not others.

Most leaders don't realise the power of language. Just try using trigger words like no, disagree, wrong, but, and a range of others, and see what happens. Watch the reaction of your team member, as their amygdala fires and sends a message to their pituitary gland to release cortisol, which triggers the adrenal gland to release adrenaline so that the team member can be ready for a fight or to flight. Or to freeze or fawn. All in about .120 milliseconds. From just one word.

As important as step one is, just try making a commitment to a team member in an area that's important to them. Like their conditions, income, leave, or even their office space. They'll remember it until you follow through. So make sure you do. (See my sections on psychological safety.)

LEADER ACTION

With leadership comes the great responsibility to understand the language you use, and understand how to be less triggering as a

leader, so you don't have a negative impact on your team members (sometimes, even without knowing it). Choose your words carefully, especially in high-pressure situations.

THREE DO NO HARM.

Be the leader who people remember for the right reasons. Not always popular decisions, but popular delivery of those same decisions.

This section is short, and the advice is simple: try not to be abusive, aggressive, or abrupt. These are the three major types of behaviour that hurt humans, and impact on their work.

Remember also that team members who aren't heard are hurt (which is why step two is important). When the team member says that they don't feel valued, it's code for 'just listen to me'. Follow step one and two, and you'll be on your way to doing no harm.

LEADER ACTION

With leadership comes the great responsibility to do no harm. Be clear on how you will and want to be remembered.

Focus on your leadership goals. Think about how you want to be remembered. If that goal and that commitment is always front of mind, you'll find the courage naturally as you work towards it.

Take some inspiration from wildly inspiring leaders—like William Wallace.

HOW TO LEAD LIKE WILLIAM WALLACE

Since the day I watched the movie *Braveheart*, I've never looked at leadership the same way. It was such a revelation, in its own way. You see, I probably don't watch movies like most people do, I watch them to learn something about the human species. And you sure can learn something from watching actors play the role of other humans.

If you haven't seen *Braveheart*, get on your favourite movie-streaming service and watch it. Don't thank me now. *Rotten Tomatoes* gave it a solid rating, and it won a string of awards. Yes, it was a little (extremely) factually incorrect if you know your Scottish history, but what it lacks in accuracy, it makes up for in action and excitement.

It's a love story, as much as it's a hero's journey. It's the story of William Wallace, who wasn't born into nobility, but who takes on the nobility, based on their poor leadership and the abuse of power. It's a story of a peasant who led a militia to take on the might of an invading nation, encouraging his own countrymen to stand and fight again oppression and tyranny.

What most people don't see, though, are the subtle leadership messages in the movie. Particularly in the key scenes. I firmly believe that movie makers are experts in the human psyche, and the producers of *Braveheart* (Mel Gibson's production company) nailed it. In this section, I'll unpack some of the hidden messages in some of the final scenes of the movie.

Let's look at leading like William Wallace—especially under pressure.

ONE LEADERSHIP IS TAKEN, NOT GIVEN.

William Wallace turned up and took control.

In one of the final scenes of the movie, the Scottish patriots (or the militia) were facing the might of the English army. Lochlan was leading the Scots, and he was trying to motivate the Scots to stay and fight. Against crazy odds. Totally outnumbered, and totally out-weaponed.

Lochlan thought he had situation covered. He was sitting atop his horse at the front of the Scottish army. And he was confident. Until William Wallace showed up. At that stage, no one knew that he was William Wallace. Not even Lochlan.

The difference was that William Wallace had a presence. William Wallace commanded respect. He told people who he was, but the Scots didn't believe him. He wasn't big enough to be William Wallace, who was apparently seven foot tall.

Once he started talking, though, the Scots listened. The pressure was on, the English were coming, and there wasn't a lot of time to motivate the Scots. But he did. And he thanked the Scots for presenting themselves on the battlefield. He was reverent, and at the same time totally committed. He was confident, and courageous. William Wallace didn't ask for permission to take charge, he just did.

Leadership is not about your job title. It's about your example, and your behaviour. Your team follow you because of who you are, not because of what your job role is.

TWO LEADERSHIP IS READING THE FIELD.

William Wallace called it as it was.

For me, this is the most important five seconds of the movie, and before I tell you what William Wallace said, let me give you the scenario. It's the very next part of the movie, after William Wallace arrives on the scene.

When Lochlan worked out it was William Wallace, he quickly shared with Wallace that the Scots were covered. They didn't need him. They told him that they had the whole situation in control. Which was interesting, because at the same time, some of the Scots were getting cold feet. They'd seen the English show up on the battlefield, and it was just a little too much for some of the Scots. They were scared. They needed to be motivated.

Ask anyone who's watched the film what the most important line in it was, and most will recite the famous line: 'They may take our lives, but they will never take our freedom!' But that isn't the most important line in the movie.

Fun fact: if you ever come to one of our leadership workshops, my favourite part (by far) is to unpack the great lines of the great business philosophers (aka, movie stars or famous humans). And when you know what the lines are from each of the famous people, you have to say it with passion. Imagine the room shouting out the freedom line from *Braveheart*. Or that unforgettable line from *Jerry McGuire*...you know the one.

If you were listening carefully to William Wallace, when Lochlan was telling Wallace that it was his army, and the Scots had it under control, Wallace said 'If this is your army, why does it go?' In other words, you're not motivating this army to stay and fight. For me, this is the best line in the movie. And leaders everywhere: if this is your team, why are they leaving?

Leadership is about being honest about the situation you're in. It's not about beating around the bush. Especially when you're under pressure, you need to be direct, and make your words count.

THREE LEADERSHIP IS NEVER GIVING UP.

William Wallace stayed committed, even on his death bed.

For me, the final scene in the movie sums up the life of a leader. To the very end of his life, William Wallace was committed to one thing. Freedom. Even when he was being tortured by the English, and his torturers wanted to hear him say one word—*mercy*.

It wasn't Wallace who said that word, though, it was the crowd. Pleading for mercy and pleading for an end to the torture. The crowd was mainly English, so it was amazing to see the impact that Wallace had on not only his own team, but also on the English.

How truthful it is, who knows. He wouldn't have been able to scream out, but he did. Instead of muttering the word *mercy*, he screamed at the top of his voice, *freedom*. That one word that had driven his life's purpose, and his life's work. He died for freedom. Like in the movie, Wallace is said to have accepted his execution without any resistance. And with a brave heart. He even made a final confession to a priest and read from the book of Psalms before his torture and execution.

Leadership under pressure is about staying committed until the situation has passed or the work is done. For some leaders, this is never. For some leaders, building their business, their team, or the organisation is their life's work. And it's work that they'll never stop doing.

Lead like William Wallace. Remember that leadership is taken, not given. Read the field, and never give up. And be courageous—especially when it's decision-making time, and people are looking to you.

I'D HAVE LESS WORK IF LEADERS DID THIS ONE THING

The more senior the leader, the bigger the decisions they have to make. But some senior leaders don't make the decisions that they need to. They put decisions off. They postpone decision making. They let decisions linger. And it doesn't help their teams.

I understand it. And I can empathise with putting off decision making. Sometimes you need more information. Sometimes you need more input. Sometimes you need more ideas.

I was sitting having a lunch chat recently with a leader, who was explaining their frustration with their leader. Their leader was sitting on some key decisions that my lunch partner was waiting on, and the person I was speaking to was beside themselves with anxiety and other negative emotions. They just weren't able to do their job properly, waiting on their leader to make key decisions. Like decisions around people, processes, or major purchases. They're the big ones.

Following our lunch chat, I went back through my coaching notes, and at least three out of four sessions discussed decisions that needed to be made by the leader of the person that I'm coaching. For most of the people I coach (well over 700), needing their leader to make a decision is a big issue.

So what stops leaders making decisions, and how can they get into decision-making mode?

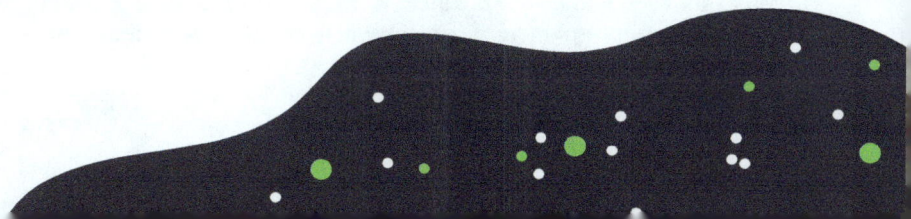

ONE LACK OF CLARITY.

When the goal of a decision isn't clear, it can be hard to make the right choice. A leader may struggle to make a decision if they don't understand the desired outcome, or are missing the parts that make up an informed decision. The goal and outcomes of every decision need to be very clear.

LEADER ACTION

Get the information, input, and ideas you need. Make a commitment to your team, that you'll make the decision after getting all of the information you need. Set a decision deadline.

TWO FEAR OF FAILURE.

Fear of failure can be a major obstacle to decision making, especially when it comes to important decisions. Leaders may be concerned that their decision could have negative consequences, or that they may make the wrong choice. This fear can be crippling enough to stop them from making a decision that needs to be made.

LEADER ACTION

Fear of failure stems from worrying about what could go wrong as a result of the decision. The trick is to reframe your thinking to work through what could go right, instead.

THREE PERSONAL BIASES.

A leader's personal beliefs and preferences can also influence their decision making. They may be more likely to make a decision that aligns with their values, even if it's not the best course of action. We lean on our values when we need to make any big decisions, so it's important to be clear on what your personal values are, and how they align with the values of the business—otherwise, you'll be prone to bias.

LEADER ACTION

Make sure you know your business's values, and your own. Knowing where you differ from your business will help you have a clearer picture of where your biases are.

Leaders need to be aware of factors that can stop them from making decisions, and they should strive to be courageous in doing it, even when it's difficult.

Take the time to gather all the information you need to make an informed decision, and be courageous enough to consider your own biases. With practice and dedication, you can overcome the obstacles to decision making, and become an effective—and courageous—decision maker.

ACTIVITY 2.5
BE COURAGEOUS

Answering the following questions will encourage you to think about what you can do to lead more courageously, in the process of upskilling your leadership. Thinking about how to be more courageous in leading your team through difficult times, and developing a stronger problem-focused coping style, can help you improve your communication and grow your confidence to get the best results from your team.

Do you have the courage to try, even though you could fail?

Can you trust your team enough to hand off important tasks? Why, or why not?

Do you use problem-, emotion-, or avoidant-focused coping? How is it working out for you?

Do you think your team members are learning effective strategies by watching and listening to you? Why, or why not?

Answer honestly. Do you think your team members follow your instructions because of your role, or because of your character and example?

Answer honestly. What personal biases are influencing your decision making?

AFTERWORD

If you're still with me, congratulations on making it this far. And thanks for finding me engaging enough that you decided not to put this book down and never look at it again.

What I hope has kept you connected to my words is the resilience with which I wrote them. I hope you can see how creating conscious control helps you to develop as a leader, to overcome the urge to lose it under pressure—no matter what's happening in that moment—and to lead your teams with emotional consistency and care factor.

I was not always a good leader. But now, I hope, I'm a leader that people will remember for the right reasons. I hope you can see how learning to respond, and not react, can help you become a better human. And that being courageous can help you to trust others enough to connect in meaningful ways, and to lead your team every day with integrity.

This book isn't the answer to all of your leadership woes. But it's the beginning of the process. A process that needs to start from within, by understanding your own triggers, fears, and coping methods, so you can put away what doesn't work, and put on what does.

If you're an old-school leader, the one that I wrote this book for, congratulations on getting through a book you probably weren't very comfortable reading. See how learning emotional literacy makes you more professional, not less? And how investing in care factor makes for a more productive team, and not a workplace in emotional chaos?

If you're a new-age leader, the one that I wrote this book for, congratulations on getting through a book you probably thought was going to be a lot less work. See how empathy, not sympathy, helps you support your team members through BOOM events without burning you out? Your consistency, conscious control, and courage are allowing your team and organisation to benefit from your growth and upgraded skills.

There's a lot more to learn about people, and yourself. Go and get stuck into whatever piques your interest: developing emotional literacy; how to manage your amygdala hijack; how to be a stoic leader. This book is the beginning, and as long as you're leading, there shouldn't be an end.

Learn more from me. I have a bunch of books and a team of people who can help you become a better leader. Or don't learn more from me. Learn from anyone whose leadership is inspiring to you in any way. Or anyone whose leadership has caused you stress, or duress, or to decide to never, ever lead your team like they led you. Go learn how to lead with care factor, and courage, and enough insight to know that leading by example is the most powerful way to guide your team towards professional development.

If you don't remember anything I've taught you in this book, remember how it made you feel. If it filled you with hope and optimism, and overwhelmed you with the urge to commit to being a better leader, good. Go do it. If it filled you with dread and shame about how bad your leadership really is, good. Go get better at it.

Either way, you got this far because you're becoming reflective. You're learning how to think differently. You're learning how to react differently. You're learning how to answer the big questions—including why you're a leader, and why you do what you do.

Congratulations on finishing this book. You're upskilling your leadership. Keep going. Every learning is getting you closer to where you want to be.

THE
LEADERSHIP
TRILOGY

BOOK 3

UPLIFT

YOUR TEAMS

LEADERSHIP LESSONS FROM LEADERSHIP SPECIALIST

ANTON GUINEA

UPLIFT
YOUR TEAMS

WITH THE UPLIFT MODEL

This model was developed as a strategic tool for putting theory into practice to uplift your teams.

The model draws on various psychological theories relating to attitude, perception, and emotional experience in the workplace, and structures this information into a practical framework to guide leaders through the process of uplifting their teams by becoming better leaders.

It was developed over nearly 20 years of theoretical analysis combined with real-world experience, and it underpins the Guinea Group's winning formula for creating effective leaders, high-performing teams, and workplaces that are both physically and psychologically safe for workers.

Refer back to this model while reading this book. It'll help you form a concrete framework in your mind that will, over time, become a natural reference point as you grow and develop in your attitudes and behaviours, and move you closer to being the leader you want to be.

To make the most of this resource, contact us via our website at antonguinea.com.au for a self-diagnostic tool and action plan to review and improve your skills against the model.

01 UPLIFT YOUR **TEAM**
Skillset: Create a high-performing and psychologically safe team

02 FACILITATE **TEAM DISCUSSION**
Skillset: Give your team members a voice, and let them challenge you

03 ROLE MODEL **LEADERSHIP**
Skillset: Lead by example, so team members do as you say, and as you do

04 DEAL WITH **DIFFICULTIES**
Skillset: Lead your team out of turmoil and into productivity

05 DEMONSTRATE **RADICAL CANDOUR**
Skillset: Care first, and show it, before you challenge directly

INTRODUCTION: UPLIFT YOUR TEAMS

When you're uplifting your teams, you have to begin at the top of the business.

Most of our work is with the most senior leader, and their team. The leadership team. And after many years, and many clients working within senior teams, we know that there are some key things that just work when it comes to getting it right at the top of the business.

Getting it right is important at the top, because it sets the agenda for the business and everyone in it. In general terms, people are a reflection of their leaders. If you aren't sure that this is the case, and you're the GM or the CEO, try changing your languaging, and watch others change. Try being calmer in your approach, and watch what happens. It's human to mirror the behaviour of our leaders.

Hence the saying that culture is driven from the top of the business. I agree with this statement (although I think it's also changed in an upward direction, too). We work with teams that are in turmoil, and we work with teams who are high performing and want to get even better results. The same applies to both scenarios.

For senior leaders who want to uplift their team culture—and their organisational culture—here are some things to consider.

ONE PROFILE THE HECK OUT OF YOUR TEAM.

If there's one piece of advice that I'd give even the most senior of leaders, it's to start profiling your senior leaders, and don't stop. Do it regularly. I've seen senior leaders either think this isn't important, or think they're all over it already. Either way, profile and profile some more.

Use DiSC, use Resicoach, use TMS, or use whatever other profiling tool your business is comfortable with. And as part of the profiling, use your team meetings (at times) to discuss the profiles, and discuss how everyone on the team is unique. They all have their own style, and their own reasons for why they do what they do.

It's good to understand that. It's good to get into connection, and not just give direction. Take the time to understand your team and what makes them tick. Yes, they're humans, too. They're engaged to lead a department, or a unit, or a product line, but the better you know your leaders, the better they'll be able to do their jobs.

The first part of our leadership workshops is about learning (LEAD: learn, engage, articulate, demonstrate), and the learning piece is such an important element of any team. Learn about self, and learn about others.

When I say profile the heck out of it, I mean regularly. Like, bi-annually or maybe even quarterly. Profiling helps everyone on your leadership team to understand each other, and it's what makes the magic happen.

TWO WORKSHOP THE HECK OUT OF PROBLEMS.

Have idea-generation sessions. Do root-cause workshops as a team. Think critically. Challenge paradigms. Spend one hour a month working on very discrete and defined problems or decisions that only the senior leadership team can address.

And maybe even bring in some other organisational experts to work on the issues. This approach is a focused defect-elimination approach, and not only solves big problems in the business, but also brings the senior leadership team together. It creates a bond. It creates trust. If done properly, that is. With respect for each other and with the right intent.

Problem-solving workshops are not just to solve problems—they're team building workshops. They're a way for the senior leaders to connect, and to talk through things are important. The process is to schedule them, to follow up on last month's actions, and to come up with a new problem to address. Or you might address the same problem for two or three months in a row, to go deep on it.

I've seen this make a massive difference for organisations. They generate a massive return on investment, especially when driven by the most senior leader. If it's important to them, it'll be important to the leadership team.

THREE COACH THE HECK OUT OF THE SENIOR LEADERS.

Yes, as a leadership coach, I know how valuable this is for your team. The teams that I work with go from where they are to where they want to. With support. And that support might be one-on-one support for one or more of the team members, or it might be group coaching.

Our process is specifically to work with a leader, if we're doing one-on-one, and then to work with their leader. I've given up coaching leaders if their own leader is not engaged. We work with the leader, and the leader's leader. Because it works. Period.

It's nearly unreasonable not to get a leadership coach for your senior leadership team now. Businesses expect leaders to work under immense pressure. To lead large teams. To take responsibility and accountability for everything in their patch. Without anyone to support them when the times are tough, or when they need someone to reach out to.

Coaching is your security blanket. It's your drop sheet. It's your fall back position. So that not only are leaders able to learn tools and skills that they can apply during the good times, but they'll also have someone to call on during the tough times. And with coaching, some of those tough times can be avoided. Coaching is such an important element of senior leadership team success. Yes, we've gone on the journey with a heap of leadership teams, and they get huge value. And a huge return on their investment.

Learn about yourself, and others, with profiling. Take a critical thinking approach to your meetings, and workshop your team's problems on a semi-regular basis. Most importantly, get someone external to the business in your corner, someone who can support you and your team through the good times—and the tough times.

SKILL 1

UPLIFT YOUR TEAM

DYSFUNCTIONAL TEAMS SUCK. THEY REALLY DO.

I've been coaching leaders and teams now for what feels like a lifetime, and I've seen first-hand the impact that dysfunction has on team members. I've seen countless people go off on stress leave. I've seen people turn to addiction or substance abuse, and I've seen leaders that sometimes don't even know how much harm they're causing. I've even seen leaders who do.

The first time I got a call about this sort of issue, the person said something like, 'Anton, do you work with teams in turmoil?' I do now, I said. Now, many years later, my response is different. My response is simply: What's their name? Who's the person? As sure as I stand here at my stand-up desk typing, dysfunctional teams are only struggling with one person. Max two. And the leader can't work out how to lead them. Or how to lose them. Both are viable options, if the situation is bad enough. It usually isn't.

For those teams, we lean into TMS (Team Management Systems) as a profiling tool for the team, and for the team members. And we work with the leader on different strategies to engage the person. Sadly, sometimes it's the leader who's the source of the dysfunction.

The other thing we do is grab the book The Five Dysfunctions of Team by Pat Lencioni.[29] That book is an absolute winner, and we work through the five things that totally derail team performance.

Quite the negative article so far, as I reread it. Let's lighten it up a bit and get more positive. The mission is always—regardless of where a team is at—to take them to higher levels of performance.

But how do you uplift a team's performance?

ONE STEP ONE IS ALWAYS ABOUT CONNECTION.

Aiir Consulting shared some research that showed that 'Connected teams demonstrate a 21% increase in profitability over their less-connected counterparts.' This is such a simple statistic, but one that reveals so much.

But what does it mean to be connected?

> **For some, a connected team means that all team members are on the same page technologically, each taking advantage of the latest collaboration software to get work done. For others, it means a team that has deep emotional connections with each other and operates more 'like a family'. (Credit: Jostle)**

Both of these definitions sum up connection. It means that team members are communicating clearly, and consistently. Simple. There are strong relationships formed within the team. Team members aren't afraid to share information, they're not afraid to share bad news, and they're certainly not afraid to be vulnerable. Connected teams have high trust factor, and high morale, because with connection comes care factor.

If your team isn't performing, or can be higher performing, consider how connected they are, both online and in person.

TWO STEP TWO IS ALWAYS ABOUT TRUST.

Aiir Consulting also shared some research that showed that '45% percent of people said that a lack of trust in leadership was the biggest issue impacting their work performance.' Another simple statistic, that reveals so much.

A lack of trust also happens to be one of the five dysfunctions of a team. That's at team level. But when a team doesn't trust their leader, that can be next-level disastrous for a team and their performance. The issue with trust is that it takes a long time to gain it, and it only takes one moment to lose it.

In my experience, perhaps the saddest thing that I see is a leader throwing a team member under the bus. Or not supporting them, when it matters. And when a team member doesn't feel supported, there's only one way team's performance is heading. Sadly, it's never a one-sided situation—if you watch a team member who feels supported, they'll walk over broken glass for their leader (a bit of a blood analogy for our visual learners, sorry—just making a point). Decisions get made. Conversations get had. Communication happens, when leaders support their team members.

If your team isn't performing, or can be higher performing, consider how to increase the level of trust the team has in their leader.

THREE STEP THREE IS ABOUT PSYCHOLOGICAL SAFETY.

This is the big one.

I've written and spoken about this topic relentlessly for about three years now. This is the concept that Amy Edmondson[19] started to make famous in 1999[19] by studying it in organisations, and Google made even more famous when they did a two-year study (Project Aristotle) that found that psychological safety was the one thing that made Google teams successful.

Yes, Google put this concept on the map. But since then, the concept has gone nuts, and there's even a guideline in Australia now that mandates how it'll be implemented in organisations. If you fail to maintain psychologically safe teams, you're now breaking the law. A big step. And a good one.

In short,

> **Psychological safety is about creating an environment where staff can speak up, share ideas, ask questions, and make mistakes without fear of humiliation or retribution. Creating this environment supports genuine participation and contribution by all staff as they feel valued and respected. (Credit: WA Gov)**

If your team isn't performing, or can be higher performing, consider how to increase the level of psychological safety in your team.

To sum it up, uplifting your team is about getting connected, getting trustworthy, and getting psychologically safe. But the work doesn't stop when you get there.

When your team is high performing, what do you do then?

THE QUANDARY OF THE HIGH-PERFORMING TEAM

The quandary for high-performing teams is: how do they get even MORE high performing? When your team is at the top of its game, how can you elevate it even further? Yes, it's a good quandary to have, but what's the solution? Glad you asked.

Luckily for our business, we've become somewhat of an expert in this area—because most of our work is with high-performing teams. I know, right? For every call we get from a team in turmoil (or a leader in turmoil), we get three calls from a high-performing team, asking for help to take them to the next level. (Which is a beautiful thing for us.)

We've often reflected, inside TGG, on why that's the case. We keep coming back to the fact that we're quite positive about life, positive about the potential of teams and their leaders, and positive in our languaging. We seem to attract more of what we put out.

The other thing we think is that it can be hard for leaders to reach out if their team is in turmoil. It's like admitting defeat. I get that, too. Just make the call—you'll be glad you did. Never be too proud or to fearful to ask for help.

But back to taking high-performing teams to the next level.

Firstly though, what makes up a high-performing team? There are a few models out there for those readers looking for the details and research behind this section. We default to the Lencioni Model (2002),[29] which includes building trust, constructive conflict, commitment, accountability, and attention to results. And yes, we could survey your team, and measure your level of achievement in each of these areas.

Let me make it simpler.

High-performing teams only do two things. They have a high level of output. This is about what they do—they get work done. And they have a high level of relationships. This is about how they do it—they get work done, while caring for each other. And while doing no harm to each other along the way.

OUTPUTS

For outputs, think measurables. Some of our clients are in the project management and construction industries, and their measurables are around safety, schedule, cost, and quality. Your outputs might be KPIs, or daily, weekly, monthly, or quarterly targets. They're the items discussed when you talk about deliverables with your team, as their leader.

RELATIONSHIPS

For relationships, think team dynamics. Think communication styles. Think empathy, and think psychological safety. Think care factor, and connection. Relationships are very intangible, and they're not as measurable as the outputs, but they have more impact on the performance of your team. How your team delivers its outputs is more important than what it delivers.

When we survey lower-performing teams, outputs are generally higher than relationships. Relationships are their area for potential improvement.

And regardless of whether the team is high- or low-performing, high outputs are not sustainable if relationships and care factor are low (you might need to reread that last sentence).

So, how do teams become even more high performing? They focus more on outputs than relationships. They're already working well together, so the question becomes 'how we can we leverage how well we work together to get more done?' A great question—as long as the team already works well together.

Because uplifting teams begins at the top of the business, what you might need to look at is increasing the bandwidth of your senior leadership team.

HOW TO INCREASE YOUR SENIOR LEADERSHIP TEAM'S BANDWIDTH, AND WHY

'Why can't we ever get anything completed?!...' a distraught senior leader asked me during a coaching session. 'As a senior leadership team, we seem to get a lot of things started, but we never seem to really see these things through to completion. It's like we hit the ground running when the starter's gun goes off, but we can't seem to finish the race. It's a never-ending cycle of incomplete action, items and projects,' the leader went on.

The leader was obviously at their wits' end, and was struggling to understand what was at play in their senior leadership team that they just couldn't create the accountability and the responsibility that's needed to complete game-changing projects.

I asked the leaders about the bandwidth of their leadership team.

That question was met with raised eyebrows, and I explained that bandwidth is just as it sounds. Bandwidth is about the breadth of skills of the team, and the senior leaders in it. Think of bandwidth like a sine wave or waveform, which has an amplitude and a frequency (and can oscillate between high or low, depending on the situation). In short, leadership bandwidth is about having broad leadership skills that are capable of dealing with a range of issues in the organisation.

The concept of leadership (even management) bandwidth is not a new one, but my personal take on bandwidth is that it's about individual bandwidth, leadership bandwidth, and organisational bandwidth.

Let me explain.

INDIVIDUAL BANDWIDTH (OF SENIOR LEADERS)

Leaders need to be flexible, and they need to adapt. The most important thing they need to adapt to is the different communication styles of the members of their teams. And if you need to understand more about this, please reach out so we can assist with DiSC profiling, to help you understand the communication preferences of your team members.

For leaders, the better they can understand communication styles, the more they can adapt to different styles.

But it's not just communication styles that they need to adapt to. Leaders need to be able to deal with internal and external stakeholders. They need to be able to talk to the cleaner with as much respect as other senior leaders.

They need to manage every conceivable emotion, and they need to do all of that with conscious control, connection, and courage.

In other words, leaders need to develop a wide bandwidth of skills to deal with various communication styles, personality styles, emotional styles, and everything in between. Leadership is a dynamic process, not a static one.

Without a wide individual bandwidth of personal interaction skills, leaders will struggle not only to connect, but to inspire others to follow through and hit their goals, objectives, and the completion of major projects.

The solution to this issue really is external leadership training and coaching, with a focus on people skills and leading under pressure.

LEADERSHIP BANDWIDTH (OF ALL LEADERS)

Leadership bandwidth (called management bandwidth by some scholars) is about the ability of the leaders in an organisation to lead their teams. That is, to do all the things that engage, energise, and enable others to aspire to greatness and to work at a high-performing level.

Leadership bandwidth starts with the senior leadership team. If they don't have the bandwidth to start, follow through, and complete projects, then things will either not get started, or not get finished. And yes, being a starter or a finisher is a personality trait.

Or the senior leaders don't provide the coaching that's needed to develop other leaders in the business to become better versions of themselves.

Or the lower-level leaders don't understand how to create a culture of completion. Of high performance. Of project delivery.

Or the lower-level leaders don't have the skill sets in their teams to deliver on the project requirements, which always require a diverse range of skills (see the next point on organisational bandwidth for more of an explanation on this point).

The solution to this issue is internal leadership training and coaching, with a focus on senior leaders supporting their leaders, and ensuring that they're developing the skills—and are given the support—to deliver on their responsibilities and accountabilities.

ORGANISATIONAL BANDWIDTH (OF ALL HUMANS IN THE BUSINESS)

Some businesses suffer with a bandwidth issue. Imagine for a moment that your project was a technology-based project, but you don't have a developer or software engineer on your team, and you don't know what to look for in a developer. Your team's chances of successfully implementing a technology project are Buckley's and none.

Or imagine that your key team members are on parental leave or long service leave for the duration of a key project. Or that the server keeps crashing when people work from home, or that the sales team has overcommitted and made promises that the operations teams cannot deliver on.

These are organisational bandwidth issues. And yes, some of these are temporary. In fact, any bandwidth issue can be viewed as temporary, if it's understood and addressed.

The solution to this issue is to put some time and effort into project planning, project resourcing, and project scheduling. Including what's realistic and what's not. And what resources are required, that aren't currently available to you and the team.

In summary, senior leaders need a wide bandwidth, due to the wide array of circumstances, situations, and humans they're required to deal with on a daily basis. Leadership bandwidth is about every leader in the business, and whether or not they're able to lead their teams to greatness. Organisational bandwidth is about the organisation's ability to deliver on major projects.

And yes, all of these helped my coaching client, though time will tell if they can get more key projects completed.

Sometimes, you might need to switch things up. Sometimes, new humans are needed to increase the bandwidth of the senior leadership team. But how do you find, and hire, the right humans?

HOW TO HIRE THE RIGHT LEADERS FOR YOUR ORGANISATION

If you want to create a nightmare in your organisation, hire the wrong leader. If you want to upset everyone, and lower morale, hire fast and fire slow. If you want to demonstrate that you're more worried about bums on seats than hiring quality leaders, hire the first applicant. Or even worse, promote someone just because they're a good technician, and not necessarily because they're a good leader.

On the other hand, if you want to hire great leaders, who care about your business, and who are aligned with your values and vision, here are my top three hiring tips.

ONE HIRE FOR VALUES.

Here's what can happen.

You're a senior leader. You hire a leader, for your leadership team. They like your organisation for a while. Then, there's a tough decision to make. Or you need them to implement a change that they don't entirely agree with. They're not happy anymore. They leave. When you ask why they left, they say very simply: 'Because my values don't align with the values of the organisation.' Ouch.

So, the challenge is, how do you prevent this process from playing out in your organisation? It's not easy, but the one thing you can do is to be very clear on values in the job interview.

In my leadership coaching sessions, I encourage senior leaders to ask applicants for their top three values, and then ask how they align with the organisational values. This will tell you if they've done that thinking around why they really want to work for you, and if they feel like you're going to be a good fit, from a values perspective. It also shows if they've done some research into your values, which is important.

LEADER ACTION

Before you ask about values, be clear on what your own values are, and what the organisational values are.

TWO HIRE FOR FIT.

The old saying is that we hire on attitude, we don't hire for skill. Yep, that used to be relevant. And it you're hiring a salesperson, or a tradesperson, or an administrator, great strategy.

But if you're hiring a senior leader, it's just not that simple. Senior leaders need to have the right attitude, and the right skills. You don't have the time or the effort to train your senior leaders to be good leaders. You'll coach them, but you just can't be running around after them, doing their job. Which will happen if you don't hire the leader that best fits into your team, or organisation, or culture.

Hire senior leaders on fit. Cultural fit. Because culture is driven from the top of the organisation, the leader that you hire will be expected to drive the culture. And you might want an inclusive culture, and engaging culture, a proactive culture, or even just a positive culture.

What's a positive work culture? Simply put, a positive work culture is one that prioritises the wellbeing of employees, offers support at all levels within the organisation, and has policies in place that encourage respect, trust, empathy, and support (Credit: Wiki).

If you get the feeling that the languaging and the behaviour of the applicant you're considering won't drive this type of culture, say to yourself: NEXT.

LEADER ACTION

Before you ask about culture (like values), be clear on what culture you're trying to drive in your business, and what you expect of your leaders in that space.

THREE USE THE COFFEE CUP TEST.

This is my favourite, and there are two stages to this one.

Firstly, be aware of how the applicant treats others, either on their way to the interview, or just as they enter the building. Ask the receptionist for feedback on how they were treated by the applicant when they arrived. If they don't treat people with respect, because that person is not seen by them as being important, that should be a red flag.

The second thing to do—this is my favourite, and I've used it on multiple occasions—is to make sure that your applicant has a coffee or a drink of water during the interview.

The kicker: watch what they do with it at the end of the interview. See if they take it back to the kitchen, or to the sink. You can tell a lot about a leader just by watching their behaviour, and it's something that most people either don't notice, or don't think is important.

LEADER ACTION

This takes no effort at all. It's about being observant. Be observant of all elements of body language, because what the leader does, the team will follow.

If you've read the first book in this series, you'll know how important it is to have a future focus in leadership, especially when you're hiring new leaders. Think about where you're taking the team and the organisation, and who'll be among the best leaders for the job.

But once you find them, how do you use them to uplift the team?

That's where systems leadership comes into play.

HOW TO USE SYSTEMS LEADERSHIP TO UPGRADE YOUR TEAM

Systems leadership was made famous by MacDonald, Burke, and Stewart,[33] in the book of the same name. That book unpacked the key elements of systems leadership and described the elements of human decision making.

Human decision making is about being charismatic, technical, and academic. Part of that decision making relates to culture and beliefs, hypotheses, and action testing.

Ultimately, it's how leaders facilitate these, and the other components of dealing with the humans in their teams (at the same time, increasing productivity and output) that's the focus of systems leadership.

As a side note, the book references the work of Elliot Jaques,[24] who authored The Requisite Organisation, which looks at layers and levels of organisations. Jaques was a psychoanalyst, who focused on organisation hierarchy and organisational structures. These are important elements of systems leadership of course, but systems leadership, to me, is more about making the job of leading a more systematised process.

And that's the reason I was compelled to write this section. Too many leaders that I speak to, and coach, struggle with time, business, and pressure. They miss the 1:1 meetings they should be attending, and they don't have the ability or the time to prioritise people. Systems leadership takes care of that. In short, it takes the people part of leadership, and turns it into a system that can be scheduled, planned, and prioritised.

So how do you do systems leadership, from the perspective of this leadership coach?

ONE REMEMBER THAT LEADING AND MANAGING ARE BOTH IMPORTANT.

This is the key premise of systems leadership (and mind you, the topic of many blog posts and possibly books for me). For some reason, people are fascinated by the dichotomy between managing and leading—without really understanding that a great leader needs to be a great manager, and vice versa. It does frustrate me (just a little) to read post after post about leaders and managers, from people who just don't get how the two come together.

They come together in systems leadership.

In essence, people are the most important thing in a leader's life. But the challenge is that a leader's time is not their own, and they're pulled from pillar to post. They're busy humans, and they need to go to endless meetings, just to keep up with what's happening in their organisation.

So, how do they make people their priority? Simple. Diarise it. If it's important enough to attend all the other meetings in the business, it must be important enough to attend meetings with team members, right?

Here is systems leadership 101 (don't thank me now): 1) Work out what meetings (or time) you need to dedicate to your team, or your team members individually. 2) Put these in your calendar. 3) Commit to them, and never miss one or reschedule.

Voila, you've applied systems thinking to your leadership. Done. Systematise the people work that you need to do.

TWO MEASURE YOUR OUTPUTS AND RELATIONSHIPS.

Have I mentioned that we at TGG are very simple humans, and actually, we are the masters of simplification? Our business has a process for determining whether or not a team is high performing. And it's simply this.

If you look at a team, and what's required for it to simply function (not be high performing), there are two elements. Outputs: what the team does; and relationships: how the team does it.

In our experience, working with over 150 businesses over 18 years, what we know is that most teams will say that they're good at getting their outputs delivered, but they aren't great at delivering their interpersonal stuff (like connection and communication).

From a systems leadership perspective, systematise how you measure and mange this aspect of your team performance. Use KPIs to measure team performance, and use a morale meter, or similar, to systematically measure the relationships in your team.

Come up with a minimum level or performance—say, 70% for each. And then aim for 70% in each area, outputs and relationships. Create a system for understanding how your team is performing together, not just what they're achieving. Yes, a novel concept for some, but try it and watch the magic happen.

FYI, the relationship piece is way more important than the outputs piece. It's hard to have a high-performing team if they're at each other's throats constantly, regardless of whether the KPIs get hit.

THREE MAKE IT VISUAL.

How will the team know how they're progressing, from an output or a relationship perspective, if they can't see it? How will they even know what's important to you as their leader, if they can't see it?

As a leader, here's a key mantra of mine: if your team can't see it, you can't have it. Make it visual. It really is that simple.

If your team needs to guess what you're measuring, or how you're measuring it, forget it. They'll never buy into something they don't get, and they'll never care about that metric. Period.

So, how much do you make visual? Enough is the answer. Enough to ensure that key metrics, both outputs and relationships, are visible to all team members—and that it's updated regularly. Please don't put something on a wall somewhere and never go back to it. Put it up, and have stand-up meetings around it, to reinforce how important the metrics and the measures are to you, and why they should be important to your team.

Have somewhere between three and seven metrics (why this number? Because the human frontal lobes, and their working memory, and can only store three plus or minus two units of information at any one time). Three to seven is the magic number of anything. Whatever you do, make it visual. Especially when you're going through the bad weeks or months!

Systems leadership is not new. It's based on the premise that humans make decisions, and leaders facilitate those decisions. For me, this takes putting the people stuff into a system and calendar entries. Then, measure the outputs and the relationships in your team, and make the results visual.

But once you've got the system in place, how do you make it happen? And how do you make sure the right person is on the right task, at the right time?

The answer is a dirty word for some—allocation.

HOW TO DO ALLOCATION VS DELEGATION

One common senior leader challenge is doing all the work themselves and not delegating. Or even worse, micromanaging. Which is a recipe for disaster. And burnout.

But it doesn't have to be that way. When senior leaders realise that they have to be resourceful, and not the resource, their world shifts. And their leadership team, and all the teams in the business, are uplifted.

Delegation is a word that has a negative connotation for most leaders, and for their teams. It feels like they're doing something nasty to their team members. Or that it only happens when things are going badly and everyone is stressed. But it's precisely then that we need to delegate.

No one likes being delegated to. It feels abrupt, it feels aggressive, and it feels aloof. Especially when it's delivered in a delegation type of way. Which is very one-way.

Unlike task allocation, which is more of a consultative process (and a business process), that involves a discussion and agreement. It's a two-way, collaborative conversation.

Let me explain why you should allocate, not delegate.

ONE ALLOCATION IS ENGAGING.

Leaders need to assign work. They need to ask for support. They need to allocate tasks to individual team members, particularly when the pressure is on. Allocation takes time, because it's about the conversation, it's about the dialogue, and it's about the consensus.

The allocation of tasks and projects should include a conversation about why that task or project is important, what milestones need to be achieved, and when exactly those deadlines are. Your team members might even have some ideas to share about what could be modified or changed as part of the current plan. Then you get the opportunity to listen, learn, and lean into some optioneering. Engaging.

TWO ALLOCATION IS EFFECTIVE.

Allocation is most effective when delivered as part of a process. That process should outline the allocation of tasks with something like a RACI matrix (which states clearly who is responsible, accountable, consulted, and informed, about all of the activities completed by the team members). Too often, roles and responsibilities get blurred, and the term 'swim lanes' comes up (i.e., 'you need to stay in your swim lane').

Allocation is effective as a team activity, as well as a one-to-one activity. By its very nature, it spreads the work, assigns the activities, and aligns the tasks with the RACI matrix. It's effective because it creates clarity, consistency, and commitment. Team members are aware of their roles and responsibilities, and can talk to progress and project updates. Allocating activities to teams reduces ambiguity and uncertainty. It sets the team up for success, and it sets the team up for high performance. Effective.

THREE ALLOCATION IS ESSENTIAL.

With a RACI matrix in place, allocation becomes easy. If tasks need to be modified or managed in a way that's not aligned with the matrix, further task allocation is required, to walk the team through what needs to be modified and why. Having good business processes for the allocation of tasks is a key element of effective and high-performing teams. Essential.

Allocation is engaging, it's effective, and it's essential to a high-performing team and a high-performing leader. Unlike delegation, and the process of telling team members what to do, allocation is about engaging with them to help every team member know what the team is doing, and why. It might sound like splitting hairs when I unpack allocation versus delegation—but you only have to sit in a coaching session with me to see the emotional shift when we change that one word and share how it's done properly.

And it's a shift that helps the whole team, especially the C-Suite team, to be more attuned and aligned to the values and goals of the organisation.

HOW TO BE MORE ATTUNED AS A C-SUITE TEAM, AND WHY

C-Suite teams are living entities, which grow and reshape themselves over time. That growth is sometimes forced. Forced through the engagement of a new CEO, the implementation of a new change process, or the impact of a negative internal or external crisis event.

Gallup described attunement as 'the affective way a human is sensitive to the demands of a situation.' There are some subtleties in that definition. Affective means with emotional control. Sensitive means having acute awareness to the needs of others. The demands of a situation implies that your emotional state will be challenged by a range of situations (potentially major changes). These situations might be crisis events, or internal or external events, some with the potential to affect business continuity.

When these events occur, the C-Suite team need to be attuned. Having attunement therefore means to be adaptable, agile, and aware. Agility to take the organisation on a new journey, in a new direction. Adaptable to the changes that are occurring, and aware of how this might affect each team member. It means to be a team who shows up with energy, engagement, and enterprise thinking.

As a note, it would've been easy to include 'aligned' in the above paragraph. For me, alignment is a result of leadership, not a cause of it. In other words, if the attunement is in place, the alignment will take care of itself. Alignment is the by-product of attunement.

A C-Suite team that's attuned demonstrates to the organisation that all is well. That all is in control. That all is being managed in the best interests of the organisation and the best interests of the people in it.

But how do you become attuned as a C-Suite leadership team?

ONE BY STARTING WITH A GROWTH MINDSET.

Regardless of the situations you're currently facing the C-Suite senior leadership team, the biggest issues that the CEO will face are entrenched, embedded, and instilled ways of thinking and ways of leading. Aka: a low level of adaptability to anything new.

With change comes growth and with growth comes challenge. For some of the team, this growth, and the associated challenge, will be too much. It'll be too far to stretch, in terms of mindset, and in terms of the willingness to adapt to a new norm or to a new structure or strategy.

The research around having a growth mindset is over 35 years old now, and was carried out by Dr Carol Dweck to understand why some students (who were the study participants) bounced back after failure a lot quicker than others. Dweck's research[18] has since informed leader behaviours around having a fixed mindset (in short: stuck in the past), versus a growth mindset (in short: looking forward).

Leaders and teams with a growth mindset learn from their mistakes, and look to learn something from what has happened previously, to ensure that they get better results in the future. But having a growth mindset can be a real stretch for some of the C-Suite. Especially those members that are entrenched in fixed ways of thinking and behaving.

LEADER ACTION

If you want to get your C-Suite attuned and able to adapt to the situation, especially during or after a challenging period, step one is encouraging every member of the team to think forward, not backward. To think big, not small. To think growth, not status quo.

TWO BY CONTINUING WITH AN IMPLEMENTATION MINDSET.

The organisation is watching. They're waiting. And they're willing to follow. Especially if the C-Suite are ready to implement change and make the decisions necessary to be highly efficient, highly effective, and highly agile.

The entire organisation is ready for the change. They're ready to be led, and they're ready to be part of an upgraded and upskilled future state. And they generally don't want to wait. They want to get there quickly. Or, at least, they want to see steps in the right direction. They don't want to hear talk about what's going to happen. Words are cheap. They want to see action— from the top of the organisation—that demonstrates that the C-Suite is committed to organisational growth and change.

C-Suite teams that don't take action promptly following a demanding situation lose credibility, and quickly. A C-Suite team should act. Especially when the organisation knows that action is required.

The sign of progress is demonstrated by implementing changes. Not for the sake of change, and not as a knee-jerk reaction, but because it's the right thing to do given the situation. Agile decision making, and action taking, is a sign of an attuned C-Suite team. Particularly when the C-Suite are all committed to the decision, have the same languaging around it, and share the message with the business in a way that explains what's happening, why it's happening, and what the C-Suite are willing to do to make sure the change is successful.

LEADER ACTION

If you want to get your C-Suite attuned, step two is about being agile in decision making and action taking, to ensure that situations and organisational demands are addressed in a timely manner.

THREE BY FINISHING WITH AN AWARENESS MINDSET.

Let's bring that affective element into the attunement process.

In psychology, affect is a term that encompasses a broad range of feelings that people can experience. It embodies both emotions and moods.

An emotion is an intense feeling that's short term and is typically directed at a source. A mood is a state of mind that tends to be less intense than an emotion, and doesn't necessarily need a contextual stimulus. Moods last longer than emotions, from hours to days (Credit: DBT Centre).

When it comes to attunement, affect means being aware of one's emotions or moods, and ensuring that they're regulated in a way that those emotions are used for good, and not as an excuse for doing harm to humans through emotion-driven behaviour like aggression, abuse, or abruptness.

Self-awareness is the first and most important element of C-Suite attunement, as it demonstrates that all senior leaders are in control of their state. This allows them to have a level of situational awareness, and to clearly understand what the situation demands. It helps them to be aware of what the organisation is experiencing, because they're also experiencing the impact of the situation.

Leaders with high scores on the positive affect scale are perceived as being more connected and attuned not only to the situation, but also to the impact on others. With positive affect comes conscious control. With conscious control comes behavioural control. And with behavioural control comes situational control. It all starts with affect.

LEADER ACTION

If you want to get your C-Suite attuned, step three is about being in conscious control of your emotional state and the moods that you're experiencing. So you do no harm. And so that you can maintain control of yourself and the situation.

An effective and efficient C-Suite team is about attunement, adaptability, agility, and awareness. When those attributes are present, the team and the organisational alignment will increase. That alignment, the key element of highly effective SLTs, is what will uplift your team.

ACTIVITY 3.1
UPLIFT YOUR TEAM

The series of questions on the following pages will encourage you to think about what you can do to uplift your leadership team, and apply what you learnt in the last chapter to the process.

Can you think of ways to facilitate connection and trust among your team members, and with you as a leader?

Do you think you need to improve the psychological safety in your workplace? Why, or why not?

Is your team high performing? What measurable output targets (safety, schedule, cost, and quality) are you meeting or not meeting?

As a leader, are you flexible and adaptable? Why, or why not?

Do you think your leadership team shares your values, or the values of your organisation? Why, or why not?

Can you think of visual ways to help your team see how they're progressing, from an output or a relationship perspective?

Answer honestly. How well do you use allocation to share your workload with your team members?

What could you do to make your allocation more effective and engaging for your team members?

How could you improve your growth mindset? What about your implementation mindset, or awareness mindset?

SKILL II

FACILITATE

DISCUSSION

IN 2004 I SHARED WITH MY AMAZING WIFE THAT I HAD QUIT MY JOB AND DECIDED TO BECOME A 'MOTIVATIONAL SPEAKER'. SHE WAS NOT OVERLY IMPRESSED.

To say the least. Especially for the first few years, when speaking work was somewhat hard to come by. Mostly because I wasn't very good at it. I hadn't really learnt how to engage an audience. Several years later (and thank you, Marc McLaren), an early mentor of mine shared that 'if you're going to get great at public speaking, the thing you need to learn is how to talk with an audience, not at an audience.' Some of the best advice I've ever received.

But what does that mean, and how does it apply to leadership?

In my humble opinion, engaging your team—really engaging them—is the key leadership skill of the future. Aka, workshop facilitation (or, in essence, good meeting management). FYI: how to masterfully facilitate a workshop or meeting is all summed up in an e-book available for download here.

Since the COVID pandemic started, we've moved online. We've moved work to home. We're still working through the great resignation. Which was quoted by several sources (MIT Sloan Management Review study, as an example) as being caused by 'Toxic Workplace Cultures'. Which is code for team members not being heard, and hence not feeling valued.

The most frequent query I get from our leadership coaching clients is why their teams have stopped making decisions, and how can I help them be decisive and act. The theory was that the 'water cooler' conversations were no longer happening, and team members no longer have anyone to bounce ideas off. Makes sense.

So how do we, as leaders, be a sounding board, or give team members the ability to share ideas and opinions in either one-on-ones or in group discussions? By facilitating great workshops and great meetings. By talking with team members, not at them. By giving team members a voice—a real voice (online or in person).

Here's how to do it.

ONE   LEADERS, YOU DON'T NEED ALL THE ANSWERS. YOU NEED TO HAVE ALL THE QUESTIONS.

Leaders still tell me that they feel like they need to have all the answers.

And my first thought is, how is that humanly possible? Which I sometimes verbalise (on the rare occasions I haven't got my filter on). When leaders understand that all sources of information and knowledge are embedded in the collective experience of team members, and that it's a simple (sometimes not easy) process of asking for help, the answers will present themselves. Especially in areas like:

- Goal Setting,
- Idea Generation, and
- Problem Solving.

LEADER ACTION

Never undervalue the knowledge in your team, and how the right engagement and facilitation (workshop or meeting) will give team members the forum to share information and answer questions that you'll have as the team leader. Ask the right questions.

Back to learning how to be a better public speaker.

Great public speakers are generally great facilitators. To talk with an audience is simply to be able to 'curate the conversation.' To be able to thoughtfully choose great questions that will keep the dialogue in motion. Same with leadership. Keeping dialogue in motion is the fine art of facilitation, and the even more fine art of thinking fast and talking slow (yes, it's a learnt skill).

TWO   LEADERS, THE MORE YOU LISTEN TO IDEAS, THE MORE IDEAS YOU'LL GET.

Listening to your team is key, especially when you're facilitating a workshop with a purpose. For those leaders who aren't yet adept at the fine art of facilitation, start with listening, and writing. Yes, writing. Writing things down and following up on ideas and opportunities.

You might not agree with an idea or opinion, but it gives value to your team member's input if you take the time to acknowledge them. Then you can close the loop on the idea (during the workshop or meeting), or on why the idea will or won't be implemented.

The challenge for some leaders is that they get too many ideas and opinions. I get that, too. The challenge here is to prioritise and work through what's achievable, and what's biggest bang for buck. And having the group conversational skills to articulate all of that.

LEADER ACTION

Workshop facilitation can be an exercise in creating conscious control, especially when you don't agree with ideas, or when the conversation is getting animated. Listen, listen, and listen some more to what's really being said, and listen for any underlying issues that might be showing up. You might even have to take some of that offline.

THREE LEADERS, DON'T THANK ME NOW. HERE'S THE PROCESS—AND A GREAT RESOURCE.

Part of the fine art of facilitation is following a process. The clearer the process, the better the outcome. (It's the same with most things in life, really, not just workshop facilitation.)

So here's the 5P process for facilitating great workshops:

- **Purpose**: clearly define it, and share it prior to the workshop or meeting;
- **Process**: how will the workshop be run, what resources will be used (preparation);
- **People**: who needs to be at the workshop or meeting;
- **Performance**: the fine art of facilitation, following the above steps of having great questions, curating conversation, and listening to and documenting what's said; and
- **Polish**: the close out process, to add value to the time that your team has committed to the process.

LEADER ACTION

The best leaders that I've encountered are engaging. They're conversation specialists, and they can curate a one-on-one chat with as much purpose and ease as they do in a group scenario.

I'm sharing this information because it was game changing for me when I learnt it. And just being told that facilitation matters didn't mean that I could do it well, right off the bat. It takes work, it takes practice, and like most things in life, what's worth having doesn't come easy. But as promised, you can learn more about information-driven workshops **here**.

If you follow the process, your team will give you answers, and they'll give you ideas. But that depends on an important thing: are you willing to let them contribute? Or are you going to keep micromanaging?

'IF YOU WANT SOMETHING DONE, YOU HAVE TO DO IT YOURSELF' IS SO 1900s

I went from being a stressed leader to a calm leader by working out that I couldn't do everything myself. And that I didn't have to.

My team is capable, and courageous. They can do things that I can't and shouldn't be doing. And they do them well.

Let me share with you how I learnt to trust my team—so you don't have to keep stressing out about your workload.

ONE SHORT-TERM TIME FOR LONG-TERM DIME.

Most leaders would be ready for me to write 'short-term pain, long-term gain.' But I just don't think that putting time into your team and coaching them is pain. It might be inconvenient for you at the time, but it's certainly not pain. And the dime bit refers to the return on investment that you get for the investment of your time into your team's skill set.

Take a coaching approach to your team's work. Most leaders will tell me they're time poor—and then they take on more work, instead of delegating.

LEADER ACTION

Understand that coaching your team to be able to do a task every time from now on is an investment, and one that will get you a great return. It WILL reduce the pressure on you, and on them.

TWO YOU'LL BUILD YOUR CREDIBILITY, AND TRUST IN YOU.

Trust is a beautiful thing. It's a self-fulfilling prophecy: the more trust you give, the more you get. Being trustful is good for your credibility, as your team sees you having faith in their skills and abilities. And it's an integrity thing. When you say you'll trust your team, and then follow through on that, you're winning.

Say it, then do it. Integrity and credibility are two halves of the same apple. And trust is the core that holds them together, and the core that holds your team together. Two-way trust.

LEADER ACTION

Step into being a trusting and trusted leader. Make the call to allow your team to shine or learn. Be of high integrity, and in doing so you'll reduce the pressure on you, and on them.

THREE IT ANNOYS YOUR TEAM WHEN YOU DO THEIR WORK FOR THEM.

Seriously! We can tend to think as leaders that we're helping (or at least, that's how some leaders justify dealing with stress and pressure). 'I'll help' is like having your two-year-old 'helping' you take the rubbish out. It feels good in the moment, but doesn't really add much value. In fact, it does more harm than good. And sure, you might be quicker, or better, at that task, but think about your team members for a moment. What does your behaviour say to them? I'd spell it out, but I think it might be self-explanatory.

LEADER ACTION

Understand that doing your team's work is not cool, or quicker. It's disheartening for them. Support your team if they need it. Reduce the pressure on you, and on them.

And yes, it does take conscious control to delegate tasks in the right places, and to move past the old thinking of doing it yourself. There are so many better ways to lead in this day and age, that will uplift instead of hinder your team. And your team members want to contribute—that's their greatest need on planet earth!

But what happens when you give them the space they need, and something goes BOOM? And how do you deal with team members who go BOOM when something goes BOOM?

DEALING WITH A TEAM MEMBER WHO GOES BOOM WHEN THINGS GO BOOM

Is there anything more challenging for a leader than a team member who's explosive, and who goes BOOM when the pressure comes on? This is a situation covered a lot in coaching conversations, because it's real, it happens, and it needs to be managed. With control, of course. And care factor. And courage.

One of our coaching clients (R) recently encountered this situation, and at the end of this section, I'll let you know exactly what changed his life, and why. But he had to go on a little journey to get there.

Let's unpack the process using a real-life example.

ONE DON'T IGNORE IT.

The important thing to do is to be upfront about the situation. When a team member goes BOOM, leaders need to address it straight away. If it happens in a team situation, you can address it in that forum if you're comfortable to do that. Otherwise, take it offline, and have a one-on-one conversation.

That conversation should be about unpacking what's going on for the team member, and what was driving the behaviour (care factor first). If there are other issues at play, offer support. If it's a lack of control, and going BOOM is the team member's M.O. (which it was in R's case), read on.

TWO DON'T PRESUME THEY KNOW.

Don't presume that the team member knows what they look or sound like (which is generally very ordinary). If they don't know how they're being perceived, share it with them. Share what it looks and feels like to you as their leader, and to their team (this was the case with R). Be honest with them. Be courageous enough to lay it out.

If they know, but don't care, that'll require a whole other conversation. One that's about expectations, and commitments around behaviour change.

THREE DON'T GO BOOM.

The human species has mirroring neurons, and these neurons mean we mirror the emotional state of other humans. Someone goes BOOM, we go BOOM. But that can't happen if you want to model the right behaviour and diffuse a BOOM situation.

I promised to share the secret sauce that R worked out was the big ticket item, and the one thing that changed R's life and the behaviour of that one team member.

R learnt to breathe, and to stay in control. R created conscious control. R controlled his emotions. Which meant he was in control of the situation. It was a top-shelf outcome. And if you ask R now, he'll say it's about breathing. Breathe and respond. Don't react.

In short, R is a perfect example of how to demonstrate control, care factor, and courage. And it resulted in a successful outcome for R and his team, and you can uplift yours in the same way—with conscious control.

And positive communication. Now's the time to ask yourself: are you uplifting your team by facilitating positive discussion, or are you hindering them by being part of the 'deficit dialogue dilemma'?

ARE YOU PART OF THE 'DEFICIT DIALOGUE DILEMMA'?

Maybe there are times when all you can think about is the things you don't have. The deficits. Just ask Aussies about their life, and they're always 'not bad' or 'not great'. They have no time, or not enough minutes. They're doing not much or not a lot. Which is not great as a conversation starter, and even worse as a leader, when we've got no wins, no runs on the board, no clients, or no success to celebrate.

And yes, there are leaders who are in deficit mode. Deficit dialogue is a thing. Now that you know about it, you'll start to notice it, and I'm going to note that I'm noticing it more in recent times, than in the past...pandemic maybe? Or leaders are just not choosing their language well?

So, what's the opposite of deficit? Surplus, maybe? Or abundant, or adequate, or plentiful (none of them rhyme with dialogue, though). Let's use the word 'positive'. And no, this is not just a positive thinking section, it's a positive dialogue section. It's about using language—leader language, more specifically. Which is important, because it sets the mood, and it sets the culture for your team.

The more that speak is deficit, the more that deficit shows up. And the more that deficit shows up, the more your team will focus on deficit. Or what they don't have or haven't achieved. Instead of what they do have or have achieved. It's a self-fulfilling prophecy.

Deficit dialogue can show up in one-on-ones; it can show up in team meetings; it can even show up in written communication. It's a big deal, because it instantly changes the mood or the tone of the conversation, and even of the culture of the team or organisation.

And it can become habitual. Then, one day, you'll ask yourself (or your coach, when you're sitting with me) why everyone is so negative all the time.

Here are some strategies that you can try if you're caught in the deficit dialogue dilemma. Sadly, none of them are new or groundbreaking— but they remain current, and useful, for changing the mood of your conversations, or your team.

ONE START WITH CELEBRATING SUCCESS.

This is an easy one. And in any good meeting, it's the first agenda item (or it should be). Start with a positive, and some recognition of personal or team achievement. Too fluffy for some leaders, but essential for all teams and team members (high performing ones, at least). This is also the first thing to get dropped from the agenda, when we have 'bigger fish to fry.'

TWO CONTINUE WITH SOME SOLUTIONS.

Lots of people, leaders included, have got lots of problems for every solution and not a lot of solutions for problems. As a leader, be firm on your commitment to talk in solutions and steer the conversation around to what you have to do to move forward, instead of looking back. This is a skill set.

THREE FINISH WITH SYMBOLS.

Remember that everything you say, and do, makes a statement. Know what your body language is doing and ensure that it lines up with your words. This is called being congruent. Incongruence is saying one thing, and either meaning another, or worse—doing another thing. Your team will see right through you. And no, you can't hide what you're thinking. Too many people think they can, and they end up sending the wrong message.

Other symbols include making a commitment to avoid deficit dialogue. Or rewarding positive results in general. Yes, there are times when we need to address a deficit. I get that. It's not every conversation, though. Make a commitment to surplus speaking, and see how it uplifts your team.

Then it's time to move on to another way of facilitating discussion. One that's so uplifting, it's worth more than gold.

HOW TO APPLY THE PLATINUM RULE OF COMMUNICATION

Most people have heard of the Golden Rule. Which is the principle of 'treating others as we would like to be treated'. This is a simple premise that was first noted in the big book that was penned several thousand years ago, and which contained a range if parables and testaments that were designed to help us live a more compassion-filled life.

And the Golden Rule is as current now as it was when it was first written. Imagine if everyone on the planet really bought into the Golden Rule and applied it in their own lives, and treated everyone how they would like to be treated. Yes, that's drawing a long bow, but it's a nice thought, right?

Here's another thought—when it comes to leadership, and leading under pressure, your team members don't actually want to be treated how you want to be treated. I know...breathe...

They want to be treated how they want to be treated. Yes, every team member has different requirements and a different communication style—and they'd prefer that you communicated with them in their style (not yours). This is called the Platinum Rule.

The Platinum Rule is about personal connection and productive relationships. It's about communicating in a way that's meaningful to the other person, and it's about understanding their style so that you can adapt yours. And although you change your style, you don't have to change your personality. You don't have to roll over and submit to others. You simply have to understand why people communicate how they do and understand your options for increasing the effectiveness of your communication with them, so that you can better connect. After all, communication should be for connection, not just direction.

But how do you know what someone else's communication style is? Great question, and glad you asked.

We use a personality profiling tool call DiSC, which some of my readers will be familiar with. DiSC stands for Dominant, Influential, Steady or Conscientious. From the DiSC Profile site, here are what the four personality and communication styles refer to:

- **Dominant**: A person primarily in this DiSC quadrant places emphasis on accomplishing results and 'seeing the big picture.' They're confident, and sometimes blunt, outspoken, and demanding;

- **Influence**: A person in this DiSC quadrant places emphasis on influencing or persuading others. They tend to be enthusiastic, optimistic, open, trusting, and energetic;

- **Steadiness**: A person in this quadrant places emphasis on cooperation, sincerity, loyalty, and dependability. They tend to have calm, deliberate dispositions, and don't like to be rushed; and

- **Conscientiousness**: A person in this DiSC quadrant places emphasis on quality and accuracy, expertise, and competency. They enjoy their independence, demand the details, and often fear being wrong.

Part of doing your DiSC profile is understanding how to communicate with each of the different styles. There's a great page in the profile booklet that unpacks the dos and the don'ts of each style, and how to better connect with them. How to apply The Platinum Rule, essentially.

For a leader, this information really is priceless. It cannot be overestimated how valuable it is for a leader to really understand how their team members want to be communicated with. This is especially true for new team members, who we don't know yet. Or that one team member that we haven't quite connected with.

Our leadership workshops include DISC profiling and helping leaders and team members to firstly understand their own style, and then understanding others' styles, so they can be more effective in their interactions.

The aha! moments that leaders and teams experience when they start to understand themselves and others at a different level is amazing to watch. That's when we get to see how The Platinum Rule helps to facilitate discussion, and how uplifting it is to the team.

Once you've learned the tools of facilitating discussion, you can use them right to the end of your entire leadership journey—including when it's the end of a team member's employment.

HOW TO SEND TEAM MEMBERS OFF THE RIGHT WAY

I didn't have many jobs before I quit work to start my own business. When I think back on the roles I did have, the two periods that I remember most are the engagement period and the exit period. Basically, when I started, and when I finished. And more importantly, how I started, and how I finished.

To me, these are the two most important periods of the employment tenure. And yes, there are many positive and negative times that you remember about your experiences in organisations, but how you come in and go out of an organisation is important. And the experience is driven by your leader.

Spare a thought for the Twitter staff who are or have been 'freed up for industry' by Elon Musk. Think about the excitement that they would have felt starting their employment journey with a global organisation. Then, think about what they would have experienced as they were fired by email, or by Twitter post. Imagine how those employees would feel about their experience of being let go.

I once had a manager who said that it's just as important to send team members off the right way, as it is to bring them into the organisation the right way. And I agree with that. But I understand that it's a challenge. I get that team members are usually leaving leaders, not businesses, so when team members do leave, it can hard for the leader to stay positive, and focus on providing a good leaving experience. Especially if the employment has been ended prematurely, by termination.

Here are some tips to facilitate discussion to send team members off in a professional and caring way.

ONE MAINTAIN THE RELATIONSHIP UNTIL THE END.

If the relationship is still intact when the decision is made (by you or the by the team member) to end the employment tenure, do what it takes to maintain it until the very end. Be personable, be professional, and be approachable. No matter what.

Find a way to practice what Deepak Chopra[11] calls Emotional Freedom. Which means to be emotionally free. Which is about being free of guilt, resentment, grievances, anger, and aggression. Emotional freedom is accepting the situation, whatever may have led up to it, and moving forward. Reframe the situation, find the positive, and carry on regardless.

Most team members need to provide between two and four weeks of notice and work this period after they've submitted their resignation. As a team member, that period is painful, and in my experience, most team members mentally check out. For the leader, not only do you need to be scrambling to replace the position, but you also need to be dealing with a team member who hasn't only formally resigned, but has mentally resigned too. Be patient, be accommodating, and be ready to support the departing team member, as well as your other team members during the notice period.

If you don't think you can, end the notice period early, pay the person out, and end on a positive before it gets you down too much and you say or do something that isn't good for anyone. The message is to be firm, fair, and friendly, right through to the end of the relationship. And, if it's possible, maintain it, and end on a positive note.

TWO DO AN EXIT INTERVIEW.

This is such a key step in the process of ending an employment agreement with someone, but it needs to be done properly.

It needs to be done by another person in the business, probably HR (if they've been adequately trained in doing exit interviews, because like everything, it's a skill set). The skill is related to creating a safe space for the team member to say what they really think. To give us all the good. And to give us all the bad. So you can work on improving the organisation for the next time you're ready to hire someone.

As a leader, have the courage to ask the person doing the exit interview to focus on the LMX (leader team member exchange). Ask the interviewer to focus on the relationship that the team member had with their leader. And what their experience of being led by you was like. This is crucial information, as it can determine what you could and should be doing differently as the team leader.

If this section scares you, revert to point one, and detach emotionally. Regardless of whether the team member was in your in-group or out-group, you need to hear what their experience was. You might not think that you do, but if you're open minded, and the interview is open and honest, you'll get some tips to work on as a leader. And who doesn't want that?

The message is to get the exit interview done properly, to have it focused on your leadership, and to be willing to get the feedback from that interview and integrate it into your leadership style.

THREE MAKE IT AN EVENT.

Bring in a cake. Buy muffins. Bang out some donuts. Do a morning tea. Do something special. Make it an event for the team member, so that they get the chance to celebrate the moment. Which most people want to do, regardless of the reason for their departure.

It's so uncool when leaders just let people leave without an event of some sort. Or a speech or a few kind words. Because it's not about you as the leader, it's about the team member. They want to say goodbye to their team members, they want to know that they were valued, and they might even want to have the opportunity to say thank you for the experience of working with you and the team. Never deprive a team member of the chance to say goodbye and to be farewelled in the right way.

The message is that a small event on the team member's last day will send them off the right way. They'll get the chance to end on a positive and with their head held high. They'll maintain their dignity and their self-esteem.

Put as much time and effort into helping someone leave as you do helping them join the business. How handle the exit process will say more about you as a leader than it'll say about them as a team member.

Facilitating discussion around leaving is important—even when it's only for the business's holiday break.

HOW TO CLOSE THE YEAR OUT AS A SENIOR LEADER

I've tried everything as a business owner at year's end. We've closed early, we've worked right up to Christmas Eve, we've done something in between. All the while with a focus on our team, and our clients. Our clients are generally flexible, so it's easy enough to make timing work with them.

Our staff are flexible, too. Everyone is keen to break, while at the same time knowing that we can still hustle for a few more days. Because I never really stop hustling. And I'm more in the Gary Vee School,[58] where no one loves your business as much as you do. I get Elon's strategy of sacking people that aren't working twenty-four hours straight, but that doesn't seem right. Just because the owner wants to hustle, doesn't mean everyone has to.

In saying that, the leader needs to finish the year off well. And properly. Yes, we only have a small team that's been up and down over the years.

But here's what I've learnt over time about facilitating communication during the year-end process, and what leaders should keep in mind.

ONE DON'T OVERDO THE PARTY.

Regardless of the size of your team, the Christmas party (or end of year party—whatever your terminology is) can get out of hand.

Remembering that the Christmas party is a work function, the things that happen at the party are actually happening at work. Add alcohol, which increases the risk factor, and watch things go horribly wrong. You might get lucky, and nothing bad happens. But if it does, what's talked about at that party could be talked about in the office for the next few years, and there are just some things co-workers don't need to know about each other.

As a leader, by all means, celebrate the year and the wins with a party—just do it at lunch time, or in a more controlled way. Set some ground rules, finish the party at a reasonable hour, and never ever let anyone drive home. A wild party isn't worth the risk. You won't forgive yourself if something happens.

TWO CELEBRATE THE BUSINESS SUCCESSES.

Over the course of a year, there will be massive wins to celebrate, so celebrate strong. Thank everyone for their efforts and contributions. Congratulate them for their successes. Share the excitement of another successful year with your staff.

Review the goals that you set for your business or your team, and talk about what worked and went well, what didn't, and what you'll change into the new year. And include the team in your review. After all, they were the ones responsible for the team's success.

As a leader, remember to thank your clients. Send Christmas cards, send personal notes, send Dan Murphy's vouchers (not to government-owned corporations—be aware) and be generous. Remember that you don't have a business without clients, or a team without team members.

THREE PLAN YOUR HOLIDAY OR DOWNTIME.

This is the big one. Plan your Christmas holiday. Travel, read, take downtime. Go to the beach, unwind, and let your hair down (if you still have some).

This is a big deal for me. My wife and I try to get away every January and take at least one or two weeks where we go overseas and go touring. Recently, we visited orangutans in Borneo. We went to Borneo for two weeks to see some of the wild animals in that country with the goal of unwinding, unworrying, and unburdening.

Fun fact: Researchers have discovered that humans and orangutans share approximately 97% of their DNA. This compares to about 99% sequence similarity between humans and chimps. The orangutan is the third non-human primate to have its genome sequenced, after the chimp and rhesus macaque (Credit: National Institute of Health).

However you do it, enjoy your end of year!

ACTIVITY 3.2
FACILITATE DISCUSSION

Take some time now to think about what you've learnt in the last chapter.

The series of questions on the following pages will encourage you to assess how effective you are in facilitating discussion with your team members, and in helping them find ways to contribute positively to the team and the organisation. It can also help you to generate ideas about how you can better facilitate discussion in the process of uplifting your team.

Alternatively, spend some time thinking about how you can better create a work environment conducive to cooperation. Thinking about how you can better assist your team members to communicate and participate in the workplace will go a long way to strengthening you as an inspiring and supportive leader for your team.

Answer honestly. Do you listen to the ideas of your team members? Why, or why not?

When facilitating workshops, how well do you adhere to the 5 Ps (Purpose, Process, People, Performance, Polish)?

Answer honestly. Do you still believe that if you want something done right, you have to do it yourself?

Do you have a team member who goes BOOM when things go BOOM? How do you address it, and how can you do this better?

What practical ways can you help to overcome the deficit dialogue dilemma?

Do you understand the different needs and communication styles of your team members? How can you better address or employ them?

How do you think DiSC profiling could benefit your team and your organisation?

How do you send your team members off? Do you maintain a relationship to the end, or simply close the door?

In what ways can you better conduct exit interviews? Are there any important elements missing from this process?

What business successes can you plan to celebrate when closing out this year of work?

SKILL III
ROLE MODEL LEADERSHIP

YOUR TEAM MEMBERS ARE ALWAYS WATCHING AND LISTENING TO YOU.

What you do matters to them, and it affects how they perform in the workplace. Every one of your actions has the potential to help, harm, hear, or hurt your team members.

They're looking to you for guidance in the quiet times, during crisis events in their private lives, and even during crisis events in your life. They're looking for predictability—even when you're under the pump.

So how to you guide your team in times when your leadership matters the most? And what leadership skills do you need to uplift your team, and turn them into a high-performing people machine even during BOOM events?

WHEN LEADERSHIP MATTERS THE MOST

On August 5, 2010, a mine cave in trapped 33 miners 700 metres underground. It would take 17 days for rescuers to establish communications with the trapped workers (with a note taped to a drill bit). That note said 'We are well in the shelter, the 33 of us'. It would take 70 days for the miners to be rescued.

Luis Urzúa (54) was the shift foreman at the time of the mine cave in. Immediately following the incident, Urzúa took control. He got his team to a safe location, he managed the few resources that the team had, and he worked closely with the rescuers to evacuate the 33 miners.

But what did Urzúa do, specifically, to lead that team through such a dire situation right to the end?

'It's been a bit of a long shift', foreman Urzúa joked. A man whose levelheadedness and gentle humour is credited with helping keep the miners under his charge focused on survival during their 70-day underground ordeal, Urzúa kept his cool in his first audio contact with officials on the surface. He glossed over the hunger and despair he and his men felt, saying, 'We're fine, waiting for you to rescue us'. (Credit: Wiki)

A mine cave in is a situation when strong leadership is required. It's an example of when leadership matters most.

ONE LEADERSHIP MATTERS MOST DURING MAJOR CRISIS EVENTS.

Crisis events mean different things to different leaders. My definition is 'an event (or series or events) that results in a risk manifested, that causes or has the potential to cause the loss of psychological or physical safety in an organisation, or the loss of business continuity for the organisation.' I know, way too technical, but it summarises the concept.

It's during these events that our teams need strong leadership. Think Dreamworld (2016), COVID-19 (2020), and CS Energy (2021) as examples. Imagine for a moment being at Dreamworld on the day of that tragedy.

In your team or your business, a crisis event could be the economy tanking, your business struggling, or an injury or fatality on your site.

During crisis events, emotions are high, and our teams are in a state of panic. As leaders, we need to remain in conscious control, and we need to take a leaf out of Urzúa's playbook and remain calm and in control. The simple strategies that you can use to stay in control include breathing, counting to ten, and reframing the situation. Yes, they sound simple, but they work a treat—don't discount them until you've tried them!

LEADER ACTION

Because crisis events are risks manifested, you can do some preparation work to help you and your team be ready for such eventualities. Regardless, no matter how much prep work you do, as a leader you'll still need to stand up during times of crisis. Your team needs you to.

TWO LEADERSHIP MATTERS MOST DURING TEAM MEMBER CRISIS EVENTS.

Your team members have all got personal lives. They're having experiences on a daily basis that challenge their ability to cope and to function. These situations can be overlooked by leaders in relation to their importance, but have no doubt that it's how leaders support their teams during their personal crises that demonstrates the character and values of the leader.

The very best leaders understand that if their team members are struggling, it's time for the leader to step up. And step into empathy and care factor. To understand what the team member is experiencing, and be willing to support them through it.

Whether it's the death of a loved one, the death of a pet, a cancer diagnosis, or some other personal crisis event, team members will have times when they just can't be at their best. And that's part of leading a team.

Empathy is the most important tool in the leader's toolkit during these times. Empathy requires the leader to think about what it would be like to be going through the same thing. Empathy requires an emotional connection with the team member, and it takes compassion. Compassion is about taking action to support someone. That might include reducing someone's responsibilities for a period, providing time off, or reducing their hours. I'll give you a little tip here: the leadership that you display during these times for your team members will never be forgotten (the leadership response will be internalised by your team members, because they're going through such an emotional time).

LEADER ACTION

Make sure that your team members remember how much you supported them, not how much you neglected them, during their personal crisis events. Spend a moment or two, now, reflecting on how you could demonstrate empathy, the next time you need to.

THREE LEADERSHIP MATTERS MOST DURING LEADERS' CRISIS EVENTS.

This point is one that can be quickly and quietly overlooked. Leaders are just expected to get up, dress up, and show up, regardless of what's happening in their own lives. The old rule is that leaders can't show any emotion; they need to 'take a teaspoon of cement' and get on with it, because they have work to do and a team to lead.

This is an interesting approach, and one that's partially true, but it forgets that leaders are human, too. The reason that these are the most important times for leaders to be in control is because when leaders aren't thinking clearly, they don't make great decisions. They make mistakes. I've seen leaders having to step out of their role (for a period, or forever) during these times. And that can be the right thing to do—for the leader and for the team. Making a bad decision during a tough personal time is not an excuse.

If you're a leader, and you're struggling personally, reach out for help. Let your team know what's happening for you (if you can share it) and get into coping mode. Coping mode requires you to take a problem-focused approach to your crisis (getting into action, and getting it sorted out as best you can outside of work). Take an emotion-focused approach (where you reduce the negative emotions you're experiencing, by reframing the situation) or taking an avoidant approach (not a great approach, but it might work for some crises).

Some leaders need to lean into some personal development during these times. That helps the leader to process what's happening for them, and it helps them to refine their coping skills.

LEADER ACTION

The next time things go BOOM for you, remember Luis Urzúa. And remember how he was able to remain calm, to keep 33 others calm, and how he followed his team out of a collapsed mine after seventy days of coping with a major crisis event.

Your team members are looking to you for guidance. Unfortunately, they're sometimes also looking to you to see what they can get away with. That's when it's critical do say, and do, what you expect them to.

DO AS I SAY, AND DO AS I DO

Why do some leaders still not understand that team members don't listen as much as they watch? Why don't leaders realise that they're always on show? They're being analysed for how to behave, and their example is the most important thing that they have to influence others.

We had a client that was big on 'do as I say, not as I do.' Seriously. Their belief was that it was OK to say one thing and do another. Which is OK, if you want your team to be totally confused about the standards you're trying to maintain.

We've used this story as a case study in the past, as this leader went from being incongruent (saying one thing and doing another) to really understanding what it takes to lead by example.

Here's what she learnt.

ONE TEAM MEMBERS ARE WATCHING YOU ALL THE TIME.

This leader didn't get the importance of the behaviour that she was exhibiting. There was a lack of understanding that team members directly reflect the example of their leader. It wasn't until we were unpacking specific examples of team behaviours that it became clear just how much impact her example was having on the team—a massive learning.

When leaders get this message (emotionally, I mean; like, 'feel' it), they can be clear on the standards that they're setting. Which might be lower than they're trying to set. There's nothing like a deep understanding of 'behavioural impact' to help you out of incongruency.

TWO WHAT YOU WALK PAST, YOU CONDONE.

This was another area we worked on. Being willing to clearly set an expectation and stick to it—and hold others accountable. It's difficult to turn the incongruency ship around, but not impossible. It takes effort, and it takes honesty. And it takes being willing to call out behaviour that's not aligned with the right values or standards.

The challenge is that team standards drop to the lowest level demonstrated by one team member. And it's about having caring conversations (not robust conversations) that unpack why a certain type of behaviour is inappropriate—especially when it comes to attaining and maintaining psychological safety.

THREE DON'T DO SOMETHING THAT YOU DON'T WANT YOUR TEAM TO DO.

It's actually pretty simple.

At the end of the day, it's about integrity. The opposite of incongruence. When you say you're going to do something...do it. Follow through. That's integrity. (Aka: the most important leadership character trait, according to most team members.)

And when you've got integrity, you can role model leadership in one of the most important ways: leading to help and hear, not harm and hurt.

HELP NOT HARM, HEAR NOT HURT

I was recently in Perth speaking at the *AusIMM International Mining Conference*. Being back in WA gave me an opportunity to reflect on my time in mining there, and what I learnt from those experiences. And the thing that keeps coming up for me is that in the teams I worked in, we wanted to be heard by our leaders.

My mining career started at the ripe young age of 21. I was a young tradie who had just been released from a burns unit after more than a month of healing from a BOOM event. In the burns unit, I remember making the decision that I wouldn't be working as an electrician for any longer than I absolutely had to. That meant I needed to find something else to do with my career, and find it fast.

So, when the 'Employee Representative Role' came up, to represent the workforce in the workplace agreement negotiations, I jumped at it. A side note: this section will trigger some people in the mining industry, because it's about workplace agreements, and not unions.

For whatever reason, I've never been part of a union. Not because I didn't want to, just because I've always ended up on sites that weren't unionised, and that were termed something like 'WPAs' (aka: workplace agreements). Robe River was one of those sites.

Back to the story. My role in the process was to meet with the trades teams and get their feedback on what they were prepared to negotiate on, and what they weren't. What conditions they were chasing, and what wasn't important to them. Then, to communicate that to the management team.

And because I've never been part of a union agreement negotiation, I can't speak from that experience. I can only speak from the experience that I had, which was really very positive. It was a cool role to be put in at such a young age, and I loved every minute of it. It was my first taste of what it's like dealing with senior leaders in mining. Yes, they were tough, but they listened, were open to ideas and open to negotiation (within reason).

It was a lifetime ago, but I still have such positive memories of sitting in the equivalent of the boardroom on that mine site talking with senior leaders about the conditions for all the trades teams. And I remember constructive conversation. Not arguing or shouting. It was a calm process that required giving a bit and getting a bit.

There were other representatives, from other sections of the mine, like operations, and technical. Overall, it was a predominantly positive experience (some of the tradies gave me a hard time about not getting us enough money—to be expected), but the leaders were great to deal with. We always felt heard. We were left feeling that the WPA was helping us, not hindering us (and I must say that I could never understand how people could whinge about working in mining, when our conditions and pay were so good—even back then).

Looking back on that particular experience, it's left a lasting impact on how I approach some of the coaching sessions that I do now with leaders. Regardless of the situation, team members just want to be heard. They want to be helped. It's not just about productivity or getting the job done, it's about psychological safety. Team members that are not heard are hurt.

Leaders, always remember to help, not harm. Hear, not hurt. Yes, that's not always possible; but let it be your default position. Be consistent enough in it that you're predictable—and just a little boring.

HOW TO BE OK WITH BORING

I couldn't work out how one of my clients just kept their stuff together. Always. Never lost it. Ever. So cool, calm, and collected. Unlike me (at times). My emotions seem to fluctuate wildly, and I feel like I get the full human experience, going through all the emotional states.

So, I asked my client what was going on for them. Even when things were going south. When things weren't right. When things weren't ideal.

After some considered reflection, my client said that in their mind it was as simple as 'being OK with boring.'

Quite the insightful response. Quite the measured response. Quite the unexpected response.

I asked him to clarify it for me. He said, as a leader, you don't need to be all over the place. You don't need to be inconsistent, and you don't need to be unpredictable. You just need to be boring (not as a human), but as a leader.

Here's what else we discussed.

ONE LEARN TO BE PREDICTABLE IN YOUR EMOTIONS.

In short, don't be the leader whose team have to wait until you're in the right mood to approach.

Don't be the leader whose team have to worry about your emotions being out of control when they deliver bad news.

Don't be the leader who's unstable, unpredictable, or unreliable emotionally.

Be boring. Get in control of your emotions so that regardless of the situation, you're able to 'take it in your stride.' You're able to engage your frontal lobes and talk yourself down before responding. You're able to name your emotional state, which is the first step in the emotional intelligence process (Credit: Daniel Goleman[22]).

TWO LEARN TO BE PREDICTABLE IN YOUR BEHAVIOUR.

When we survey team members (or leaders) and we ask them what's the most important character trait that they'd like to see in their leaders, there are several commonly used words (like charisma, care factor, consistency, commitment, or communication).

What would you answer to the question of what's the most important leadership character trait? The most common response we hear is consistency. Consistency of response. Consistency of mood, and consistency of behaviour.

Team members need leaders to behave consistently. Why? Because leadership behaviour is reflected by team members. Leadership behaviour becomes the example to follow. Leadership behaviour has an impact on others. Leaders need to have the courageous conversations at times. And they need to have those in a way that's not aggressive, abusive, or abrupt. If they're any of these things, the conversation is not courageous, it's counterproductive.

Be boring. Be the leader who is so consistent that your team knows what your decisions will be before they ask you. Be the leader who has words or phrases that you use consistently. Be the leader that's in control of their behavioural patterns.

THREE LEARN TO BE PREDICTABLE IN YOUR FOCUS.

Too many leaders have too many priorities. Too many leaders are chasing their tails. Too many leaders have a daily focus instead of a monthly, quarterly, or annual focus.

One of our favourite clients picks a focus for every year. This year it was simply 'happiness.' Be happy at work. Be happy at home. Be happy at life (as much as you can—not always achievable, but a great goal). Every month, my sessions with that team are focused on content that supports the mission critical focus of happiness.

When working with that team, it's pretty simple. Is what we're doing making us happy? Is what we're doing making our team happy? Is what we're doing making our clients happy? If not, it's time to change something.

Be boring. Have a consistent focus. Have a consistent priority list. Have a consistent approach to delivering your priorities. Have punctuality (watch how much your credibility increases, just with that small change).

In summary, be boring (if I haven't mentioned that already). Yes, leadership is about firefighting. And most leaders get some excitement from reacting, rather than responding. But the more boring and consistent you can be, the better your team will respond.

Being predictable is a good thing. It means you've got the conscious control to ensure your actions are serving and positively influencing others, rather than hurting them—just like in the story of the Old Man and his Grandson.

THE OLD MAN AND HIS GRANDSON IS A LEADERSHIP STORY

Have you heard of Cinderella? Have you heard of Rapunzel? Have you heard of Snow White? Me too. But have you head of The Brothers Grimm?

Jacob and Wilhelm Grimm were two brothers that wrote the fairy tales (in the early 1800s) that we still get enjoyment from today. Their original works were quite dark, even violent, and some of those stories have been rewritten to soften them up a little. But every one of their fairy tales has a great message, and messages that are relatable and relevant to us all...in a fairy tale kind of way.

Just like the tale of *The Old Man and His Grandson*. As you read this tale, think about who you are in the story—and more specifically, how important your behaviour is and what it's saying about you.

> **There was once a very old man, whose eyes had become dim, his ears dull of hearing, his knees trembled, and when he sat at the table, he could hardly hold the spoon, and spilt the broth upon the tablecloth or let it run out of his mouth. His son and his son's wife were disgusted at this, so the old grandfather at last had to sit in the corner behind the stove, and they gave him his food in an earthenware bowl, and not even enough of it. And he used to look towards the table with his eyes full of tears.**
>
> **Once, too, his trembling hands could not hold the bowl, and it fell to the ground and broke. The young wife scolded him, but he said nothing and only sighed. Then they brought him a wooden bowl for a few half-pence, out of which he had to eat.**
>
> **They were once sitting thus when the little grandson of four years old began to gather together some bits of wood upon the ground. 'What are you doing there?' asked the father. 'I'm making a little trough,' answered the child, 'for father and mother to eat out of behind the stove when I'm big.'**
>
> **The man and his wife looked at each other for a while, and presently began to cry. Then they took the old grandfather to the table, and henceforth always let him eat with them, and likewise said nothing if he did spill a little of anything.**

This is the story that I use a lot in my sessions, and it never ceases to get the desired reaction of making people thing about their behaviour and how it impacts on others.

ONE OUR ACTIONS CAN HURT OTHERS.

And it can hurt others either intentionally or unintentionally.

A big part of our leadership training programs is about intention. I ask leaders what their intentions are. Are their intentions to help or hurt, to harm or heal? The majority of leaders have the right intent.

In the moment, when the pressure is on, or during a crisis event, things can change. And intent can change quickly. And your team might not be your priority in the moment.

It's in those moments that you could metaphorically 'put someone behind the stove.' Out of sight, out of mind! Or you could exclude them. Or put them in your out-group. Like the son and his wife did.

LEADER ACTION

The message is to be aware of your intent before you make people decisions or have courageous conversations.

TWO OUR ACTIONS CAN INFLUENCE OTHERS.

And it can influence others either intentionally or unintentionally.

Leading by example is not an important element of leadership; it's the only element of leadership. Your teams don't listen to you as much as they watch you. Your teams are continuously observing your behaviour for the signs and signals of how to behave.

They're looking for the minimum line of what's acceptable. And the maximum line of what's expected. So that they can stay within those lines and avoid falling below what's accepted, while aiming to perform above what's expected (exceeding expectations).

And you don't have to say anything to influence behaviour at times. You just have to act. Like the four-year-old grandson did.

LEADER ACTION

The message is to always behave in a way that's in alignment with your values. That's legal, moral, and ethical, and that has high integrity.

THREE OUR ACTIONS CAN SERVE OTHERS.

And it can serve others to see them succeed.

There are times when you might need to swallow your pride. Change your mind, change your decision. And that's OK. It's sometimes better to change your decision than to continue to argue or fight for an outcome that's not possible. Changing your decision is a sign of courage, not a lack of it, but most leaders don't see it that way. They see it as a sign of weakness or a lack of conviction, when the opposite is the case.

Being in service, even if it means implementing a change, or a changed decision, is important. You can be in service, like the son and his wife were.

LEADER ACTION

The message is to be aware of what your teams are experiencing, and what you might need to change to upgrade their experience.

Your behaviour matters. It can impact others—in their experience as a team member, and in how they behave as a leader. And this is particularly important when you're leading at the top of the corporate food chain, which is always going to be one of your biggest challenges.

LEADING LEADERS IS THE BIGGEST LEADERSHIP CHALLENGE

I went from leading a team to leading leaders. I'll never forget how hard that was. Really, really, hard. Here I was, leading great humans that lead their own teams, who have their own styles, leadership goals, and career goals. It was tough going, and I had to update, upgrade, and upskill my leadership skills. And Quickly.

Now that I work with CEOs and C-Suite teams, I still hear from senior leaders that their biggest leadership challenge is the leadership of other senior leaders. And I can relate.

So, what are the skills that are required to lead senior leaders? Read on to find out what my own experience is, and what over 700 1:1 coaching sessions has taught me about leading other leaders.

ONE MICROMANAGING DOESN'T WORK.

One of the most common issues that senior leaders have is that they're micromanaged. Yes, the CEO, sometimes knowing exactly what they're doing, chooses micromanaging as a strategy. And the C-Suite don't like it. They don't respond, and they don't buy in.

Micromanagement is where managers feel the need to control aspects of their team members work and decision making—to an extreme degree, more than is necessary or healthy for a usual working relationship. Many people will have experienced micromanagement and its impact at some point in their careers. As much as it might appear to be working, it doesn't.

For leaders who've climbed the ladder of corporate success, who are sitting in the C-Suite, they feel like they've got a handle on leadership. They feel like they're building a high-performing team, and they feel like they're absolutely capable of leading others and making decisions. Micromanagement just doesn't do it for them.

LEADER ACTION

CEO, give your leadership team the chance to shine, to decide, and to develop professionally.

TWO THE PERSONALITIES ARE BIGGER.

Senior leaders are more confident. They're more committed. They're more courageous. And they're bigger personalities. With big personalities come big opinions, and big ideas. Which takes a solid CEO who's capable of dealing with big personalities.

Yes, leading big personalities is a big job. CEOs with a range of big personalities on their senior leadership team need, above everything else, to take on the role of facilitator. That means to make sure that everyone on the senior leadership team has a voice, has a value, and has a vested interest in the team as an aligned unit.

CEOs who can facilitate have the ability to question, listen, and decide. They have the ability to engage everyone in conversation, and they have the ability to get all opinions prior to make a decision.

LEADER ACTION

CEO, give your leadership team the ability to contribute, to be heard, and to add value.

THREE THE SILOING GETS WORSE.

For me, the biggest challenge that I see CEOs having is that their senior leaders forget that they're also part of a team. The C-Suite can get focused on their own patch, their own department, their own business unit. Even when decisions impact other senior leaders and other departments. That's called building empires, or becoming siloed.

Siloing is a big issue in organisations, because it doesn't just occur at the most senior levels of the organisation. Issues with siloing flow down through the business, and team members at every level pick up on it. They know that the senior leaders aren't aligned, and it does nothing for morale, motivation, and making things happen.

Siloing stifles creativity. Siloing stifles cultures. Siloing stifles commitment. And siloing generally starts at the upper echelons of the organisation.

LEADER ACTION

CEO, encourage your leadership team to work together, talk together, and decide together.

Remember that role modelling leadership to leaders is about showing them how to be a good leader. A good leader isn't just a fair and suppportive boss; it's one who supports team members to grow and develop professionally, to contribute meaningfully to the team, and to work together seamlessly in achieving common goals.

Your job isn't just to support leadership roles; it's to create more leaders. Let your behaviour demonstrate that. Because people and their wellbeing should be your focus, always.

ACTIVITY 3.3
ROLE MODEL LEADERSHIP

Take some time now to think about what you've learnt in the last chapter.

The series of questions on the following pages will encourage you to think about what you can do to develop your capacity for strong leadership during crisis times, and ways you can effectively role model that leadership to others to positively influence both their work life, and their development.

How have you led your team through crisis events?

How predictable to your team do you think you are in your emotions, behaviour, and focus?

Can you detail times where your actions as a leader have hurt, influenced, or served your team members?

Answer honestly. Do you micromanage your team members?

How well do you lead leaders, especially ones with big personalities?

Answer honestly. As a leader, are you working in a silo, or are you fully integrated into the team?

Answer honestly. Do you condone bad behaviour in the workplace by walking past it?

Introspect honestly. Think of what your team members have seen and heard you do, and whether you can be proud of that or not.

a survey) that their outputs are going well. They get their work done. A team in turmoil might even rate themselves as being high on outputs. The challenge is that outputs are at risk if relationships aren't strong. In my experience, a team in turmoil is just not able to sustain high output for a long period of time, when the team members struggle to work together—and struggle to deal with each other.

From a 'how to' perspective, if you have a high-performing team, focus on outputs because your relationships are in good shape and your team could work together to get more done (if they're not already at capacity). If you have a team in turmoil, it's time to really lean into the relationships in your team, and how to improve them.

But how do you do that? Glad you asked. Here are some thoughts, and three things you might consider.

ONE A TEAM CHARTER SESSION WILL REALLY HELP.

Team charters are a winner. But the message here really is don't try this at home (or alone) without a strong and capable facilitator. This could be a TGG facilitator (reach out) or someone from HR or from BI. Please, as the leader, if you have a team in turmoil, don't take this on yourself. You need to lead the session, not run it. Facilitating a team charter workshop with a team in turmoil is a learnt skill, and one that takes a significant amount of conversational control. And conversational management. Because, unfortunately, there will be conflict.

So what's a team charter? Glad you asked that question, too. A team charter is an overview of things like team beliefs, behaviours, or visions or values. Team charters help connect teams back to both purpose and people.

It's what we all commit to doing, and how we commit to being. How we'll treat each other. How we'll communicate. And what happens when we don't follow through on our commitments to treat each other with respect and high care factor. We don't have to be best friends with our teammates, but we do need to be able to work with them in a respectful way. If you'd like an enjoyable work life, that is. And don't want to work in a team in turmoil.

From experience, a team charter would be the best way to create alignment in a team that's not working together. Don't thank me now.

TWO LEADERSHIP CONVERSATIONS ALSO HELP.

One of the biggest issues with teams in turmoil (in my experience) is that the leader is avoiding the conversations that matter. The leader doesn't want to address the team members that are causing the challenges.

You see, what can happen is that the team member/s causing others grief can be the highest performers. These team members are high in the output section. The leader is afraid that if they take on the high performer, even when they're disrespecting others, the team member might drop off on performance, or might leave.

Remember this: you can't lead someone you need. Your highest performers don't have the right to hurt others, just because they're high performers. Leaders, have the conversation. It's not a performance conversation; it's a values-based conversation. It's a code of conduct conversation.

Also remember this: what you walk past, you condone. The more the leader ignores the behaviour, the more the team loses faith in their leader. Because the leader is not addressing the issue. And the team is still in turmoil. And yes, sometimes I get the job of talking to all team members to understand what's happening in the team. Which is cool, I can be unbiased—but at the end of the day, with or without the information I provide, the leader will have to have leadership conversations, and need to set behavioural boundaries.

THREE PAY ATTENTION TO TRIGGERS.

Understand the concept of triggers. And how both leader behaviour and team member behaviour causes unwanted and negative emotions to show up. And to show up in a way that drives poor behavioural response patterns. What I mean by triggers is those words or actions that cause team members to lose their cool. In other words, they lose their marbles, and say or do things are uncool.

If you're a leader, consider understanding more about Daniel Goleman's[22] work on triggers. One thing that's worth researching is his list of them. He identifies the top five negative emotional triggers in the workplace as the following:

- Condescension and lack of respect,
- Being treated unfairly,
- Being unappreciated,
- Feeling that you're not being listened to or heard, and
- Being held to unrealistic deadlines.

These areas tap straight into the Amygdala, and the limbic system—the structure in the brain that deals with fight, flight, or freeze—and thus is responsible for instant emotional reactions such as high levels of stress and panic. And anger.

As a leader, or even as a team member, these triggers are important to understand. The more you can avoid doing or saying something that would cause a team member to react badly, the smoother your team will run. Being consistently alert to them will go a long way in helping you deal with difficulties—including insidious problems like office politics.

WHAT THE ACTUAL...IS GOING ON WITH ALL THE OFFICE POLITICS HAPPENING RIGHT NOW?!

What is it with the amount of workplace politics that seem to be happening everywhere? Politics are hard to cope with at times. Until you understand what's really going on, that is.

Firstly though, this section was prompted by a trend that's showing up in my coaching conversations around how stressful office politics can be. And there really is a lack of understanding of why people form alliances or groups to increase their own personal or professional power. When you look at it from a psychological viewpoint, why wouldn't you play politics, if it helps you get ahead? Because it makes you look like a twit, that's why. And because it's not fair on the humans that can't understand why you favour some people and not others, and why some get the royal and special treatment, when others don't.

You usually only get to really understand office politics when you've made a decision that offends someone, who then rallies the posse in support of why it was such a bad decision. Or you might say something to someone who's aligned with someone else, or who's related to so and so, or who only spends the training budget on one team, so don't bother asking.

The two things about office politics are that they're generally not process related (they're people or power related), and they create a stressful working environment. It's hard to create conscious control when you're always on guard for what you might say that might get back to someone else, right? And it affects people's ability to advance their career and get ahead. **Business News Daily** notes that:

> **Politics is bubbling over into nearly every aspect of our lives; and the office, it seems, is not immune. Research from Robert Half's Accountemps revealed that political discord plays a significant role in today's office life.**
>
> **Overall, 55% of employees say they partake at least somewhat in office politics, with most of those doing so to advance their**

careers. The study found that 76% of workers believe that office politics affect their efforts to get ahead, an increase of 20% within four years.[57]

So, what can you do to deal with difficulties when you're working in a political work environment?

ONE ACCEPT IT.

Reconcile within yourself that there are things and people outside of your control (sorry if that's too blunt, or too boring, or too hard). There are some things at work that we just can't change, things that we just have to live with (or leave). Accept the fact, and understand that some people are just political by nature (or nurture) and that they'll act like that, regardless of what you say or think. Get your head around the fact that some people are just not great at doing human stuff (see **The Dark Triad** by Paulhus & Williams[42] for more information on the personality types that might be prone to political kinds of behaviour).

TWO STAY IN CONTROL.

This should be self-explanatory, but with all the other pressures out there right now, I'm hearing from coaching clients that politics is another stressor, and sometimes the proverbial straw that breaks the camel's back. I get it. It can be the thing that sets you off, especially when the politician thinks they're putting one over you. Watch your self-talk and watch your emotional state—it comes out in your behaviour, even if you don't think it does.

THREE WORK WITH IT.

And I mean that in the right way. If you can use the situation to your advantage, without compromising your values and your dignity, go right ahead. If you need to get a decision made, and you think the grapevine will help you, go right ahead, I say. This point is not so much 'if you can't beat them, join them' as it's 'anything that's done legally, morally, and ethically can't go too wrong.' Remember to have the right intent. If you hurt others to get your way, you're becoming complicit in the politics yourself.

FOUR OVER-COMMUNICATE.

If I had only two words to help you deal with office politics, these are the two words I'd share with you: Over-communicate. Yes. Over-communicate (you need to hear those two words seven times for it to sink apparently, or so the org psychs tell us). I won't write it seven times. Maybe read them seven times either quietly, or out aloud. If you read them aloud, and others ask, share this section with them, in case they're struggling too. But what does it mean to over-communicate? It means this—and I cannot emphasise how important this is, in case you haven't noticed—think before you act.

Ask yourself this question: who will be affected, or interested, or impacted, by what I'm about to do? The decision, or the action. Over-communicating means being ahead of important communication and decisions, so that you can ring the person first. Email them, to let them know what you're up to. When someone asks you to stop over-communicating, you'll know you're doing it right! Over-communicate. And you can use this strategy in general terms, if you want to, depending on your business, your leader, and your team. But please be in front of the game on any big decisions or actions. It'll help. (And I got it in seven times—yay!)

FIVE STAY CLEAR.

Yes, this is the hard one. Hard, not impossible. The more you can stay clear, the less you'll be embroiled in the tragedy and the impending catastrophe that can come from office politics. Or not. Some of the time, people (and leaders, sadly) get away with hurting others because they're—wait for it... you've heard these words before—a protected species. As well as over-communicating, please do whatever you can to remove yourself from any office politics going on around you.

These strategies are really important in dealing with the difficulty of office politics, and they're yet another reason why it's so important for you to have conscious control. With it, you'll become as adept at navigating office politics as you are at avoiding other minefields in the workplace—including the age-old issue of groupthink.

HOW TO AVOID GROUPTHINK, AND WHY YOU SHOULD

On 28 January 1986, NASA made the decision to launch *The Challenger*. That decision resulted in what's called to this day 'the Challenger disaster.'

What was the disaster? The Space Shuttle Challenger disaster was a fatal incident on January 28, 1986, in the United States space program where the space shuttle *Challenger* (OV-099) broke apart 73 seconds into its flight, killing all seven crew members aboard. (Credit: Wiki).

It's amazing when you read the story about the disaster and the review into what happened. The saddest part of the tragedy is that it could (and should) have been avoided. An engineer told his wife the night before the launch that it would blow up. And the part that failed, causing the explosion, was one (or two—depending on which website you read) O-ring, that wasn't rated for the cold temperatures that it was exposed to.

What does an O-ring cost? Not much. But what does it cost when leaders don't listen to their teams, when they have great ideas? In this case, the costs—human and financial—were significant, and tragic.

And, from all reports, there wasn't just one engineer, but four, that voiced their concerns about what could happen if NASA followed through with the *Challenger* launch that day—a day that was both colder than other launches, and too cold for the O-rings on the *Challenger*.

But the senior engineers (and the contractor engaged by NASA at the time) made the call to launch, even after having been told what might happen. After all, the US President was going to address the American people, to tell them how well it went, and how great America and NASA were at launching space craft into the thermosphere.

The investigation into the *Challenger* disaster coined the phrase 'groupthink', which means that the group has more power over the discussion (and the decision) than those (individuals) who might know better. Investopedia describes it this way:

> **Groupthink is a phenomenon that occurs when a group of individuals reaches a consensus without critical reasoning or evaluation of the consequences or alternatives. Groupthink is based on a common desire not to upset the balance of a group of people.**

In other words, groupthink doesn't consider all opinions. Some of which might be valid. Very valid, in the case of the *Challenger*.

So, just for a moment, put yourself in the position of the contractor or chief engineer in 1986, and ask yourself what you would have done. What decision would you have made? What would your priorities have been? Fame, fortune, and media exposure, or life preservation?

What's important, as we learn from tragedies like the *Challenger* disaster, is thinking about how they can apply to our situations. Most of the time we aren't responsible for the lives of seven humans, but at the same time, we have responsible decisions to make.

Here's how to avoid groupthink.

ONE TAKE A PRIORITY AWARENESS APPROACH.

Decision making is a key requirement of leaders. Especially leaders under pressure, when they might not have all the information, or they need to decide quickly. When the human brain is in decision-making mode, all that's happening is that it's processing possibilities based on priority propositions.

That means that all decisions are priority based. What your priority is in the moment will ultimately determine how you make the decision. Let's take safety for a moment, because that's the easiest was to describe this topic (and it relates to the *Challenger* disaster). Are you focused on the safety of humans, or are you focused on production, or some other priority that you probably shouldn't be focused on in the moment?

This paragraph could be called 'be aware of your values', as most of the time, our priorities in the moment of decision making are a subset of our values. The way to be aware of your priorities is to be very clear, and very aware of the rationale for your decision—and to be able to explain that clearly.

LEADER ACTION

If you feel like you're trying to convince yourself or others with words like 'the risk is worth the reward', or 'we should get away with it', rethink your priorities and rethink your decision. Then, when you're aware of your priorities, share them, and ask for feedback or input to ensure that others get the chance to contribute. Don't let your priorities drive a groupthink mindset for the team that's making critical decisions.

TWO HAVE A DEFERENCE TO EXPERTISE APPROACH.

As part of the review of the *Challenger* disaster, and a range of other major catastrophic events, the term 'High Reliability Organisation' (HRO) was coined. HRO theory flowed out of Normal Accident Theory, which led a group of researchers at the University of California, Berkeley (Todd LaPorte, Gene Rochlin, and Karlene Roberts)[28] to study how organisations working with complex and hazardous systems operated error free. And how events like the *Challenger* disaster could have been avoided, and how similar high-risk organisations did avoid those types of tragedies.

At the core of a HRO, there are five key principles, which are essential for any improvement initiative to succeed: deference to expertise, reluctance to simplify, sensitivity to operations, commitment to resilience, and preoccupation with failure.

Although all these principles are super important, the most important principle is the deference to expertise. What that means is to defer to the person who has the most expertise to make the decision. Or defer to the group of people who have the most expertise to make the decision. In the case of the *Challenger* disaster, there were four engineers who all came to the same conclusion about the O-ring temperature rating, but none of their opinions were considered (they were ignored) when it came to deciding to launch the *Challenger*.

And it doesn't matter how low you go in the organisation to defer to expertise. If it's a junior person that you need to involve in the decision, so be it. If they have the information that could help, or that could save a life, leaders are obliged to consider their input.

LEADER ACTION

Deferring to expertise is the quickest and easiest way to prevent groupthink, because you overtly and openly encourage input from the right people. If you're prepared to listen to that input, you'll notice how much value is added to the decision-making process.

These strategies aren't just effective in avoiding groupthink. They're strategies that uplift your team members, by giving them a voice and inviting them to use their valuable skills in dealing with difficulties. Commit to the strategies of uplifting your team—and you might never have to hear some of the worrying things that team members say to their leaders.

THE 5 THINGS LEADERS NEVER WANT TO HEAR FROM THEIR TEAMS

I've had some great leaders. One of my favourite leaders of all time is a person called Pat (let's use that name—it happens to be their real name). Pat was the human that shared with me the power of languaging, and how to listen to what people are really saying. Pat shared that sometimes it's blatantly obvious, and at other times, not so much. Pat's coaching is some of the reason that we now focus so much on languaging as part of our leadership workshops and training. In relation to the blatant comments that team members make, there are some that should move you to action, Pat explained. And they really are things you don't want to hear from you team.

Here's some of the big (and worrying) things that team members say to their leaders.

ONE I DON'T FEEL VALUED.

This is a tough one, and it goes straight to the solar plexus. If you follow any of my work at all, you'll understand how importantly I take the word value/s. Our values drive our behaviour, and one of our greatest human needs is to feel valued. Particularly by our leader.

What feeling valued is all about is feeling heard. This section could be 'I don't feel heard', but not feeling valued is a more common statement made by team members who don't feel like they have a voice.

Feeling valued is related to the psychological safety aspect of leadership, and it's about making it safe for team members to both contribute (with ideas or opinions) and to challenge the norms (being creative and innovative). Leaders that lead with low psychological safety will end up with team members that don't feel valued, because they don't feel like what they say ever matters.

LEADER ACTION

When you're with your team, either 1:1 or in a group setting, please be present. Be focused. Be a listener. Listen with an open heart and an open mind. You might not like what you hear, but it helps your team members feel valued if you're able to hold the space and listen to their ideas and concerns without judgement.

TWO I DON'T FEEL CARED FOR.

This is another tough one. It's not as common as the first one, but it happens, and leaders hear it (or team members tell it to other team members, and the leader might not even know). Being cared for is another human need, and one that, when violated, has an adverse impact on the team member. Who might check out or give up.

Feeling cared for is related to the psychological connection aspect of leadership, and it's about making time for team members. Yes, making time. Scheduling time with team members (both 1:1 and as a team) is a critical element of leadership, and when that's ignored or forgotten, your team feel like their leader doesn't care. Team members might say that they're not a priority for their leader, or that their leader is too busy for them. Ouch.

LEADER ACTION

Jump into your calendar and schedule 1:1 meetings with your team members. And schedule team meetings. Schedule those meetings for the same time each week, month, or fortnight, and aim to attend every meeting. And please don't reschedule them, or reschedule them AGAIN (yes, that happens).

THREE I DON'T FEEL SUPPORTED.

This is an interesting one, that can relate to a range of issues. The main area is in career progression—for the team member who has big ambitions, this is really important. And it's tough for the leader team member dynamic when there's a misalignment on career progression and pathways.

The other situations that might leave a team member feeling unsupported are during times of big projects or big decisions. With big projects or big decisions, team members need some level of direction. Yes, it might be minimal. But direction is important. I work with leaders at all levels of organisational charts, and they all need direction from their leaders—and they all struggle without it.

In our coaching sessions, I always ask our coachees if they feel like they have their leader's support. Most of the time it's a yes, but at times it's a no. And in these situations, my coaching is to not go out on a limb too far when making a decision, or taking an action, in case the branch breaks. Without leader support, team members can become very isolated very quickly, and can overstep boundaries or levels of responsibility. For more guidance on this one, see the book **Radical Candor** by Kim Scott,[49] where she talks about the balance between caring and direction.

LEADER ACTION

If a team member doesn't feel like you support their career, have a career conversation to help you get clearer on how you can support them. If it's a big project or big decision, don't say 'I'll let you decide.' If they ask for guidance, please give it to them, as best as you can.

FOUR I DON'T FEEL LIKE I MAKE A DIFFERENCE.

This is more sad than anything. It's another statement around human needs not being met. We all want to feel like our work matters to someone, particularly our leaders and our organisation.

Feeling like we make a difference is related to the psychological empowerment aspects of leadership, where team members feel like their work makes an impact and has a level of meaning. I know I've felt like this in the past, in some roles, where I questioned how much of a difference I was making to the team or the business. It's hard to show up each day when we feel like we don't really matter, and when we feel like no one would notice if we weren't there.

LEADER ACTION

If a team member doesn't feel like they're making a difference, it's important to find out why, and consider how that can be addressed. There might be an explanation around why the team member's work matters, or why it's valued.

FIVE I DON'T FEEL EMPOWERED.

This is perhaps the easiest of the big five listed here to deal with as a leader. Feeling unempowered means not feeling like you have the right level of responsibility. Not being trusted. Or not given adequate decision-making ability. Sometimes, this statement can relate to not feeling fully utilised in the role. The team member might be saying that they've got more to offer.

Feeling empowered is also related to the psychological empowerment aspects of leadership (competence and self-determination), and it's related to team members feeling like they're hamstrung in their role, and that they can't act without the direction of their leader, instead of being trusted by their leader to make decisions that relate to their role. A lack of empowerment can be the result of very transactional leadership styles.

LEADER ACTION

If a team member doesn't feel empowered, this is a sign they feel like you don't trust them to step up and make the decisions that they need to make. And that might be the case, so work out how you can develop more trust in that team member, or how you can give them more decision-making responsibility.

Think about which one of these is most important to you, which one you might have heard from a team member, and what you can do about it. It'll help give you perspective on how to move forward and effectively deal with difficulties with team members, as well as difficulties with other leaders— like leaders who go BOOM when things go BOOM.

DEALING WITH YOUR LEADER WHO GOES BOOM WHEN THINGS GO BOOM

Leaders seem to be going BOOM more often. Or at least that's what our coaching clients are telling us. We're hearing a lot of 'when the pressure comes on, my leader loses it.'

So, how do we coach our clients to deal with a leader who can't create conscious control? Let's unpack.

THE OUT-OF-CONTROL LEADER

Firstly, we need to understand what's going on for the leader who goes BOOM when things around them go BOOM. And there are both reasons and rationales, but they are in no way excuses for their behaviour.

Some leaders, as young or as old as they are, have never made the effort or taken the time to learn the skills of conscious control (aka: emotional and behavioural control).

Some leaders are born (or bred) in a way that predisposes them to going BOOM. For more information on personality traits like narcissism (a little overused these days, but a relevant term), see **The Dark Triad** by Paulhus & Williams[42] and see if your leader's behaviour is listed there.

Finally, some leaders just don't care how they impact other humans. I've worked for one of these, and they don't change their style easily. And no amount of feedback will change them.

BOUNDARIES ARE IMPORTANT

You need to have very clear boundaries relating to how you'll allow yourself to be treated by your leader, and you need to share those boundaries with your leader. Either when they go BOOM (hard), or when things are quiet and you can create the expectation (easier, but not easy). Without boundaries, you're not being clear on what you will or won't tolerate, and you won't be able to communicate those.

CREATE CONSCIOUS CONTROL

The most common reaction I hear from our leadership coaching clients is that when their leader goes BOOM, so do they. It's like 'if you can shout at me, I can shout at you.' Which is uncool. Sorry. I know your leader has gone BOOM, but it doesn't help to react in kind (which is a natural reaction, by the way). It takes conscious control not to react like that. The trick with conscious control is to respond not react. Use your frontal lobes (smart), not your limbic (emotional) brain.

ALWAYS DEBRIEF THE BOOM

If your leader goes BOOM—and most people don't do this one, because they're just happy it's over, but you must, it's critical!—debrief.

After a BOOM event, things will settle down. When they do, it's time to unpack what happened, and ask for a commitment that you won't be treated like that again. And get that commitment.

CHANGE ROLES OR LEADERS

Don't threaten to leave. That's never a good look. Just do it (like Nike)! Just move out of the team or the organisation and leave with integrity. Share at your exit interview why you've left, and the fact that you've been hurt once too many times. You never know what change it might effect.

But dealing with difficulties isn't just about dealing with difficult people. You cause difficulties too, albeit unintentionally—difficulties like committing the cardinal sin of leadership.

HOW TO NOT COMMIT THE CARDINAL SIN OF LEADERSHIP

The cardinal sin of leadership is not doing one-on-ones (1:1) with your team members. Even worse than that is scheduling those meetings every week, fortnight, or month, and either not attending them, or continually rescheduling. These behaviours are very damaging to the relationship between the leader and team member.

There's only one thing worse than either not scheduling, or rescheduling, those meetings—and that's to use the excuse that you're just too busy. Any leaders out there that say they're too busy for their team are just saying that their team member (and connecting with them regularly) is not a priority for the leader. 'I'm too busy' is translated (subconsciously, by the team member) as 'my leader has higher priorities than our relationship.' Which is uncool.

And the reality is that leaders are busy. They have too much to do. They're stretched, and for some, taking the time to have the regular 1:1s that they need to can be a real challenge for their time and their calendar.

Here are some real practical tips and tricks to help you stay committed and focused on your one-on-ones.

ONE KNOW HOW IMPORTANT THOSE MEETINGS ARE.

1:1 meetings are highly valued by team members. Sometimes, a 1:1 meeting is the only quality time that a team member gets with their leader. Most team members prepare well of these meetings, have a list of things to discuss with their leader, and generally make great use of the time. Obviously, some team members don't take them that seriously, but the message is that 1:1 meetings give employees face-to-face time to discuss the things that are important to them.

During COVID, Microsoft[3] surveyed their leaders and teams to understand how important 1:1 meetings really are, and if the business benefits from them as much as the employee does. Their findings were published in a blog post titled **The New Manager 1:1: Nurturing Employee Resiliency During Disruption and Change.**

In short, and to unpack just how important 1:1 meetings are for a leader and team member, these meetings actually lead to less meetings overall. Winner. They lead to better collaboration and less work hours for team members. Winner. They lead to more resilient team members. And they lead to a better work life balance for team members, because the meetings are not just work related. Winner. The data is conclusive, and it demonstrates that if 1:1 meetings work during a high-stress time like during a global pandemic, imagine how well they'll work in your business now, all these years later.

And sometimes just knowing and acknowledging how important things are—like 1:1 meetings—can mean that you put higher priority on them, and don't reschedule or miss them.

TWO TAKE OWNERSHIP AND RESPONSIBILITY FOR YOUR CALENDAR.

This means not changing or rescheduling 1:1 meetings. It's hard to put it any other way, sorry.

I was going to leave this paragraph there, but that would be uncool, because I know that there are things that pop up that need your urgent attention. I get that, but I also get how your team members feel when they're 'rescheduled.' The big thing here is to have the conversation firstly about what else is happening that's preventing you from attending the 1:1 meeting. And it's not just being too busy. And if you do reschedule, make sure you attend the rescheduled meeting (and yes, you won't believe how many leaders I know that are in a perpetual cycle of rescheduling).

Also, if you have someone that coordinates your calendar, like I do, ask them to hold you accountable. Asking for their commitment also helps you to hold yourself accountable.

Also consider the use of notifications or other push prompts, to make sure you're in your office, or the meeting room, when your next 1:1 meeting is due to begin. At Microsoft, tools like MyAnalytics have manager-focused features that remind managers to maintain 1:1 connection with employees through nudges. If it's good enough for Microsoft, it should be certainly be good enough for us.

THREE KNOW THAT IT'S NEVER TOO LATE TO START.

Again, from the Microsoft study, When manager 1:1s hadn't been a long-term habit, increasing them had an immediate benefit. An IMMEDIATE benefit.

Imagine, as you sit and read this section, what else there is at your disposal that you could implement right now without much effort. And that'll help you create happier, more resilient, and better-balanced team members. If you can think of something, please feel free to send it to me, and I'll study it and write a post or book sections about it in the future.

Also in the future, we can unpack how to have great 1:1 meetings. Some leaders take the entire meeting, and give directions. Or in the last five minutes, ask 'and how are you going?' This is not optimal. But that's a conversation for another day.

I just can't think of anything else that's as good as 1:1 meetings for changing the dynamics in your team. They're extremely important. They create engaged team members and teams. They allow the leader to focus on building the relationship. And in my humble opinion, to reschedule or to not value 1:1 meetings is THE cardinal sin of leadership.

Dealing with difficulties is extremely important. But rather than just focusing on putting out fires, it's important to implement strategies before they're needed—strategies that underpin effective working relationships.

LEADERSHIP TEAMS NEED THIS ONE THING TO BE EFFECTIVE

Teams need not only strong leaders, but strong leadership teams. Senior leadership teams set the tone for the business, for the culture, for the vision, and for the strategic direction.

Every day, or every week, I get asked by a leader or a team member why their leadership team isn't aligned, why they're not singing the same tune, why they're not all focused on the same things. Generally, the problem is that the senior leadership team don't know that they're not aligned. And without alignment, it's only a matter of time before there are staff issues relating to psychological or physical safety.

In my experience of coaching a large number of senior leadership teams, alignment is the big thing that's missing in less effective Senior Leadership Teams (SLTs).

Here's how you increase it with your SLT.

ONE SENIOR LEADERS NEED BELIEF ALIGNMENT.

When we do SLT workshops, to help senior leadership teams to come together in a unified way, the first thing we work through is belief systems and belief alignment. This is a crucial part of the alignment process, because our beliefs drive our behaviour in an unconscious way. They drive our languaging, they drive our decisions, they drive our team leadership.

And they're deep down in our unconscious mind. They come from our conditioning, from our nurturing, and from our environment as we've gone through life. We are a sum of our experiences, and those experiences shape how we lead.

If senior leaders have different belief systems, and that shows up as different leadership behaviours, the teams will see and feel the misalignment.

LEADER ACTION

Take the time to align your belief systems. Start with what behaviours those beliefs should be driving.

TWO SENIOR LEADERS NEED VALUE ALIGNMENT.

The next part of our SLT workshops involves a personal value process. Our values drive our behaviour in a conscious way. If you asked someone to describe you, they'd use values-based words, like honest, happy, committed, motivated, or something similar.

Our values are those parts of our psyche that we call on when we need to make big decisions. Like investment decisions or people decisions. We lean into our integrity, or our respect, or our caring values.

We all have personal values. But so do organisations and leaders, and they need to align with the values of the organisation.

This is very, very, very important. Please don't underestimate how important it is for the SLT members to align their own values with each other, and with the values of the organisation. When senior leaders leave, they usually cite misaligned values as their reason for leaving.

The values need to be on the wall, visible. With bullet points of required behaviours under each value. SLTs need to lean into those values when they're making big decisions, and clearly explaining why they've been made.

LEADER ACTION

Take the time to get clear on your own values, then share them with the other senior leaders, and align those with the values of the business.

THREE SENIOR LEADERS NEED CULTURE ALIGNMENT.

The good news is that this one can take care of itself if the first two have been done properly. But even if they have, there's still a requirement for every SLT to be clear on what type of culture they're trying to drive in the business. Culture starts with the SLT.

Indeed.com writes:

> **Organisational culture refers to a company's mission, objectives, expectations, and vision that guide its employees. Businesses with a strong organisational culture tend to be more successful than less structured companies because they have systems in place that promote employee performance, productivity and engagement.**

Strong culture drives the desired behaviour at all levels of the organisation. When the senior leaders behave in a certain way, the whole business will follow suit. SLT members need to lead by example. Not leading by example is the quickest way to impact organisational culture.

LEADER ACTION

SLT members need to be aware of the impact of their behaviour on the teams. Lead by example is the key message here.

The process of dealing with difficulties doesn't always have to be reactive. Create a more aligned—and therefore, more effective—SLT, and far it goes towards creating a high-functioning, problem-free team.

ACTIVITY 3.4
DEAL WITH DIFFICULTIES

Take some time now to think about what you've learnt in the last chapter.

The series of questions on the following pages will encourage you to think about what you can do to help your team members when they're in turmoil, and to apply the lessons you've just learnt about dealing with difficulties in the process of uplifting your team.

Alternatively, spend some time just sitting and writing about how you've managed your team through crises in the past, and what skills you need to improve to overcome difficulties you're currently experiencing or are likely to experience in the future.

Do you have a team in turmoil? Can you think of skills you need to effectively lead them through their challenges?

Do you use a team charter? Why, or why not?

Do you think your team members showing or experiencing condescension or lack of respect in the workplace? If so, how can you address it?

Answer honestly. Do you think your team members feel they are being treated unfairly, or not being unappreciated?

How can you better help your team members to feel like they're being listened to—and heard?

Answer honestly. Do you believe you set realistic deadlines, or are you expecting too much from your team members?

Do you think there are unhealthy office politics happening in your workplace right now? If so, how can you better manage it?

What are your highest priorities in the workplace? Are you focused on the safety of humans, or are you focused on production, or some other priority?

Do you defer to team members with deeper knowledge and superior expertise? Why, or why not?

Answer honestly. Do you commit the cardinal sin of leadership?

SOME LEADERS REALLY STRUGGLE WHEN THEY'RE CHALLENGED BY THEIR TEAM MEMBERS.

Even if the challenge is just an idea or an opinion, and one that shouldn't warrant an emotional reaction.

It's difficult, especially for leaders under pressure, to keep it together when everyone's got an idea on what could be improved. Or on how the team should be run. But it's OK for your team to offer suggestions.

It's better than OK. It's a great thing that team members want to offer suggestions and have input into the team's functioning, because it means they care about their work. That needs to be tempered of course, because every new idea won't fly. But it's about giving team members a voice. Remember that if team members aren't heard, they're hurt.

But what's radical candour? And what has it got to do with team members having a voice?

Radical candour was coined by Amy Edmondson[20] as part of her research into how to create psychologically safe teams. **Psychological safety** was defined by Edmondson as a team or workplace culture where it's OK for team members 'to take interpersonal risks', without the fear of rejection, resentment or ridicule. Taking interpersonal risks is another way of saying 'speaking up without fear.'[20]

Radical candour is a leadership approach that doesn't only make it OK for people to share ideas and information, but actually encourages it.

In relation to leading with radical candour, there are three things to discourage in your team discussions, and there are three things to encourage. Let's start with the discourage first. Because these are the behaviours that will reduce psychological safety in your team.

When your team is sharing information, lean away from:

- **Ruinous Empathy**: insincerity in your responses, feedback, or praises, particularly the sugar-coating of criticism, so the other person doesn't feel bad (this comes from a place of caring);

- **Manipulative Insincerity**: insincerity in your responses, feedback or praises, without the sugarcoating, that's delivered with the wrong intent—to hurt or harm (this definitely doesn't come from a place of caring); and

- **Obnoxious Aggression**: this is about being clear, and not kind (some people call it brutal honesty), and unlike manipulative insincerity, it's not meant to hurt, but it does, due to the message's poor delivery.

When your team is sharing information, lean into:

- **Promoting Respect**: we don't have to agree, but we do need to respect each other;

- **Welcoming Curiosity**: even team members with ideas might not have all the information required—encourage them to ask questions as much as they provide answers; and

- **Acknowledging Ideas**: all ideas are relevant, when they're shared. It's not until they're discussed that they can be discarded (might be a short discussion, or a long one). And, if they don't fly, share why; and if they were the wrong idea, share the mistake.

If you can lean into these three leadership behaviours, you'll create a psychologically safe team, you'll be leading with radical candour, and you'll encourage your team to share and contribute ideas and opinions in a safe environment. You'll also be prepared to be challenged, in good ways.

HOW TO MAKE CHALLENGER SAFETY A THING IN YOUR TEAM

In the book The Four Stages of Psychological Safety, Timothy R Clark[12] unpacks how to develop a team that feels safe to challenge the norms. Challenger safety is the fourth and final rung on the ladder (with inclusion safety, learner safety, and contributor safety being the first three).

Inclusion safety is about how well the team includes and integrates outsiders into the team. Learner safety is how much growth, development and learning are encouraged and adopted. Contributor safety relates to how safe people feel to contribute and to do their best work. And challenger safety is about how safe team members feel to speak up, and how safe they feel to offer ideas, opinions, and views. And to be creative and innovative. To think outside the box. To try new things. Without the fear of resentment, ridicule, or rejection.

So, how does a leader achieve that in their team?

ONE MAKE IT EXPECTED.

This is an important first step. Leaders need to be able to state clearly that they would like to be challenged, and need to hold the expectation that their team should feel safe to come up with creative solutions to problems. Leader languaging should be around expecting input and expecting their team to challenge the norms.

Creating the expectation of input is providing a license to innovate. That license might include incremental innovation, or it might be innovation at a disruption level. It might take the Google approach that gives team members thinking time as part of their work, to come up with great ideas, and then to present them. Gmail is one idea that came from thinking time, and Google being willing to be challenged on their business norms.

TWO MAKE IT ACCEPTABLE.

I get that this one seems redundant given that as a leader, you've made challenger safety an expectation. But here's the challenge for leaders, as I hear during coaching sessions: team members that have a license to innovate take that license and innovate. They do come up with ideas. They do challenge the norms, and they do offer solutions to problems that may not have been thought of previously.

And that can be tough for a leader. Leaders can be inundated with improvement ideas. This really can be overwhelming. Seriously. At some stage during the development of challenger safety, leaders think that 'you need to be careful what you ask for.' Which is cool. It means your team is committed, not just interested, and they feel safe enough to be part of the future growth of the team.

The way to think about this one is to consider the Tuckman model of team development, from forming to storming to norming to performing. Here's the thing about that model—it shows that during the storming stage, the team culture deteriorates (drops) for a period, until the team can come out the other side, and make challenger safety the norm (Google that model, if you're not aware of it). What it's really saying is that during the storming phase, there are issues at a team level, due to everyone wanting to raise their ideas and opinions. This stage should be called brainstorming because that's what it is. It's a phase where leaders need to have an open mind and an open heart.

And leaders need to not react with negative emotions when they're overwhelmed with the ideas and opinions offered by their team. This is where emotional intelligence comes into it.

THREE MAKE IT RADICAL.

Making challenger safety real is to do it with radical candour (from the **book of the same name** by Kim Scott).[49] In that book, Scott unpacks the most important thing about psychological safety, and that's about having conversations with radical candour. Which means challenging directly, but challenging with high care factor.

For the leader, the biggest challenge with challenger safety is sharing with team members that some ideas won't fly, and why. This is an important part of the challenge safety process, as there will be ideas that aren't right for the team or that just aren't right at that particular time. It's how these conversations are handled that will determine whether the team members continue to challenge or if they go into an 'it's all too hard to say anything' mode. If these conversations aren't handled well, it'll feel like rejection, ridicule or resentment.

The opposite of radical candour is manipulative insincerity. That is, to not challenge and to not care about the team member. These conversations have a lack of sincerity and a lack of specificity about them, and the team member leaves the conversation with more questions than answers about their idea or opinion. This happens when a leader beats around the bush when sharing that the idea or innovation isn't or won't be implemented for whatever reason.

FOUR TAKE A SUNSET-FIRST APPROACH.

What's the sunset-first approach? It's when you let the sun set on a major decision or the execution of a major decision. And you come back to the decision the next morning and make it then, after some thinking time (and maybe sleeping time).

I'm hearing you—when you're under pressure, this isn't always possible, or achievable. The decision must be made right now, or action must be taken right now. Or does it?

The issue with taking a right-now approach, as opposed to a sunset-first approach, is that you rush into making decisions. Or you're more worried about what your leader, or someone else, will think about the decision. I've been in senior leadership roles where plant downtime equates to millions of lost production, in both tonnes and dollars. But a sunset-first approach is still the right one when it comes to making major decisions. When you can.

And it demonstrates to your team that you're willing to wait for the right information, or the right people, or the right time, to make a big decision. Explain to others why you're willing to wait until tomorrow, then make the decision in the morning.

LEADER ACTION

If you don't do any of these, just listen to people that have some value to add to the decision. Don't let groupthink affect your decision making, especially when the consequences are high.

Sometimes, things need to be changed, which means you need to be challenged. Being a good leader means giving team members a chance to contribute to good change, and making it feel safe for them to do that. The new ideas support the business—and the space to challenge goes a long way towards creating a workplace that's psychologically safe.

WHY A SAFE SPACE IS MORE THAN PSYCHOLOGICAL SAFETY

Amy Edmondson[19] called it psychological safety. **Simon Sinek**[52] called it a circle of safety. We call it a safe space. Same, but different.

In our leading under pressure model, and with the support of research relating to how important it is to give your team members a voice, I'm going to say that a safe space is part of psychological safety. But it's way more than that.

To create a safe space, leaders need firstly to stay in control. It takes only one moment of out-of-control emotions to destroy years of creating trust and credibility as a leader. It takes leaders caring for their teams, not because they're told to, but because they want to. And it takes courage to make the decisions that might be unpopular, but that are made with the right intent. And of course, psychological safety is part of that. But, again, there's more to it.

Recently, I had a meeting with a business based in the USA. The leader of a 20-person team, in a 14,000-person business, explained what he'd managed to create in his team. And it was more than just giving his team a voice, and the ability to share ideas freely. It was deeper than that. It was about the way they communicated with each other. It was the intent of the communication, and it was about how their communication impacted others.

We discussed the fact that he had created a psychologically safe team. But we took the discussion further than that, and unpacked what really happens in his team to help everyone feel safe.

There were organisational things that business did, like unlimited sick leave and the flexibility of working from home. But it was more about the leader, and his team, and what they all did to foster a safe space. Remember, it's a team effort. Because a safe space is all about communication, and how we interact with other humans.

Here are the key elements of safe space communication. Firstly, have the right intent. That's a given. DO NO HARM. Don't hurt each other. Help not hurt; heal, not harm.

Then, give your team members permission to do the following.

ONE SPEAK WITH INFLUENCE.

Part of influence is interpreting the situation. Interpreting the position of the other human and acting accordingly. Influence can't happen without engagement and information. Information sharing, in a productive way, is influence. And it's not about winning a conversation, it's about influencing someone to share, to feel safe, and to act safe. It's listening to understand and not to respond, and being caring through your wording. Speaking with influence is about communicating with passion.

TWO SPEAK WITH IMPACT.

Be honest. Have real conversations. Be robust, with the right intent. Be memorable. Be the person that thinks fast and talks slow. Let silence do the heavy lifting. Be present. Be focused on the other human, and when the conversation is finished, hope that they share what a positive experience it was. Even if you had a tough conversation. Speaking with impact is about communicating on purpose.

THREE SPEAK WITH INSPIRATION.

Firstly, make commitments and keep them. Ask for help. Ask for a favour. Craft your call to action. Let people know why you're asking them to come on the journey (humans are quite simple creatures, a lot of the time, they just want to know why). Never leave the site of a meaningful conversation without the accompanying action, and someone to take responsibility for it.

Psychological safety is about being able to speak up. You create it with radical candour, and with conscious control, care factor, and courage. In giving people a voice to speak with ideas, and giving them permission to speak with influence, impact and inspiration, results in psychologically safe workplaces—and teams.

WHAT PINK CAN TEACH US ABOUT TEAM SAFETY

A few years ago, Mrs G and I were lucky enough to go to a Pink concert (*Beautiful Trauma Tour*). She was amazing. Then recently we sat down and watched the doco (*All I Know So Far*) about that tour, and we watched an amazing mum, an amazing wife, an amazing performer...and an amazing leader! I'm even more of a Pink fan now.

Here's why. Pink was so open with her behind-the-scenes shares. There were no holds barred, there were nappy changes (Jameson, who was a character, took a lot of Pink's attention). And of course, husband Carey Hart was always on hand, to be the parental support that a touring performer needs. There were hotels, concerts, daughter Willow conversations, tears and smiles, anguish and excitement. If you haven't watched the doco, don't thank me now. You'll love it, especially if you're a leader.

Here are some pearls of wisdom from Pink.

I DON'T GO OUT THE DOOR TO WORK—MY WORK AND MY HOME LIFE ARE THE SAME THING—OUR FAMILY GOES EVERYWHERE TOGETHER.

And not once did Pink say to her children that 'sorry Willow or Jameson, I have to work.' It was amazing to see her master the balancing act of performing and parenting.

There really wasn't a separation between the two areas of Pink's life, and she explained that, as parents, her and Carey worried that the kids might not be getting a conventional upbringing. Then, it was—'but hey, look at the life experiences they're getting.'

Although there were moments of emotional turmoil during the doco, the calmness that Pink demonstrated during the whole process of filming was something to be marvelled at. Whether she was performing or parenting, Pink has this ability to remain in control. It was an example of both leadership and parenting under pressure. Nothing seemed to really phase Pink (other than one stage change that she demanded...nicely).

I DON'T GET WHY OTHER PERFORMERS ARE ALWAYS AUDITIONING NEW PERFORMERS—OUR TEAM HAVE BEEN TOGETHER FOR TEN YEARS PLUS—WE LOVE OUR TEAM.

Pink just couldn't grasp why you'd want to change your team members, just because. Her philosophy was that loyal team members should be rewarded and recognised for their contribution.

They should enjoy their work. And that their leader's role is to encourage that. The tour was hard work, but at the same time, they were rewarded with a lot of downtime, and team members got the chance to socialise and have fun with Pink and her family.

There was a feeling of family to the tour, and to the team's interactions with Pink, Carey, Willow, and Jameson. It was lovely to watch how the team interacted with the children, and the team were not 'subordinates', but were active members of the decision-making process and the relevant conversations about the tour.

Pink used the word leadership on a few occasions. When she used that word, it was really about everyone, about being inclusive, and about being caring and conversational. Pink attended one of the team's birthday dinners while on tour—she sat at the table and cheered a team member on for their birthday. A little thing, but very symbolic.

YOUR TEAM HAS TO FEEL SAFE—SAFE TO SHOW UP, AND SAFE TO BE THE BEST VERSION OF THEMSELVES.

My jaw dropped. Go Pink. Talking about psychological safety (sort of). And it was just an off-handed comment that most people wouldn't have heard. But it's critical to what Pink believes and how she behaves. Pink encourages contribution. She shared openly that her leadership strategy is to encourage people to shine.

To encourage team members to share ideas. To encourage team members to grow. To encourage team members to learn and to become more during the touring process.

One comment Pink made was around hiring people smarter than her! How good is that? Pink—super star, world renowned, crazy good at what she does (and the only person that does the type of acrobatics that she does on stage)—talking in a documentary about team member safety. Wow.

Let's summarise what team safety means to Pink, from my understanding of the doco. Pink manages her emotional states and doesn't get flustered (she did when she got pulled off stage by a rope that wasn't connected properly—oops—but even angry, she kept it together well). She had care factor for her team and went out of her way to show that she cared. And they cared back. And she made courageous decisions like trusting her team to step up. Asking for input. And hiring people smarter than her.

This documentary is a leadership training program, really. And it's an example of a human who is as vulnerable as everyone else, but who also doesn't hurt people along the way. Pink's radical candour makes her the leader that everyone wants to work for—and you can be that leader, too.

Use radical candour, but not just to avoid hurting and harming. Use it to move your leadership further along the spectrum towards transformational— by learning how to show others you care about their wellbeing.

FROM 'I CARE' TO 'I REALLY KNOW HOW TO SHOW THAT I DO'

Most of the industries we work with have male leaders. And some have been in their roles for a long time. It's changing, slowly, which is positive. Our focus has always been to deliver programs that train and coach 'soft stuff for hard blokes', and that train leaders in general terms about how to better care for their teams.

Bob was one such leader. And for Bob it wasn't that he didn't care, it was that his team didn't feel like he did. And if teams don't feel cared for, they won't care for their leader, or their team. What you give out you get back— isn't that right?

So, what did Bob need to do to demonstrate care factor?

ONE BE PRESENT.

If you asked Bob's team, he was a powerhouse. He was always moving somewhere or doing something. Bob was energetic. He was passionate. His team thought that he was a strong leader, but they didn't think they were really on the top of his priority list. The work was. And the next catastrophe was Bob's focus.

This was really apparent when Bob's team really needed his attention. For example, when they had to discuss personal issues, Bob cared (and wanted to help) but didn't know how to show that.

Leaders who can't slow down and take their time to listen and support their teams when they need it aren't demonstrating care factor.

Bob's mission was to stop what he was doing. Sit still. Look at his team member. And listen. And be present. Have a conversation. And take the time to understand what's happening in their life that they need to talk about.

TWO LEARN TO SAY 'I CARE.'

Now this one shocked Bob. 'So, you're saying I should just tell people that I care about them?' he asked. Yes, Bob. Tell people, in whatever words feel right for you, that you care about them.

It's strange that telling team members that we care for them is such a big deal. But watch the reaction from your team members when you convey with them that you care about them as humans. Not just as team members.

To be honest, I'm not sure if Bob ever really got comfortable with this one. But he did try at least.

THREE STEP INTO COMPASSION.

We are born compassionate. Compassion is an innately human trait. We start demonstrating compassion in the early months of life.

Compassion is the third part of empathy. After thinking about what it must be like for the other person, and feeling what they must be experiencing. What makes compassion important, and what a lot of people don't understand, is that compassion is about action. It's about doing something for another human who needs support. Sometimes, there's nothing we can do as leaders, but at other times there is.

For Bob, it was very much about understanding what he could do to help. Whether it was approving personal leave when required, working with HR on solutions, or anything else that helped his team to feel cared for.

Fortunately, most (not all, but most) of our coaching clients are open to improving, and to showing up differently. Bob was one of those clients. And of course, his team benefited greatly.

Demonstrate radical candour, and you'll see it yourself. But if you want to see the effects on paper in black and white, there's a way to do that, too: with 360-degree feedback—that's done right.

HOW TO GET 360-DEGREE FEEDBACK SURVEYING RIGHT

For leaders to do their best work, it's important that they get feedback from those around them. From their leader, from their peers, and from their team members. It's important that the feedback is open and honest, and relevant to the leader and the organisation. Unfortunately, it's easy to get the process wrong. As I did in the early days of doing leadership development work.

Here's how to get the process right, so that the leaders get a tonne of value from the process.

ONE GET THE PREPARATION RIGHT.

This part of the process is crucial. It sets the process, and sets the leader up for success. You need to remember that feedback can be confronting for some people, so the more information that you give them about why you're doing the survey, the better. An explanatory meeting or email should go out at least a week before the survey with an overview of how the process will work, and why it's being done. And it should focus on the fact that the survey is being done with the right intent, to support the personal and professional development of the leaders.

Part of the preparation process is to let the leaders know that the surveyor is going to sit down with each leader and deliver the survey results, to help interpret and understand them, and to ensure the leaders know that the survey will be done anonymously. This last point is key, as the feedback needs to be de-identified.

Continue your preparation with getting the questions right. Make sure the questions are focused on your organisation's values and vision. This is so the leader can be made aware of how they're living those values, or if they have some opportunities for improvement.

Once you get the questions right, you can set up the survey. How you develop the survey will make or break the success of the process. That's because the questions need to make sense and be relevant to those completing the survey. The survey needs to be easily accessible and easy to complete, including both multiple choice questions, and free text questions. Then it needs to be sent to the leader's leader, their peers, and their team members, so the surveyor can collect and collate the information. A note here: more survey responses are not always better. Aim for between ten and fifteen responses, as that's a manageable number. Also allow for one to three respondents not providing enough information on the survey.

TWO GET THE PEOPLE PART RIGHT.

You need to get the people part right, and this is about delivering the survey results. Yes, this is set up for success in the preparation stage of the process; and yes, leaders are still wary as they come into meetings with the surveyor (me) to talk through their survey results.

The biggest 'don't' here is to give leaders 360-degree survey feedback without an explanation, and without giving them the time to understand and process the information. In my experience, leaders come into that meeting not knowing what to expect, and they leave having learnt some valuable information about how those around them perceive their leadership style. And that's worth gold.

And, if you do 360-degree surveying with me[55] and **The Guinea Group**, we'll catch up again for a quick touch-base after two weeks, to further unpack or talk through the feedback, after the leader has had more time to process the information. Winner.

THREE GET THE POST-PROCESS RIGHT.

Close out the process properly. This involves thanking all respondents for their input. Meeting with the CEO or the other senior leaders, to talk through how the process went. And making sure that overall, all leaders got great value and great information from the 360-degree survey process.

And, if the business is smart, they could ask the surveyor for some feedback on what the main areas of opportunity are (de-identified, of course) overall. And then consider if a training or coaching process is required to further support the leaders and their development.

This is a part of the work we do. Yes, 360-degree surveying is a great tool to help leaders continue to learn about themselves and develop their skills. Yes, it needs to be done correctly and the business needs to get it right—like all processes, if you get it wrong you can do more harm than good, so do it properly. And yes, it's a great way to see the impact of your leadership, and your commitment to demonstrating radical candour for the benefit of your team members, your organisation, and your development as a leader.

ACTIVITY 3.5
DEMONSTRATE RADICAL CANDOUR

Take some time now to think about what you've learnt in the last chapter.

The series of questions on the following pages will encourage you to think about how you can use radical candour in your leadership, and in the process of uplifting your team.

Alternatively, sit and write about how you feel when you're challenged by your team members, and what you can do better to encourage your team members to take interpersonal risks, share ideas, and share information to help your team—without the fear of criticism.

Do you struggle when you're challenged by your team members? Why, or why not?

Do you think your team members feel free to take interpersonal risks without the fear of rejection, resentment, and ridicule? If so, how did you achieve this?

Answer honestly. When your team is sharing information, are you subject to ruinous empathy, manipulative insincerity, or obnoxious aggression?

In your leadership, do you promote respect, welcome curiosity, and acknowledge ideas? Why, or why not?

Is challenger safety 'a thing' in your workplace? If not, how could you make it 'a thing'?

Do you take a 'sunset-first' approach to making difficult decisions? Why, or why not?

In what ways could you create a safe space for your team so they can speak with influence, impact, and inspiration?

Do you think you give your team members the safety to show up and be the best version of themselves?

In what ways can you move from 'I care' to showing you care for your team?

How effective is your process of obtaining feedback? How could you better conduct 360-degree feedback surveying?

AFTERWORD

If you're still with me, congratulations on making it this far. And thanks for finding me engaging enough that you decided not to put this book down and never look at it again.

What I hope has kept you connected to my words is the radical candour with which I wrote them. I hope you can see how investing in challenger safety and creating a psychologically safe workplace can help you to get the best out of your team—both in KPIs, and in job satisfaction, for the people at every level of your organisation.

I also hope you can see how taking the time to facilitate and allocate tasks to your team members—and letting go of old habits like micromanaging—makes your work life easier in the long run. And how being more attuned to your C-suite team not only improves your capacity to succeed, but creates an atmosphere of judgement-free communication that improves your team's capacity for innovation.

This book isn't the answer to all of your leadership woes. But it's the beginning of the process. A process that needs to start from within, by understanding your own thinking, emotions, and behaviour. So that what you say is what you do, and your team respects you all the more for it.

If you're an old-school leader, the one that I wrote this book for, congratulations on getting through a book you probably weren't comfortable reading. See how helping, not harming, and hearing, not hurting, can make it your team feel valued, cared for, and empowered?

If you're a new-age leader, the one that I wrote this book for, congratulations on getting through a book you probably thought was going to be a lot less work. See how not committing the cardinal sin of leadership is just as effective in building a psychologically safe team as showing your team members that you care about them?

There's a lot more to learn. Go and get stuck into whatever piques your interest: getting 360-degree feedback to improve your leadership; how to deal with leaders who go BOOM when things go BOOM; and how to create a safe space that's more than psychological safety. This book is the beginning, and as long as you're leading, there shouldn't be an end.

Learn more from me. I have a bunch of books and a team of people who can help you become a better leader. Or don't learn more from me. Learn from anyone whose leadership is inspiring to you in any way. Or anyone whose leadership has caused you to engage in the deficit dialogue dilemma, or witness groupthink, or to decide to never, ever lead your team like they led you. Go learn how to lead with radical candour, and care factor, and enough insight to know when to shamelessly hand over the reigns to someone better qualified or more experienced than you are.

If you don't remember anything I've taught you in this book, remember how it made you feel. If it filled you with hope and optimism, and overwhelmed you with the urge to commit to being a better leader, good. Go do it. If it filled you with dread and shame about how bad your leadership really is, good. Go get better at it.

Either way, you got this far because you're becoming reflective. You're learning how to think differently. You're learning how to react differently. You're learning how to answer the big questions—including why you're a leader, and why you do what you do.

Congratulations on finishing this book. You're uplifting your team. Keep going, and you'll soon be enjoying their success—and yours.

REFERENCES

1. Alexander, F. M. (1924). Constructive Conscious Control of the Individual. The Irdeat complete edition. Mouritz.

2. Algoe, S. B. (2012). Find, Remind, and Bind: The Functions of Gratitude in Everyday Relationships. Social and Personality Psychology Compass, 6(6), 455-469.

3. Anderson, E., Singh, A., & Sherman, K. (2020). The New Manager 1:1: Nurturing Employee Resiliency During Disruption and Change. *Microsoft Latinx*. Retrieved from https://blogs.microsoft.com/latinx/2020/05/11/the-new-manager-11-nurturing-employee-resiliency-during-disruption-and-change/

4. Bingham, J. (1999). *The Courage to Start: A Guide to Running for Your Life*. Touchstone.

5. Bowman, J. (2020). *Stoicism, Enkrasia and Happiness: How Stoic Philosophy Can Bring Happiness*. Independently published.

6. Brin, S., & Page, L. (1998). The Anatomy of a Large-Scale Hypertextual Web Search Engine. *Computer Networks and ISDN Systems, 30*(1-7), 107-117.

7. Brown, Brene; see https://brenebrown.com

8. Burns, J. M. (1978). *Leadership*. New York, NY: Harper & Row Publishers.

9. Byrne, R. (2006). *The Secret*. Atria Books/Beyond Words.

10. Chamorro-Premuzic, T. (2018). 5 Ways Leaders Accidentally Stress Out Their Employees. *Harvard Business Review.* Retrieved from https://hbr.org/2018/08/5-ways-leaders-accidentally-stress-out-their-employees

11. Chopra, D. (2010). *The Soul of Leadership: Unlocking Your Potential for Greatness*. Harmony Books.

12. Clark, T. (2019). *The 4 Stages of Psychological Safety: Defining the Path to Inclusion and Innovation*. Berrett-Koehler Publishers.

13. Clear, J. (2018). *Atomic habits: An Easy & Proven Way to Build Good Habits & Break Bad Ones*. Penguin Random House.

14. Cortes, J., Barragan, R. C., Brooks, C., & Meltzoff, A. N. (2012). Compassion in Children: Its Association with Prosocial Behavior and

Aggression. *Social Development, 21*(2), 332-349.

15. Cotrus, I., Stanciu, M., & Bulborea, C. (2012). EQ vs. IQ: Which is Most Important in the Success or Failure of a Student. *Procedia - Social and Behavioral Sciences, 33*, 1105-1109.

16. Covey, S. M. R. (2006). *The Speed of Trust: The One Thing That Changes Everything*. Free Press.

17. de Botton, A. (2019). *The School of Life: An Emotional Education*. Penguin.

18. Dweck, C. S. (2006). *Mindset: The New Psychology of Success*. Random House.

19. Edmondson, A. C. (1999). Psychological Safety and Learning Behavior in Work Teams. *Administrative Science Quarterly, 44*(2), 350-383.

20. Edmondson, A. C. (2019). Psychological Safety: The History, Renaissance, and Future of an Interpersonal Construct. *Annual Review of Organizational Psychology and Organizational Behavior, 6*(1), 1-23.

21. Fitzgerald, M. (2011). *Iron War: Dave Scott, Mark Allen, & the Greatest Race Ever Run*. VeloPress.

22. Goleman, D. (1995). *Emotional Intelligence: Why It Can Matter More Than IQ*. New York, NY: Bantam Books.

23. Guinea, A., Stephens, D. J., & Humer, S. (2011). *Millionaires & Billionaires: Secrets Revealed* [E-Book]. Available at https://theguineagroup.com.au/product/millionaires-billionaires-secrets-revealed-e-book/

24. Jaques, E. (1998). *Requisite Organization: A Total System for Effective Managerial Organization and Managerial Leadership for the 21st Century*. Cason Hall & Co Publishers.

25. Kahneman, D. (2011). *Thinking, Fast and Slow*. Farrar, Straus and Giroux.

26. Lassiter, C. W. (2015). *Everyday Courage School Leaders: Taking Action in the Face of Risk*. Teachers College Press.

27. Lai, E. R. (2011). Metacognition: A Literature Review. *Pearson Research Reports*. Retrieved from https://files.eric.ed.gov/fulltext/ED518612.pdf

REFERENCES

28. LaPorte, T. R. (1996). High Reliability Organizations: Unlikely, Demanding and At Risk. *Journal of Contingencies and Crisis Management, 4*(2), 60-71.

29. Lencioni, P. (2002). *The Five Dysfunctions of a Team: A Leadership Fable*. Jossey-Bass.

30. Li, J., Wu, X., Johnson, R. E., & Wu, J. (2011). When Does Employee Empowerment Lead to Customer Orientation? A Multilevel Study of Work Unit Empowerment and Customer Orientation. *Journal of Applied Psychology, 96*(5), 1191-1201.

31. Livingston, J. A. (2003). *Metacognition: An Overview*. Online Submission. Retrieved from https://www.researchgate.net/publication/234755498_Metacognition_An_Overview

32. Lloyd, C. (2018). *Next Generation Safety Leadership: From Compliance to Care*. Routledge.

33. MacDonald, C., Burke, S., & Stewart, K. (2013). *Systems Leadership: Creating Positive Organisations*. Bristol University Press.

34. Mackey, J., Mcintosh, S., & Phipps, C. (2020). *Conscious Leadership: Elevating Humanity Through Business*. Harvard Business Review Press.

35. Marsh, C. (2003). A Psycho-Physiological Comparison of Post-Traumatic and Prolonged Duress Stress Disorders. *Behavioural and Cognitive Psychotherapy, 31*(1), 109-112.

36. Maxwell, J. C. (2007). *The 21 Irrefutable Laws of Leadership*. Thomas Nelson.

37. McCormack, C. (2011). *I'm Here To Win*. Hachette Books.

38. McGonigal, K. (2013, June). *How to Make Stress Your Friend*. [Video]. TEDGlobal. https://www.ted.com/talks/kelly_mcgonigal_how_to_make_stress_your_friend

39. Meng, X., & Sun, P. (2019). The Relationship Between Work Motivation and Job Satisfaction in Chinese Universities: The Mediating Role of Perceived Organizational Support and Psychological Capital. *International Journal of Educational Research, 93*, 1-11.

40. Mirvis, P. H., & Googins, B. K. (2010). Stages of Corporate Citizenship:

An Integrated Framework for the Study of Corporate Social Responsibility. In W. Visser, D. Matten, M. Pohl, & N. Tolhurst (Eds.), *The Oxford Handbook of Corporate Social Responsibility* (pp. 67-83). Oxford University Press.

41. Nelson-Isaacs, S. (2019). *Living in Flow: The Science of Synchronicity and How Your Choices Shape Your World*. North Atlantic Books.

42. Paulhus, D. L., & Williams, K. M. (2002). The Dark Triad of Personality: Narcissism, Machiavellianism, and Psychopathy. *Journal of Research in Personality, 36*(6), 556-563.

43. Pury, C. L. S., & Lopez, S. J. (2016). The Psychology of Courage: Modern Research on an Ancient Virtue. *American Psychological Association*.

44. Quinn, W. (2015). Transformational Leadership: Confession, Discovery, Revelation. *Journal of Applied Management and Entrepreneurship, 20*(1), 21-36. Retrieved from https://wjquinnconsulting.au/images/pdf/Transformational-Leadership-Confession-Discovery-Revelation-Jan-2015.pdf

45. Robbins, T. *Discover the 6 Human Needs.* Retrieved from https://www.tonyrobbins.com/mind-meaning/do-you-need-to-feel-significant/

46. Rossouw, P. & Rossouw, J. (2020). The Predictive 6-Factor Resilience Scale: Neurobiological Fundamentals and Organizational Application. *Journal of Business and Psychology, 35*(4), 499-511.

47. Safe Work Australia. (2018). *Work-Related Psychological Health and Safety: A Systematic Approach to Meeting Your Duties*. Safe Work Australia. Retrieved from https://www.safeworkaustralia.gov.au/doc/work-related-psychological-health-and-safety-systematic-approach-meeting-your-duties-archived

48. Safe Work Australia. (2019). *Guide to Preventing and Responding to Workplace Bullying*. Retrieved from https://www.safeworkaustralia.gov.au/doc/guide-preventing-and-responding-workplace-bullying

49. Scott, K. (2017). *Radical Candor: Be a Kick-Ass Boss Without Losing Your Humanity*. St. Martin's Press.

50. Scott, S. (2002). *Fierce Conversations: Achieving Success at Work and in Life, One Conversation at a Time*. New York, NY: Berkley Publishing

REFERENCES

Group.

51. Sheldon, K. M., & Lyubomirsky, S. (2006). How to Increase and Sustain Positive Emotion: The Effects of Expressing Gratitude and Visualizing Best Possible Selves. *The Journal of Positive Psychology, 1*(2), 73–82.

52. Sinek, S. (2011). *Start With Why: How Great Leaders Inspire Everyone to Take Action*. Portfolio. See also https://simonsinek.com/stories/the-circle-of-safety/

53. Singh, P. (2016). Influence of Leaders Intrapersonal Competencies on Employee Job Satisfaction. *Global Business and Management Research, 8*(2), 57-65.

54. Sull, D., Sull, C., & Zweig, B. (2022). Toxic Culture is Driving the Great Resignation. *MIT Sloan Management Review*. Retrieved from https://sloanreview.mit.edu/article/toxic-culture-is-driving-the-great-resignation/

55. The Guinea Group; see https://antonguinea.com.au and https://theguineagroup.com.au

56. van Cuylenburg, H. (2019). *The Resilience Project: Finding Happiness through Gratitude, Empathy, and Mindfulness*. Ebury Australia.

57. Vasconcellos, E. (2021, March 31). 6 Types of Office 'Politicians' and How to Handle Them. *Business News Daily*. Retrieved from https://www.businessnewsdaily.com/3048-coping-office-politics.html

58. Vee, G. (2023). [YouTube]. *Gary Vee social media 2023 predictions*. Retrieved from https://www.youtube.com/watch?v=mArnxXgyeQ See also https://garyvaynerchuk.com

59. Willink, J., & Babin, L. (2015). *Extreme ownership: How U.S. Navy SEALs Lead and Win*. St. Martin's Press.

GLOSSARY

Akratic. Characterised by a weakness of will, resulting in action against one's better judgement.

Allocation. A consultative process of assigning tasks and responsibilities involving engagement, discussion and agreement between leaders and their team members (as opposed to delegation).

Amygdala hijack. Coined by psychologist Daniel Goleman. Where processing emotions such as fear, anger, and anxiety, overrides the prefrontal cortex, the part of the brain responsible for reasoning and decision making.

Avoidant-focused coping. A style of coping where the person pretends the event or stressor doesn't exist and avoids dealing with it.

Bandwidth (leadership and management). The capacity or limit of an individual or team to effectively lead and manage a certain number of people, projects, or responsibilities.

Big 3 leadership mandates. The obligations of leaders to the organisation, to the team, and to the self. Also known as values, transformation, and control (VTC).

BOOM Event. An unexpected serious or catastrophic event in the workplace or the lives of an organisation's employees.

Bystander effect. Psychological phenomenon where the inhibiting influence of the presence of others affects a person's willingness to help someone in need.

Care factor. Strategy for effective leadership involving giving team members time, using conversation techniques around psychological safety, psychological empowerment, and psychological connection, and being courageous in the process.

CBT. Cognitive Behavioural Therapy. A form of psychological treatment or therapy that focuses on changing negative or unhelpful thoughts and behaviours in order to improve mental health and wellbeing.

Challenger safety. One of the four stages of psychological safety in teams in Timothy R Clark's theory on how safe team members feel to speak up, and offer ideas, opinions, and views without the fear of resentment, ridicule, or rejection.

Conscious control. The ability to intentionally and actively regulate one's thoughts, emotions, and behaviours using conscious awareness and decision-making processes. Includes emotional, behavioural, and situational control.

Conscious leadership. A leadership approach that emphasises self-awareness, personal growth, and the cultivation of positive relationships and organisational culture. Conscious leaders are aware of their own thoughts, feelings, and behaviours, and how they affect others, and create a supportive, inclusive, and purpose-driven workplace.

C-Suite team. The group of top executives in an organisation (usually including the CEO, COO, CFO, CMO, CTO, and CHRO) who are responsible for setting the strategic direction of the organisation, making major decisions, and overseeing the day-to-day operations of the business to achieve its goals and objectives.

Dark Triad. A psychological term to describe three personality traits that are characterised by a lack of empathy, a tendency toward exploitative behaviour, and a focus on self-interest and personal gain. Comprised of three traits including narcissism, machiavellianism, and psychopathy. Associated with negative outcomes in personal and professional relationships, and in mental health and wellbeing.

Delegation. A process of assigning tasks and responsibilities to team members without collaboration with or input from their leader.

Deficit dialogue dilemma. A term to describe the challenge of effectively communicating and building understanding across different perspectives and worldviews in an organisation. Arises when individuals or groups with differing viewpoints are unable or unwilling to engage in productive dialogue with one another due to factors such as ideological polarisation, social or cultural barriers, or a lack of trust or respect between groups, leading to a breakdown in communication, a lack of cooperation and collaboration, and organisational dysfunction.

DiSC profile. A personality assessment tool designed to help individuals understand their behavioural preferences and communication styles. The DiSC model categorises people into four primary behavioural styles: Dominance (direct and assertive communication style and focus on results), Influence (persuasive and enthusiastic communication style and focus on building relationships), Steadiness (patient and supportive communication style focused on collaboration), and Conscientiousness (a cautious communication style and focus on quality and accuracy).

Disciplined courage. The courage you need to stand up for your position and maintain your commitments when things are going badly.

Duress. Wrongful or unlawful coercion applied by another person (usually a leader). Distinct from normal stress, strain or pressure.

EI (also EQ). Theory of emotional intelligence heavily influenced by Daniel Goleman. Applied in profiling tools to assess social management on measures of empathy, sensitivity, and appreciation; service, compassion, and benevolence; holistic communication; situational perceptual awareness; and interpersonal development.

Emotion-focused coping. A type of stress management that attempts to reduce negative emotional responses associated with stress. Negative emotions such as embarrassment, fear, anxiety, depression, excitement, and frustration are reduced or removed by various coping methods.

Empathetic courage. The courage to challenge your personal biases so you're better placed to experience what others are going through and to understand why.

Empathy. The key skill for leading under pressure. A process beginning with cognitive understanding of what someone is going though, and ending with doing something (where possible) to support them.

Golden Rule (of communication). Treating others how you would want to be treated.

Groupthink. A phenomenon that occurs when a group of individuals reaches a consensus without critical reasoning or evaluation of the consequences or alternatives.

Growth Mindset. A concept popularised by psychologist Carol Dweck. A belief that individuals can develop their abilities and intelligence through hard work, dedication, and perseverance, and that talents and abilities are not fixed, but can be improved through effort and learning.

High Reliability Organisation (HRO). An organisation that operates in complex, high-risk environments where the consequences of errors can be severe (e.g. nuclear power plants, air traffic control centres, and hospitals). Characterised by a strong safety culture, a commitment to continuous improvement, and a focus on identifying and managing risks.

Intellectual courage. The courage you need to turn your knowledge into action in the workplace.

Lencioni Model. A popular leadership development and team-building framework developed by author and consultant Patrick Lencioni. Provides a clear and actionable roadmap for building effective teams, involving trust, productive conflict, commitment, accountability, and a focus on achieving outcomes and results through both individual effort and collaboration.

LMX (Leader-Member Exchange). A leadership theory that focuses on the relationship between a leader and their individual followers or team members. Suggests that the quality of the relationship between a leader and their team members can have a significant impact on individual and team performance.

Manipulative Insincerity. Insincerity in your responses, feedback or praises, without the sugar-coating, that's delivered with the intent to hurt or harm.

Metacognition. Described as 'thinking about thinking.' How you learn and gain knowledge, and then how you apply that knowledge.

Normal Accident Theory. A theory the field of system safety engineering that explains why complex technological systems are susceptible to catastrophic failures or accidents. Suggests that accidents are an inevitable result of the complexity and interconnectedness of modern technological systems, and that no amount of planning, engineering, or design can completely eliminate the possibility of an accident occurring.

Obnoxious Aggression. Being clear, but not kind (also known as 'brutal honesty'), and unlike manipulative insincerity. Unintentionally causes hurt through poor delivery of the message.

Platinum rule (of communication). Communicating with others in the communication style they prefer, not the style you prefer.

PR6. The six elements of resilience developed by Jurie Rossouw. Includes vision, collaboration, composure, health, tenacity, and reasoning.

Problem-focused coping. Addressing the root cause of a stressor, and taking ownership and responsibility for either solving or minimising the problem with whatever resources are available at the time.

Project Aristotle. A research project initiated by Google in 2012 to study what makes a successful team. Identifies key factors that contribute to high-performing teams and improve team effectiveness and productivity, including psychological safety, dependability, structure and clarity, meaning, and impact.

Psychological safety. A concept describing the extent to which team members feel that they are respected, valued, and that their contributions are important, and how safe and comfortable they feel expressing their thoughts, ideas, and concerns without fear of negative consequences. Encourages open communication, promotes learning and innovation, and can improve team performance.

RACI matrix. A project management tool used to define and clarify roles and responsibilities within a team. RACI stands for Responsible, Accountable, Consulted, and Informed. The matrix is used to assign these roles to team members for each task or activity in a project.

Radical candour. A leadership approach that allows and encourages team members to share ideas and information, and contributes to the psychological safety of the workplace.

Ruinous Empathy. Insincerity in responses, feedback, or praises, and sugar-coating of criticism, to avoid the other person feeling bad.

Siloing. When leaders or team members don't operate as part of a team, but focus on their work, department, or business unit without regard for the rest of the organisation.

Senior leadership team (SLT). Also called Senior leadership group. A team of leaders of different levels that manage the running of the business to help it reach its goals.

Sunset-first approach. Letting the 'sun set' on a major decision or the execution of a major decision, i.e., thinking and 'sleeping on it' before coming back the next day to make a decision.

Systems Leadership. The practice of leading and managing complex systems, such as organisations, by focusing on the interrelationships and interconnectedness of the various components and stakeholders involved. Seeks to engage all members of the system in collaborative problem solving, decision making, and innovation. Requires a range of skills, including communication, collaboration, systems thinking, data analysis, and strategic planning.

Team Charter. A document that outlines the purpose, goals, roles, and expectations of a team so all members have a clear understanding of the team's mission, objectives, and expectations for performance.

Team management systems (TMS). A set of tools and assessments used for profiling and managing teams. Provides a framework for understanding team dynamics and individual preferences, and helps team leaders to identify and leverage the strengths of their team members.

Tell courage. The courage to articulate goals and objectives to the team.

Tepid leadership. A laissez-faire, 'hands-off' approach to leadership where the leader doesn't sufficiently support the team members.

Toxic Workplace Culture. An environment in which employees experience persistent negative attitudes, behaviours, and practices that have a harmful impact on their wellbeing and job performance. Common characteristics include lack of trust, bullying and harassment, poor communication, high levels of stress, lack of recognition and reward, low morale, and resistance to change.

Transactional leadership. A contingent reward-based style of leadership where the leader expects strict compliance with business practice.

Transformational leadership. A process in which leaders and followers help each other to advance to a higher level of morale and motivation.

Trust courage. The courage to trust team members to reach a goal themselves.

Trust-less leadership. Aka, micromanagement, where the leader doesn't allow team members sufficient responsibility and room for professional growth.

Tuckman Model. A widely recognised model in the field of team dynamics developed by psychologist Bruce Tuckman in 1965. Identifies four stages of group development: forming, storming, norming, and performing.

Try Courage. The courage to try and reach a goal despite the risk of failure.

Values, Transformation, and Control (VTC). A theoretical framework developed by Cameron and Quinn in the 1980s to understand organisational change and development. Posits that culture is made up of three main components: values, transformation, and control. Based on these components, organisations can be classified into one of four categories (clan, adhocracy, market, and hierarchy cultures).

360-degree survey feedback. A type of performance appraisal tool that provides an individual with feedback from multiple sources. Feedback is gathered from various sources, including the individual's manager, peers, direct reports, and customers or stakeholders.

5P process for facilitating workshops. Involves purpose (clearly define and share), process (how to run it and what resources are needed), people (who needs to be there), performance (facilitating questions, encouraging conversation, listening and documenting discussion), and polish (close out process to add value to the time the team has committed to the process).

7 states and traits. Skills for effective leadership that include learning, engaging, articulating, demonstration, empathy, resilience, and safety.

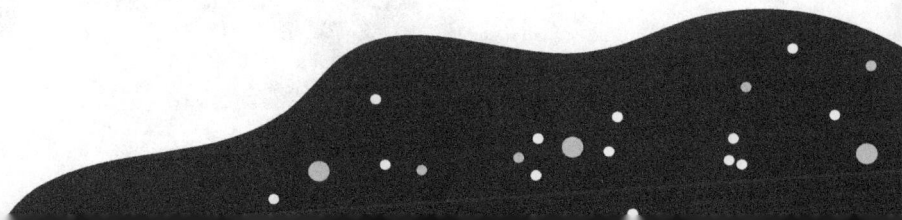

UPGRADE YOUR LEADERSHIP TEAM

We can help you to amplify your impact, through the principles and processes of:

01

SELF AND SOCIAL AWARENESS

[COACHING]

02

ON PURPOSE, UNDER PRESSURE, WITH PASSION

[TRAINING]

03

TAKING TEAMS TO THE NEXT LEVEL

[CONSULTING]

> I am amazed at how much value I got from the program, from the one-on-one sessions, and from the 24/7 support. Nothing was ever too much trouble.

Over the course of one year, I feel like I have reduced my leadership learning curve by at least 10 years. It has saved a lot of uncomfortable situations and painful lessons. I have gained so much insight, so quickly, into how the human mind works and reacts.

—Frontline Leader, and Coaching Client

ABOUT *ANTON*

Anton's life and work experiences have led him to become a visionary thought leader, delivering the right mix of empathy and enthusiasm in all his programs. His energy, engagement, and enterprise thinking is helping leaders develop into transformational and inspiring role models, who uplift the people in their care, and create high-performing teams.

Anton is a widely regarded keynote speaker. But he is also a qualified Resilience Coach, and a graduate of psychology and human resources. He's supported by The Guinea Group team of professionals, who share his commitment to service and over-delivering for leaders and organisations within Australia and across the world.

This valuable experience, paired with his unshakeable commitment to his 'why'—leaving people better than he found them—underpins his truly transformative programs.

LOOKING FOR A
WORLD-CLASS SPEAKER
FOR YOUR NEXT LIVE OR VIRTUAL LEADERSHIP EVENT?

A professional speaker since 2005, Anton has worked with global organisations within Australia and across the world.

With a noteworthy ability to help people to think differently, Anton's speaking packages also comprise pre- and post-event support and resources, helping leaders and their teams to maintain their commitment to growth and development in the lifelong process of upgrading their mindsets.

Anton is a skilled keynote speaker. But he's also a researcher, and a former tradesperson experienced in working under pressure and for poor-performing leaders. This valuable experience, paired with his unshakeable commitment to his 'why'—leaving people better than he found them—underpins his truly transformative performance as a speaker.

To find out more about how Anton can help you to find your purpose, and to build a meaningful and rewarding career, visit us here.

◢ ANTON GUINEA